AF324342

Competing Schemas Within the American Liberal Democracy

Washington College

STUDIES IN RELIGION, POLITICS, AND CULTURE

Joseph Prud'homme

General Editor

Vol. 8

This book is a volume in a Peter Lang monograph series.
Every volume is peer reviewed and meets
the highest quality standards for content and production.

PETER LANG
New York • Bern • Frankfurt • Berlin
Brussels • Vienna • Oxford • Warsaw

Shannon Holzer

Competing Schemas Within the American Liberal Democracy

An Interdisciplinary Analysis
of Differing Perceptions
of Church and State

PETER LANG
New York • Bern • Frankfurt • Berlin
Brussels • Vienna • Oxford • Warsaw

Library of Congress Cataloging-in-Publication Data

Names: Holzer, Shannon, author.
Title: Competing schemas within the American liberal democracy:
an interdisciplinary analysis of differing perceptions of church and state /
Shannon Holzer.
Description: New York: Peter Lang, 2016.
Series: Washington college studies in religion, politics,
and culture; vol. 8 | ISSN 2151-7010
Includes bibliographical references.
Identifiers: LCCN 2016016366 | ISBN 978-1-4331-3382-4 (hardcover: alk. paper)
ISBN 978-1-4539-1854-8 (ebook pdf) | ISBN 978-1-4331-3717-4 (epub)
ISBN 978-1-4331-3718-1 (mobi)
Subjects: LCSH: Church and state—United States. | Rawls, John, 1921–2002.
Political culture—United States. | United States—Politics and government.
Classification: LCC BR516 .H635 2016 | DDC 322/.10973—dc23
LC record available at https://lccn.loc.gov/2016016366

Bibliographic information published by **Die Deutsche Nationalbibliothek**.
Die Deutsche Nationalbibliothek lists this publication in the "Deutsche
Nationalbibliografie"; detailed bibliographic data are available
on the Internet at http://dnb.d-nb.de/.

The paper in this book meets the guidelines for permanence and durability
of the Committee on Production Guidelines for Book Longevity
of the Council of Library Resources.

Printed in Germany

To my dad
Thank you for being my hero

Contents

Acknowledgments

I am deeply grateful to all those who encouraged me throughout the process of writing this dissertation. I specifically want to thank Suzanne Sellers for goading me on to finish. I also want to thank Alexandra Coolidge for her confidence in me when my own confidence was absent.

I am especially thankful to William Mitchell for the help and support he gave me in moving through the final phase of my degree.

Finally, I want to express my thanks to Francis Beckwith for inspiring my work throughout the program. I hope to continue that which you began in me.

CHAPTER ONE

Introduction

1.1 Schemas: Perceiving *As* Versus Perceiving *That*

Psychologists use the term schema to represent the different ways individuals perceive the world around them. There are two possible analogies of schemas; first, a schema is like a type of filter that allows certain beliefs to enter one's noetic structure while disallowing other beliefs to enter. Second, schemas can be likened to a doxastic sieve that strains out certain beliefs while retaining others. These filters or sieves affect one's beliefs about the nature of noetic structures as well. Schemas are epistemically prior to as well as included in comprehensive worldviews. More importantly, schemas are psychologically prior even to one's philosophical assumptions, and they often go unrecognized. Schemas can sharpen the focus on one philosophical position and blur it out on another. These are not worldviews; they are dispositions by which one develops his worldview. One's worldview, however, can reinforce one's schema.

While schemas influence how one perceives the entirety of the world and one's place in it, psychoanalysts are often more concerned with how their clients perceive society and people, and in what relation they are to these two. The analyst recognizes that his client's schema causes him to focus on certain features of the world, ignore or reject other features, and to draw inferences from his skewed perception. Because of this, the client perceives the world around him inaccurately; this wrong perception causes many of the client's troubles.

The therapist's job is to show the client that the perceptions of his relations to other people as such and such are not necessarily perceptions that such and such. The therapist asks the client to attend to that which he had ignored or rejected and to amend his conclusions. The therapist's goal is to align the client's perceptions of the world as such and such as closely as he can to perceiving that about the world. Individuals may go to psychologists to help them with this; however, societies do not.

1.1a Schema of the Theologico-Political Problem

Leo Strauss framed the discussion of church and state as a problem. The majority of literature on the subject works from this perception. This perception of the interaction of church and state as problematic focuses on certain correlatives, such as civil strife, irrationality, close-mindedness, and oppression. According to Pierre Manent, much of the history of liberalism has been the attempt to escape "decisively the power of the singular religious institution of the Church…"[1] Much like a beat reporter who knows that controversy arouses the passions and is much more likely to hit the front page than the fact that society as a whole is intact, those who tell the story of church and state often tell the sordid tale of crusades, inquisitions, and witch trials. Whereas these direct the focus towards division, power plays, and irrational beliefs, they equally direct it away from religion's ability to unify, encourage charity, demand justice, and provide hope. It is very rare indeed that one hears the positive accounts of religion's interaction with the state. This is especially true inasmuch as the issue comes in contact with the American federal courts.

1.1b Schema of the Secular-Political Solution

Given the aforementioned schema, many have perceived the secularization of government as the solution to this problem. Secularists imagine a government that operates independently of the notion that God exists, that there is "no Heaven…, no Hell bellow us, above us only sky"; from this they "imagine living life in peace."[2] Just as one has areas of focus and neglect when perceiving issues of church and state, the same is true for the one's perceptions of the secular and the state. Whereas a secular state may be perceived as freeing the autonomous individual from oppression, the granting of liberty, and the protection of matters of conscience, it could also be perceived as fragmenting, encouraging selfishness, and stripping one of hope.

I do not believe either of these schemas contains the whole picture. Many who are unaware of their schematic disposition claim to perceive that such and such is the case about issues concerning church and state when in fact they merely perceive as such and such about these issues. This is not to say that perceptions as cannot be perceptions that; it is merely to say that those who are unaware of the distinction between the two are more likely to make inaccurate judgments.

1.2 Rawlsian Schema of Liberal Democracy

John Rawls perceived liberal democracies as social contracts among individuals who use public reason to enact coercive legislation. Rawls perceived public reason as the overlapping consensus of comprehensive worldviews among reasonable citizens.[3] The social contract depends on people treating other citizens as "free and equal." In order to do this, citizens are required to withhold support of legislation that is dependent upon reasoning that is exclusive to one particular comprehensive worldview.

Rawls believed that one can see his justification for adopting his theory by conducting a thought experiment from behind what he called the "veil of ignorance." The citizen is to imagine himself stripped of all his knowledge of what position he holds politically, economically, and socially in life. From here, he is to imagine what coercive legislation best serves his interests. Not knowing whether he will be born into a wealthy or poor family or a religious or non-religious family, the citizen embraces a system that affords equal treatment to all. This is much like the mother who assigns the older child to cut the one piece of cake into two pieces and allows the younger child to have first choice. The older child wants to maximize his cake eating liberty, so he cuts the cake as evenly as he can. In the same way citizens should operate from the "original position" when enacting coercive legislation since this maximizes everyone's liberty.

Rawls argued that there are beliefs over which citizens will never agree; thus, they should not use these beliefs to enact coercive legislation. The citizen is free to act on these divisive beliefs—inasmuch as they do not interfere with the primary goods of other citizens—in private, but he should not ask the government to make others do the same. To do so would violate the respect of others as being free and equal. Rawls perceived religions as comprehensive worldviews; thus, citizens should refrain from using them to form coercive legislation. Rawls also included philosophical comprehensive worldviews that are independent from religious reasoning in those sources that should be left out of coercive legislation.[4]

If legislators evenly applied the foregoing to all legislation, the legal landscape would be very different indeed. For example, there is much legislation that uses certain comprehensive doctrines of science that are quite controversial; yet, there is no attempt at a separation of science and state. For that matter, I do not advocate that there should be a separation of science and state. History is replete with doctrines that originate from within larger comprehensive paradigms, and yet there is no suggestion that these doctrines or the comprehensive worldviews from which they come should be held at bay.

Those who subscribe to Rawls' schema often perceive knowledge claims originating from religious sources differently than knowledge claims from other comprehensive doctrines. It is certainly possible to perceive science as a divisive doxastic practice from which the enactment of coercive legislation has violated the treatment of humans as free and equal. One can point to the correlation between Darwinian theory and Hitler's master race, or to the American eugenics movement to show that governments have used scientific theories in violation of these Rawlsian principles.[5] Yet, legislators and jurists rarely perceive science in such a negative fashion. Neither Congress nor the federal courts have called for the American citizenry to separate science and the state.[6] People perceive science as a positive enterprise, as progress towards a better life, and convergence upon the truth; I agree with this.

Even though there is disagreement in subjects such as history, science, literature, and the health sciences that creates controversy, jurists and legal scholars do not claim that one should restrain the use of them to enact coercive laws. It seems that beliefs that originate from controversial sources of justification are included in public reason despite their propensity for division and the violation of rights. Jurists and legal scholars accept science, history, literature, and other controversy laden disciplines as public reasoning—even by Rawlsians—because they perceive these as rational sources of knowledge.

The federal courts' perception of acceptable doxastic practices is consistent with an understanding that a belief is rational *iff* its reasoning can be observed and understood. Rationality does not entail that one must believe the proposition or that it must be true; it merely means that subject of the discussion is somehow open to objective observation. Conversely, many jurists and legal scholars believe—especially Rawlsians—that religious reasoning is irrational. They believe that the subjects of religious propositions are not open to the public, and that religious reasons are not demonstrable and recognizable.[7]

In general, those who perceive religious reasoning as irrational often do so because of their presuppositions about the nature of knowledge. Epistemologists and academicians are divided over what types of evidence count as justifiers for knowledge. This division is evident especially when it comes to religious knowledge. Many theorists of knowledge and scientists believe that religious claims are by nature unable to be proven. Thus, any argument that supports the truth of a religious proposition is by definition irrational. With this schema one perceives the structure of knowledge as a certain type of thing that excludes the ability to possess knowledge about religious claims.

On the other hand, there are many epistemologists and academicians who do believe that religious premises and conclusions can be rationally justified. The religious epistemologist and academician use a broader scope of justifiers when examining religious statements. This schema allows for an understanding of the structure of knowledge that includes rational religious reasoning.

1.3 Purpose of This Book

The purpose of this book is to determine if the legal community has—as a result of a societal or personal schema—accurately perceived the subject of church and state. This purpose also includes answering to what extent any schema affects the courts' understanding of the American framers' intentions concerning the relationship between church and state. In doing this, I will provide a specific type of religious claim, and I will evaluate its status before the federal and state courts. I will ascertain how the courts and legal scholars perceive religious claims, and then I will ask if these jurists perceive any religious claim as worthy of public reason. I will examine two contrasting perceptions of church and state regarding this definition, and I will reveal that interlocutors select, ignore, or redefine evidence to support their schema. I will do this in order to bring awareness to the lens that colors the debate over church and state. From this, I endeavor to provide a template for future jurists to think about religious reasoning and how it influences public policy.

1.4 Methodology

The study of church and state is interdisciplinary by nature. As such, my task will require many different academic tools that come from many different disciplines. First, given that the purpose of this manuscript is to evaluate the status of religious claims before the legal community, especially the state and federal courts, I will focus much of my work on case law. Most of the cases I will use are well known and well cited, and have guided the decisions in other cases concerning religious reasoning and practice. I will also include cases that are not as well known; I will use these cases because they were determined by precedents from past religion cases.

In analyzing the courts' perceptions of church and state, I will include and evaluate differing legal definitions of religion. I will also discuss the courts' use of religious tests. I will apply a general hermeneutic to state and federal court decisions to give the best explanation as to how they perceive knowledge in general, religious knowledge in specific, and religious reason's place in the formation of public policy.

I will also use history as another disciplinary tool for my analysis of the legal community's perception of the relation between church and state. Because the framing of discussions of church and state is rooted in historical discussions, I will explore at least two dissenting accounts of the history of the American constitutional experiment. On the one hand, I will give a separationist account of the experiment as the intentional detachment of religion and state. *The Godless Constitution*, by Isaac Kramnick and R. Laurence Moore, provides a good example of a separationist schema of history.[8]

On the other hand, there are historians whose attention is not drawn to the constitutional framers' ambition for separation; instead, many purveyors of history perceive the architects of the American constitution as highly motivated by their religious beliefs. I will use Garrett Ward Sheldon's book *The Political Philosophy of Thomas Jefferson* as an example of a history that is more perceptive of the framers as using and promoting religious reasoning in the public square.[9]

In addition, I will also rely on Michael Sandel's critique of the federal courts' tendency to perceive religious beliefs as a matter of choice rather than conviction.[10] If Sandel is correct, the federal courts do not perceive religious beliefs as matters of conscience as did the framers. This understanding of religious belief has a profound effect on the courts' decisions relating to church and state. The schema by which the federal courts analyze history limits how they perceive the framers' original intent. One of my goals is to determine which historical perspective the courts use to guide their decision making.

Along with law and history, I will also incorporate theological discussions. The central theme of studies concerning church and state is whether theological concepts should be part of coercive public policy. I will ask if the federal courts are willing to accept any theological construct or do they obligate all legislation to be stripped of anything related to God. I will contend that the language of the American constitutional experiment is steeped in theological constructs. I will then discuss how the courts understand this language and use or ignore it when they make legal decisions.

Finally, and most of all, I will be using philosophical tools to assess the courts' and legal scholars' reasoning. My goal is not necessarily to correct any of the experts; instead, it is to determine whether the courts and legal scholars have acted consistently within the framework of their perception of epistemology, metaphysics, and ethics as these subjects pertain to issues of church and state.

Ultimately, I believe that some judges and scholars start from certain philosophical assumptions. These assumptions determine what judges and legal scholars accept as reasonable and useable to form coercive legislation. There are also some judges and legal scholars who embrace particular philosophical positions to support their prior held conclusions. For instance, some scholars merely presuppose that religious reasoning is irrational. Upon reflection, the judge or legal scholar tries to identify a feature that religious beliefs have or lack to support the forgone conclusion that religious reasoning is irrational. On the one hand, schemas affect the federal courts' perception of knowledge, which in turn is applied to religious reasoning. On the other hand, schemas may not affect the judges' perception of knowledge in general; schemas may affect only the judges' perception of religious knowledge. I believe that these unchecked schemas have resulted in federal court decisions that show inconsistent reasoning. My use of philosophy will serve to provide what Hadley Arkes referred to as "First Things."[11] These are first principles from which one can discuss issues of knowledge, religion, and coercive policy without having to suffer from the cognitive dissonance schemas may cause.

If it is true that societies and individuals perceive the world around them—particularly that which justifies the enactment of coercive legislation—through schemas, then it is not necessary to frame the discussion about church and state *as* a problem and absolute secularization *as* the solution. Also, if schemas shape one's psychological disposition to accept some doxastic practices rather than others, then by recognizing and reflecting on this disposition one may—if necessary—free himself from it. If legal federal court judges understood the influence schemas have on their legal decisions, they could take steps to keep these tendencies in check. From this, the courts could operate with a wider understanding of knowledge and how to use it in deciding cases concerning religious reasoning and actions.

1.5 Chapter Breakdown

I have used this opening chapter to suggest that discussions of church and state have been framed as a problem. As I have mentioned, though there are historical accounts of problems that accompanied the interaction of church and state, there are also accounts of great success. Similarly, there are historical accounts of successes and failures in all institutions and belief forming practices. Framing the entirety of the discourse concerning church and state as a problem is a sweeping generality.

I have used the term schema to mean that there is a psychological or even a social disposition to focus on certain features contained in the discussion in order to create or protect certain conclusions. I will use the following chapters to support the thesis that legal scholars, jurists, and much of the general population perceive religion differently than they do other doxastic practices. This schema directs the independent subjects as well as society as a whole towards dispositional perceptions of church and state.

In chapter two, I will discuss the differing perceptions of religious reasoning that undergird judicial decision making. In doing so, I will address certain philosophical principles the court has employed in religion cases. If these principles are sound, they should be used universally. If these principles fail in some sort of way, it is possible that they should be abandoned. I will use several cases that came before the state and federal courts to reveal how judges have used these philosophical principles to determine issues of church and state. I will consider to what degree the courts have consistently applied these principles, and I will determine to what extent they have exclusively used them to support their perception of religious claims. I will then take note of how the courts' decisions over issues of church and state correlate with how they perceive religious reasoning. I believe that the courts' use of language will reveal how the judges perceive religion and to what understanding of history they subscribe.

In chapter three, I will compare and contrast two sides of contention regarding the history and development of the American constitutional experiment, the role religion played in its development, and the framers' original intent. While doing this, I will highlight the fact that there exists myopia on both sides of the debate. This is especially true when it comes to the concept of separation. Daniel Dreisbach writes the following about Jefferson's letter to the Danbury Baptists:

> The Court's use of the metaphor has polarized students of church-state relations and, in application, has frequently excluded religious citizens from public life and discourse. Jefferson's figurative language, detractors continue, has not produced the solutions that its apparent clarity and directness lead the wall-builders to expect. It has obfuscated our understanding of constitutional principles. Indeed, it has unnecessarily infused the church-state debate in modern America with inflexibility and fostered distortions and confusion.[12]

This supports my claim that there exists a lens—so to speak—through which scholars perceive the subject of church and state.

I will pay particular attention to how the framers and their antecedents used language about religious reason and practice in the grounding of rights and formation of public policy. Given that separationists and accommodationists differ in their interpretation of the historical data, I will compare both of their answers to the framers' language and reasoning. From this, I will point out where the two sides are consistent with the original language and where each side's interpretation departs from it. I will determine to what extent the separationist interpretation of the historical documents and accommodationist interpretation of the historical documents accept or reject the framers' language. I will also take account of which schema practices or avoids the framers' type of reasoning. Just as chapter two argues that schemas affect how federal judges define religion and treat religious claims, chapter three shows how schemas affect the interpretation of historical events, the portrayal of historical figures, the meaning behind their language, and their intentions.

Chapter four will further the previous chapters' work by showing that the courts understand the framers' original intent through a separationist schema. In light of this, I will use this chapter to discuss Michael Sandel's critique of the federal courts' treatment of religious claims. Sandel makes a distinction between voluntaristic belief and matters of conscience, and he shows that the framers understood religion as the latter. On the other hand, Sandel points out that the current legal culture has a voluntarist conception of religion. If Sandel is correct, then the courts have perceived religious reasoning inaccurately. Moreover, if the courts have perceived religious reasoning inaccurately, then their construal of church and state is something other than the framers intended. As such, their decisions about the relation of church and state may have followed suit.

I will use chapter five to address the challenge of Rawlsian liberalism. By "challenge," I mean that there are those who perceive a religious position that becomes law *as* unjust because it is based on a disputed view of the good life that dissenters are not unreasonable in rejecting. There are several scholars who share similar perceptions of the interactions between church and state as Rawls does; Stephen Macedo, Ronald Dworkin, and Robert Audi are a few. I will interact with these scholars' work and ask if their perception of church and state is guided by a pre-determined schema that creates problems of inconsistency within their noetic structure. I will also contrast the manner in which these Rawlsian type scholars perceive religious reasoning with the perceptions of those who disagree with Rawls; these scholars include: Francis Beckwith, Michael Sandel, Nicolas Wolterstorff, Christopher Wolfe, and Robert George.

Though I will highlight the similarities between these intellectuals, I want to point out that the two sides do perceive issues concerning church and state differently. Of course, I maintain that this difference in perception is because of the lens through which they observe the subject. This is not to say that all perceptions are equal; I am saying quite the opposite of that. Just as people use psychotherapy to align their schema to properly perceive reality, so too should legal scholars, historians, jurists, and philosophers align their schemas. The recognition that one perceives the world through schemas is merely the recognition of a perceptual problem; it is not the solution to it. There are those who perceive the world more accurately than others perceive it. I maintain that this is true with whole segments of society as well. If I am correct, then to some degree either the separationist schema or the accommodationist schema allows greater convergence on reality.

In chapter six, I intend to show that individual and societal schemas have allowed judicial perceptions of church and state to morph into religion and state, morality connected to religion and state, and philosophy supportive of or by religion and state. Specifically, I will use the structure of scientific revolutions that Thomas Kuhn gave as a model to show that a similar event has occurred in the intellectual history of liberal democracy. It is because of this, I will argue, the federal courts have sharpened their focus so tightly on the subject of church and state as a problem and secularization as a solution that the judges have extended this perception of religion to anything that is associated with it.

My intention is to draw the attention away from the separation of religion and politics and draw it back towards issues of church and state. I will make it clear that there is a distinction between churches and persons. Churches are ecclesiastical entities with governing bodies; people represent themselves. Churches, religious propositions, and politics inform people how to live their lives. If the federal courts have perceived religious individuals as identical to ecclesiastical bodies, then religious citizens who represent a large segment of the American population will be alienated from voting or enacting legislation according to their conscience.

Chapter seven will ask to what extent the schema of the current legal culture is accurate regarding theologico-political issues. If I am correct that the legal community's perception of religious reasoning as irrational, divisive, and oppressive is not necessarily the perception that religious reasoning is irrational, divisive, and oppressive, then strict separation may not be the solution to church state issues. Though some people, reasons, and laws are irrational, divisive, and oppressive, they are not these things because they are religious. The people, reasoning, and laws will need to be judged on their own merit. If truth is the goal of our epistemic endeavors, then doxastic practices that direct our beliefs towards the truth should not be curtailed. If religious reasoning can inform us how to become a more virtuous society, then there is no need to restrain it as long as it reliably accomplishes its task.

I will also use chapter seven to address the prevailing perception of religion as divisive and dangerous. My intent is to challenge this notion and to suggest that it is an inaccurate caricature of religious beliefs, people, and history. This is not to deny that there have been dark spots on religious reasoning or practice. It is merely to suggest that the legal culture has overlooked the good that religious reasoning has brought in light of some of its misuse.

I will use chapter eight to give a summary of the proceeding chapters. I will show that all of these chapters support the thesis that there is a schema by which the federal courts, legal scholars, and individuals perceive matters of church and state and religious reasoning. I will then provide what I believe to be a wider and more accurate way to guide our perceptions over the issues of knowledge in general, knowledge about coercive legislation, and religious reasoning about such things.

CHAPTER TWO

The Courts' Perception of Religion

I will use this chapter to show that many American court judges perceive religion in such a way that has resulted in strict separation as the default position in matters concerning church and state.[1] This observation is not new; Daniel Dreisbach writes:

> Jefferson's "wall" is accepted by many Americans as a pithy description of the constitutionally-prescribed church-state arrangement. More important, the federal judiciary has found the metaphor irresistible, elevating it to authoritative gloss on the First Amendment religion provisions.[2]

However, I will argue that their reasoning is guided by a schema that construes religion as irrational and subjective. For, if the judges perceive religious reasoning as irrational and subjective, then they may *de facto* rule out all religious claims. Judges and legal scholars further perceive—because of this subjectivity—the divisive possibilities of religious beliefs. The courts and many legal scholars—I will argue—perceive the use of such reasoning for the enactment of public policies as unjustified acts of coercion. According to this schema, coercive laws that are founded on religious reasoning result in division and strife. Thus, I will argue that this line of thought guides the courts' and certain scholars' pursuit of the separation of religion from legislation as a solution to this problem.

2.1 Religious Reason as Irrational and Subjective

Two scholars, James Hitchcock and Francis Beckwith, have made the case that the courts perceive religious reasoning as irrational. In doing so, they glean statements from individual judges that reveal their personal understanding of religion and its place in public policy. Hitchcock and Beckwith show decisively that a politically influential number of federal and state judges perceive religious reasoning as an irrational and private practice.

2.1a James Hitchcock

Hitchcock devotes an entire section of his book *The Supreme Court and Religion in American Life* to the Supreme Court's perception of religion. Much of his work relies on quoting the justices, which allows them to make his case. In the opening sentence of Hitchcock's section on the rationality of religion he writes:

> The Court's finding in the Ballard case established the assumption that belief could be validated solely on the basis of individual subjective apprehensions, which were of such a nature as to be incredible, even incomprehensible, to others. Religion was seen as lacking objective foundations and resting on a purely personal view of reality.[3]

This opening statement frames the rest of his argument that progresses chronologically case by case.

Hitchcock writes that federal court judges often speak with disdain for religious belief. He states that Justice Robert Jackson "allowed himself to speak of appellants with contempt even as he was voting to uphold their rights…"[4] Jackson's disrespect for religious reasoning can be seen in his dissenting opinion in the case *Kedroff v. Saint Nicholas Cathedral* when he writes:

> [I] would not wallow throughout the complex, obscure, and fragmentary details of secular and ecclesiastical history, theology, and canon law in which this case is smothered. To me, whatever the canon law is found to be and whoever is the rightful head of the Moscow patriarchate, I do not think New York law must yield to the authority of a foreign and unfriendly state masquerading as a spiritual institution."[5]

Hitchcock interpreted Jackson as saying that this discussion is "a morass beneath the notice of rational man."[6]

Hitchcock says that this trend can be seen in a similar case that took place twenty-two years later in 1976 in an inner church dispute. This case was *Serbian Orthodox Diocese v. Milivojevich.*[7] Justice William Brennan showed that he perceived religion much in the same way as Justice Jackson when he wrote, "indeed, it is the essence of religious faith that ecclesiastical decisions are to be reached and are to be accepted as matters of faith whether or not rational or measurable by objective criteria."[8]

According to Hitchcock, this position of religion as irrational has become the opinion of the majority of Supreme Court justices. He states that they perceived religion as resting "on foundations that were not even comprehensible to people outside the faith and could not be governed by ordinary rationality."[9] Support for the claim that this perception of religion has become firmly engrained in the mind of the courts can be seen in Justice Stevens's 1977 opinion in *Wolman v. Walter* when he wrote, "the realm of religion…is where knowledge leaves off, and where faith begins."[10] If Hitchcock is correct, then one could predict with a certain level of accuracy how cases that rest on religious premises will be decided.[11]

2.1b Francis Beckwith

Francis Beckwith furthers Hitchcock's work on this subject in his article "Must Theology Always Sit in the Back of the Secular Bus."[12] The title of this article plays off the concept of the "separate but equal" laws that segregated people by race. Just as it was shown that the black race was treated as inferior to the white race, Beckwith argues that religious reasoning too is treated as inferior compared to secular reasoning.

Beckwith starts out with a scenario of a U.S. Senate Judiciary committee where a recent Supreme Court nominee is answering questions. The nominee shows that she is highly qualified academically in the disciplines of law and science. She further answers questions regarding her views on policies that would overlap with her academic expertise. In doing so, the nominee impresses those who question her. Beckwith adds that she is also a "devout Roman Catholic and has published several law review articles critical of the Supreme Court's reproductive rights jurisprudence…"[13] From this, the committee asks her how her religious views will affect her decisions from the bench. Beckwith points out that "such a question, of course, is not asked of the nominee's beliefs about biochemistry or the issues in which law and science intersect on which she has opined…"[14] His point is that religion is perceived in such a way as to relegate it to an inferior status, and that many believe that it should have limited influence over important decisions concerning policy.

Beckwith's story illustrates Hitchcock's observations of the Supreme Court's perception of religious reasoning as irrational. Because the process of appointing federal judges weeds out those who might use religious reasoning, those who do find a place on the bench tend to be those who share the same hegemonic perceptions of religious reasoning. Because of this, it is natural that religious reasoning takes a second seat to reasoning from any secular source.

In the same manner of Hitchcock, Beckwith uses the Supreme Court justices' language to exemplify his point. For example, Beckwith quotes Justice William O. Douglas' opinion in *U.S. v. Ballard*, which states:

> Men may believe what they cannot prove. They may not be put to the proof of their religious doctrines or beliefs. Religious experiences which are as real as life to some may be incomprehensible to others. Yet the fact that they may be beyond the ken of mortals does not mean that they can be made suspect before the law. Many take their gospel from the New Testament. But it would hardly be supposed that they could be tried before a jury charged with the duty of determining whether those teachings contained false representations. The miracles of the New Testament, the Divinity of Christ, life after death, the power of prayer are deep in the religious convictions of many. If one could be sent to jail because a jury in a hostile environment found those teaching false, little indeed would be left of religious freedom.[15]

Beckwith asserts that the "Supreme Court's assumption of religion's irrationality has been subtly smuggled" into cases "where citizens try to shape policy."[16] Because of the Court's perception of religion as irrational and subjective, judges tend to dismiss arguments that include reasons that are connected to theology in any way. Instead, the courts use a boiler plate of irrationality that covers all religious cases. From this, their task is not to assess the truth of any claim that includes religion, but it is instead merely to discover the religious element and weed it out.

Beckwith argues that the courts and legal scholars[17] perceive all religious statements as "equally irrational."[18] This is unlike their perceptions of knowledge claims from other areas of inquiry. For example, scientific and historical claims are individually assessed, whereas religious claims are lumped together as collectively irrational, and they are therefore unjustified. Because of this negative perception, Beckwith asserts that the courts fail to treat religion and secular reasoning neutrally. In fact, he claims, that this reasoning *a priori* rules out "all religious claims from serious consideration in policy disputes."[19]

The courts have certainly had a problem with the use of religious reasoning for coercive policy. Given their stance on the rationality of religion as a source of knowledge, the courts see little reason to cede authority to that with which they disagree. Justice Blackmun expressed this when he stated that with democracy there is a "demand for discussion and dissent" and that there is a clash with religious "faith's bowing to higher authority beyond human discussion."[20]

2.2 Religious Reason as Divisive and Dangerous

Just as before, Hitchcock points out a trend that a majority of the judges have followed. He argues that the courts have operated from the perception of religion as divisive and dangerous. Again, Hitchcock uses a section of his book to bring to light this attitude that he believes the courts share.

Hitchcock speaks of the fact that for over sixty years there were several cases concerning religion and that the issue of religious strife was not raised.[21] Hitchcock says that Justice Frankfurter, however, found "in the dangers of religious conflict an argument for restraining religious expressions that threatened the public order."[22] In this case, it was held that children should not be compelled to pledge allegiance to the flag if it conflicted with their religious beliefs. In his dissenting opinion Justice Frankfurter expressed his perception of the relationship of the church and state when he wrote:

> The great leaders of the American Revolution were determined to remove political support from every religious establishment. They put on an equality the different religious sects—Episcopalians, Presbyterians, Catholics, Baptists, Methodists, Quakers, Huguenots—which, as dissenters, had been under the heel of the various orthodoxies that prevailed in different colonies. So far as the state was concerned, there was to be neither orthodoxy nor heterodoxy. And so Jefferson and those who followed him wrote guaranties of religious freedom into our constitutions. Religious minorities, as well as religious majorities, were to be equal in the eyes of the political state. But Jefferson and the others also knew that minorities may disrupt society. It never would have occurred to them to write into the Constitution the subordination of the general civil authority of the state to sectarian scruples.[23]

For Frankfurter where there is disagreement between religion and state laws the state wins, lest there be civil unrest.

Hitchcock refers to another case that was decided a year later. This case, *Prince v. Massachusetts*, involved children passing out Jehovah's Witness literature as their religious duty, which clashed with child labor laws. Justice Murphy expressed his perception of religion in his dissent by writing:

> No chapter in human history has been so largely written in terms of persecution and intolerance as the one dealing with religious freedom. From ancient times to the present day, the ingenuity of man has known no limits in its ability to forge weapons of oppression for use against those who dare to express or practice unorthodox religious beliefs.[24]

According to Hitchcock, it was around this time that this type of religious perception entered into court reasoning.

The trend to perceive religious reasoning as divisive continued, and it fueled separationist attitudes. Hitchcock believes that since *Everson v. Board of Education* the courts "adopted a consistent view that religious strife was a danger to the nation and needed to be controlled."[25] In delivering the Court's opinion over state-funded transportation of children to Catholic schools Justice Black wrote:

> A large proportion of the early settlers of this country came here from Europe to escape the bondage of laws which compelled them to support and attend government favored churches. The centuries immediately before and contemporaneous with the colonization of America had been filled with turmoil, civil strife, and persecutions, generated in large part by established sects determined to maintain their absolute political and religious supremacy. With the power of government supporting them, at various times and places, Catholics had persecuted Protestants, Protestants had persecuted Catholics, Protestant sects had persecuted other Protestant sects, Catholics of one shade of belief had persecuted Catholics of another shade of belief, and all of these had from time to time persecuted Jews. In efforts to force loyalty to whatever religious group happened to be on top and in league with the government of a particular time and place, men and women had been fined, cast in jail, cruelly tortured, and killed. Among the offenses for which these punishments had been inflicted were such things as speaking disrespectfully of the views of ministers of government-established churches, nonattendance at those churches, expressions of non-belief in their doctrines, and failure to pay taxes and tithes to support them.[26]

Justice Black's Old World history is nightmarish to say the least. If one perceives the history of church and state in this fashion, one would conclude that the solution or prevention of such atrocities would be strict separation. Black goes on to suggest that the very same horrific events caused by religion came to America with the colonists. Black writes:

> These practices of the old world were transplanted to and began to thrive in the soil of the new America. The very charters granted by the English Crown to the individuals and companies designated to make the laws which would control the destinies of the colonials authorized these individuals and companies to erect religious establishments which all, whether believers or non-believers, would be required to support and attend. An exercise of this authority was accompanied by a repetition of many of the old world practices and persecutions. Catholics found themselves hounded and proscribed because of their faith; Quakers who followed their conscience went to jail; Baptists were peculiarly obnoxious to certain dominant Protestant sects; men and women of varied faiths who happened to be in a minority in a particular locality were persecuted because they steadfastly persisted in worshipping God only as their own consciences dictated. And all of these dissenters were compelled to pay tithes and

taxes to support government-sponsored churches whose ministers preached inflammatory sermons designed to strengthen and consolidate the established faith by generating a burning hatred against dissenters. These practices became so commonplace as to shock the freedom-loving colonials into a feeling of abhorrence. The imposition of taxes to pay ministers' salaries and to build and maintain churches and church property aroused their indignation. It was these feelings which found expression in the First Amendment. No one locality and no one group throughout the Colonies can rightly be given entire credit for having aroused the sentiment that culminated in adoption of the Bill of Rights' provisions embracing religious liberty.[27]

This strong language continued to influence cases that specifically reached for strict separation.[28]

The Supreme Court utilized the ideas of separation from *Everson v. the Board of Education* in *McCollum v. Maryland*. The Court's majority believed that the "commingling of sectarian with secular instruction in the public schools"[29] violates the Establishment Clause. Justice Frankfurter delivered and partially justified the opinion on the grounds of religious divisiveness.

> The preservation of the community from divisive conflicts, of Government from irreconcilable pressures by religious groups, of religion from censorship and coercion however subtly exercised, requires strict confinement of the State to instruction other than religious, leaving to the individual's church and home, indoctrination in the faith of his choice.[30]

Given this perception of religion as irrational and dangerous, it is no wonder the courts have steered towards separation.

2.3 Religious Reason as Coercive Indoctrination

In the movement towards stricter separation between religion and state, the courts have often used language of protection. That is, the courts imply that it is their task to protect citizens from religious beliefs more than it is the protection of religious beliefs. Hitchcock argues that by 1948 "the *Engel* and *Schemmp*[31] cases developed the jurisprudence of the *McCollum* case and formulated the position that thereafter the Court would almost undeviatingly take with respect to cases involving religion in the public schools."[32] Hitchcock furthered his point, saying, "…now efforts were being made to insulate the public sector from all religious influence."[33]

Coercion is one of the most often cited fears used to justify separation of church and state. Judges have used this word on several occasions to forbid certain acts that are associated with religion. For example, in *Santa Fe v. Jane Doe,* Justice Stevens's ruling disallowed prayer at the opening of high school football games. He felt that the peer pressure to pray was strong and that students would be coerced into participation.[34] According to Hitchcock, Stevens believed that prayer at the high school football games would cause some to feel like outsiders, and he wanted to protect students from what they might think to be a "personally offensive religious ritual."[35]

In *Wallace v. Jaffree* the Supreme Court struck down a law allowing for a moment of silence in public schools.[36] Just as many cases concerning school curricula, this case was brought before the court by a secularist. Ishmael Jaffree's contention was not that the endorsement of a specific sect within a particular religion was influencing his children's particular religious beliefs. Instead, Jaffree did not want the public school directing his children away from their non-religious beliefs. He feared that by allowing moments of silence and prayer in the public school his children might be coerced into religious practice. Part of Jaffree's argument was that his "children were ostracized, laughed at, talked about, subjected to racial epithets and physically harassed."[37]

Similarly, in 1991 the Supreme Court delivered the decision over the case *Lee v. Weisman* that disallowed prayer at graduation ceremonies.[38] Justice Harry Blackmun delivered the majority opinion:

> The mixing of government and religion can be a threat to free government, even if no one is forced to participate…. When the government puts its imprimatur on a particular religion, it conveys a message of exclusion to all those who do not adhere to the favored beliefs. A government cannot be premised on the belief that all persons are created equal when it asserts that God prefers some.[39]

In both of the foregoing cases there was a low level of coercion. The students were not required to attend the graduation ceremonies to receive their diplomas. The students were also not expected to actually pray or even lower their heads. Finally, they were not required to affirm that those who were praying were actually correct in their actions. The courts perceived this coercion as coming from unspoken peer pressure.

Justice Kennedy believes that coercion is the leading principle in the Establishment Clause. He writes:

> …government may not coerce anyone to support or participate in any religion or its exercise; and may not, in the guise of avoiding hostility or callous indifference, give direct benefits to religion in such a degree that it in fact "establishes a religion or religious faith, or tends to do so."[40]

If coercion is the villain, then one should expect that it should be extended to other areas of inquiry.

The courts have not always applied the principle of coercion in a uniform manner. Recently two graduate students alleged that their state-funded universities imposed practices on them that violated their free exercise of religion. Graduate student Julia Ward was part of Eastern Michigan University's counseling program that required practicum hours to graduate. Ward, a Christian, tried to opt out of counseling a homosexual student about a same-sex relationship. As a result, Eastern Michigan University dismissed her from the program. EMU's counseling program follows the American Counseling Association's ethical standards of the counseling profession, which "requires that students demonstrate in practicum the ability to consistently set aside their personal values or belief systems and work with the value system of the client."[41] Ward stood before a formal review, where the reviewers justified her dismissal based on the "conflict between your values that motivate your behavior and those behaviors expected by the profession."[42] This case centered on the question of which source of ethics Ward ought to act upon, the American Counseling Association's or her religion. District Court Judge George Caram Steeh granted summary judgment in favor of EMU.

On January 27, 2012, Judge Sutton overturned Judge Steeh's summary judgment. Sutton made it clear that:

> The problem in this case is not a facially unconstitutional policy, as Ward submits, but the potentially improper implementation of that policy by some members of the university and not others.[43]

Sutton further stated that "the district court properly accounted for this discretion."[44] This was not a court victory; instead it was a failure of the defense to obtain summary judgment at the court of appeals. Sutton did not grant the defense summary judgment because he believed that "a reasonable jury could find that the university dismissed Ward from its counseling program because of her faith-based speech, not because of any legitimate pedagogical objective."[45] The case settled without going to trial.[46] Alliance Defending Freedom perceives this settlement as a victory.[47]

In 2010, Jennifer Keeton filed suit against Augusta State, stating that they "violated her First Amendment rights to free speech and the free exercise of religion by threatening her with expulsion if she does not fufill [sic] requirements contained in a remediation plan intended to get her to change her beliefs."[48] This action arose when Keeton expressed her desire to not counsel clients who practiced homosexuality, if that counseling required affirming the lifestyle as moral. Augusta State officials stated that Keeton could not engage in the program's clinical practicum until she "participate [ed] in a remediation plan, to help her learn how to comply with the ACA Code of Ethics" and improve her "ability to be a multiculturally competent counselor, particularly with regard to working with [GLBTQ] populations."[49] The remediation plan included these five requirements:

(1) attend at least three workshops which emphasize improving crosscultural communication, developing multicultural competence, or diversity sensitivity training toward working with the GLBTQ population;

(2) read at least ten articles in peer-reviewed counseling or psychological journals that pertain to improving counseling effectiveness with the GLBTQ population;

(3) work to increase her exposure and interaction with the GLBTQ population by, for instance, attending the Gay Pride Parade in Augusta;

(4) familiarize herself with the Association for Lesbian, Gay, Bisexual and Transgender Issues in Counseling ("ALGBTIC") Competencies for Counseling Gays and Transgender Clients; and

(5) submit a two-page reflection to her advisor every month summarizing what she learned from her research, how her study has influenced her beliefs, and how future clients may benefit from what she has learned.[50]

Keeton chose not to fulfill this remedial plan and was dismissed from the program.

In his granting of summary judgment in Ward's case, Judge Sutton commented on why he believed that Keeton's case was correctly decided. He stated that:

> ...the two claimants' theories of constitutional protection also are miles apart. Keeton insisted on a constitutional right to engage in conversion therapy—that is, if a "client discloses that he is gay, it was her intention to tell the client that his behavior is morally wrong and then try to change the client's behavior."[51]

However, for the purpose of this book, these cases are not "miles apart." Both Ward and Keeton were informed by a religious source. The court perceives that schools and professional organizations are correct in disallowing religion to inform particular practices, such as counseling. Ward and Keeton acted in accordance to their beliefs, to which the public entities pushed back. The students were both asked to change their beliefs while performing their duties as counselors. While it was settled in Ward's case that she may refrain from counseling practices that violated her religious beliefs, she could not use these beliefs to inform her counseling.[52] In Keeton's case, she was not given the chance to refrain from counseling homosexual clients. The school tried to coerce her to change her beliefs, and when she did not change she was dismissed.[53]

Ward's and Keeton's cases are as similar to Jaffree's and Weisman's as they are different. With *Wallace v. Jaffree* and *Lee v. Weisman*, there was a low level of coercion. On the other hand, with *Ward v. Wilbanks* and *Keeton v. Anderson-Whiley* the level of coercive force was much greater. With the former cases, the students were minors, whereas the latter cases involved young adults. The Jaffree and Weisman cases were part of compulsory education. Ward's and Keeton's cases were elected graduate degrees. The former cases argued that the students were coerced into religious action that violated the Establishment Clause. The latter cases argued that the students were coerced into secular action that violated their free exercise of religion.

The similarities and differences are not as important as the guiding principles in the cases. Jaffree and Weisman merely had the task of convincing the federal courts that the action of the schools was in fact religious. Once the courts recognized the actions of the schools as religious, they ruled against them. The overarching principle at work in these two cases was not the protection from coercion in general; instead, it was protection from religious coercion through state-funded education.

2.4 The Courts' Interpretation of the Establishment Clause

There are those who argue that the legal community *de facto* treats religious reason as though it is inferior to other sources of justification. Further, many scholars believe that the judges enforce secularism as the default position in any case concerning moral legislation.

2.4a Religious Reason as Private

Due to the perception of religion as irrational, divisive, and coercive, judges have often "fenced off"[54] religious reasoning from the concerns of government. Judges have often treated religion as a hobby rather than a robust part of one's public intellectual and moral life. In this sense, the courts have stated that religious beliefs are something that one chooses to believe. Justice Douglas made this point when arguing that "Americans [are] free to believe anything they choose, [and are] not obligated to prove their beliefs, which of their nature might be utterly incomprehensible to other people, the miracles of the New Testament of belief in the power of prayer being examples."[55] This is in contrast to other sources of knowledge, such as principles of mathematics that are true, whether regardless of one believes them to be so.

In one sense, the courts have used the perception of religion as being private for the protection of religious beliefs. In doing so, they greatly expanded the definition of religion to include non-theistic beliefs. *United States v. Seeger* was a landmark case that affected how later courts would perceive religion.[56] In this case, Seeger refused induction into the draft on the basis of conscientious objection. Seeger grounded his conscientious objection on §6(j) of the Universal Military Training and Service Act.[57] This section provided an exemption from military duty because of one's "religious training and belief."[58] Further, it ruled out "essentially political, sociological, or philosophical views or a merely personal code."[59] However, the Supreme Court expanded §6(j) to mean:

> ...the test of belief "in a relation to a Supreme Being" is whether a given belief that is sincere and meaningful occupies a place in the life of its possessor parallel to that filled by the orthodox belief in God of one who clearly qualifies for the exemption.[60]

One result of defining religion as "sincerity of belief" is that it stripped religion of any objective content and reduced it to merely a psychological disposition.

Welsh v. United States[61] took Seeger one step further towards the perception of religion as arbitrary belief. Whereas the Court understood §6(j) as originally ruling out "essentially political, sociological, or philosophical views or a merely personal code" as adequate to ground conscientious objection to war, they now allowed for it. Welsh admitted that he did not believe in God. Yet, concurring with Justice Blackmun, Justice Harlan wrote, "To comport with that clause, an exemption must be 'neutral' and include those whose belief emanates from a purely moral, ethical, or philosophical source."[62] Whereas other areas of inquiry have specific content, the courts took on the position that religion is merely beliefs that are "sincere and meaningful."[63] In doing so, the Court legally stripped religion of any objective content that can be scrutinized.

Seeger and Welsh may have merely exemplified that which was already engrained in the minds of those in the legal community. However, the result of treating religious reasoning in such a way secured its place in the private sphere. Just as judges use this understanding of religion to protect religious liberty, they also use it to protect society from religion. While dissenting in *McGowan v. Maryland*, Justice Douglas stated that the U.S. Constitution guaranteed "freedom from religion."[64] According to Hitchcock, though the framers intended to protect non-religious citizens from religious coercion, it is not the case that religious beliefs should be diminished in the presence of secular beliefs.[65]

2.4b Secularism as the Default Position

Some scholars argue that the courts have tended to treat secularism as the default position in matters of church and state. Robert P. George writes the following:

> On the question of the place of religion and religiously informed moral judgment in public life, orthodox secularism stands for the strict and absolute separation of not only church and state, but also faith and public life: no prayer, not even an opportunity for silent prayer, in public schools; no aid to parochial schools; no displays of religious symbols in the public square; no legislation based on the religiously informed moral convictions of legislators or voters.[66]

Many court cases illustrate George's and others' concern. Still yet, many of these cases have been arrived at by use of the principle of neutrality.

2.4b.1 The Principle of Neutrality

As stated in chapter one, those in the legal community perceive issues of church and state through schemas. Many in the legal community perceive religion negatively. As I showed earlier, the courts often perceive religion as irrational, divisive, dangerous, and coercive. Further, many judges and legal scholars have argued for the complete privatization of religion. From this negative perception of religion the courts have taken on the principle of neutrality.

In *Lemon v. Kurtzman*[67] Justice Burger formulated the Lemon test to enforce neutrality. This test consists of three prongs:

1. The government's action must have a secular legislative purpose;
2. The government's action must not have the primary effect of either advancing or inhibiting religion;
3. The government's action must not result in an excessive government entanglement with religion.[68]

Briefly stated, the principle of neutrality states that government should neither advance nor inhibit religion. However, because the rules of neutrality are drawn from a religiously negative schema, the court's concept of it arguably favors secularism. Moreover, that which motivates the enforcement of or siding with secular ideas is often the presuppositions of *potential* problems rather than *actual* problems that are occurring between church and state.

Justice Burger argued strongly for the potential religious offense to the public in *Lemon v. Kurtzman*.[69] Burger's opinion interprets the Establishment Clause as a means to prevent religious entanglement. That is, actions that have potential to lead to the establishment of a national church or religion are declared unconstitutional.

Burger argued that there was "…grave *potential* for excessive entanglement…" with the "…Roman Catholic elementary schools of Rhodes Island."[70] He went on to say "the *potential* for impermissible fostering of religion is present."[71] *Lemon v. Kurtzman* was not a case of an actual establishment of a church or religion; instead, it served as a fence to prevent the possibility of religious entities benefiting from the state.

Burger founded his prevention of entanglement on his perception of religion's "divisive political potential."[72] The justice wrote, "but political division along religious lines was one of the principal evils against which the First Amendment was intended to protect. The potential divisiveness of such conflict is a threat to the normal political process."[73] To prevent this potential set of problems, the courts have most often ruled in favor of secularism. Not only does the principle of neutrality often presuppose the schema of the theologico-political problem, but also it implies that religion is epistemically inferior, private, and a matter of arbitrary choice that can be picked up and set down at will.

John Witte argues that the "Court's first step on the path to neutrality in general came in *Jones v. Wolf*"[74] to solve an inner-church dispute.[75] Justice Blackmun stated:

> The primary advantages of the neutral principles approach are that it is completely secular in operation, and yet flexible enough to accommodate all forms of religious organization and polity. The method relies exclusively on objective, well-established concepts of trust and property law familiar to lawyers and judges.[76]

Implicit in Blackmun's argument is the claim that the principle of neutrality, which is secular, is better for solving inner-church disputes than is the claimants' own theological mechanism. The reason being is that it "relies exclusively on objective…concepts…. This is in contrast to the perception of religious reasoning to be purely subjective as Justice Brennan asserted in the *Milivojevich* case."[77] For religious entities to accept the principle of neutrality as understood here requires one to acquiesce to a particular schema that is less than congenial to religious beliefs.

Witte contends that in 1986 the Supreme Court used the principle of neutrality to interpret the Free Exercise Clause as permitting "the Air Force to prohibit a rabbi from wearing a yarmulke as part of his military uniform."[78] Rather than the religious liberty being placed in the hands of the rabbi, the Court gave it to the government entity. The reasoning was that the standards of uniformity and discipline outweighed the rabbi's religious interests. Rehnquist reasoned:

> The First Amendment does not prohibit the challenged regulation from being applied to the petitioner, even though its effect is to restrict the wearing of the headgear required by his religious beliefs. That Amendment does not require the military to accommodate such practices as wearing a yarmulke in the face of its view that they would detract from the uniformity sought by dress regulations. Here, the Air Force

has drawn the line essentially between religious apparel that is visible and that which is not, and the challenged regulation reasonably and evenhandedly regulates dress in the interest of the military's perceived need for uniformity.[79]

Like the cases of Ward and Keeton, the rabbi was faced with a strong coercive force. Rabbi Goldman had the choice of adhering to his religious convictions and facing charges from the Uniform Code of Military Justice (UCMJ) or capitulating to the coercive forces of the government and violating his conscience.

The principle of neutrality places a strong burden on religionists to prove that they have in fact been offended. Justice Souter made this clear in *Lee v. Weisman* when he wrote:

> Religious students cannot complain that omitting prayers from their graduation ceremony would, in any realistic sense, "burden" their spiritual callings. To be sure, many of them invest this rite of passage with spiritual significance, but they may express their religious feelings about it before and after the ceremony. They may even organize a privately sponsored baccalaureate if they desire the company of likeminded students.[80]

Because the students can pray in private, they are presumed to not be offended in any legal sense. This is in contrast to secularists, who by default are often presupposed to be offended by the potential of religious entanglement.

Justice Souter defended the Weisman's freedom from religious coercion by writing:

> That government must remain neutral in matters of religion does not foreclose it from ever taking religion into account. The State may "accommodate" the free exercise of religion by relieving people from generally applicable rules that interfere with their religious callings.[81]

Whereas the Court accommodated the beliefs of Weisman's atheism by disallowing public prayer and changed the meaning of §6(j) of the Universal Military Training and Service Act to accommodate Welsh and Seeger, they expected Rabbi Goldman, Julia Ward, and Jenifer Keeton to show accommodation by adopting the secular position.

2.4b.2 Secularism Enforced: *Lemon v. Kurtzman*

This case has influenced a great many cases. According to the Eastern District Court of Louisiana:

> The Supreme Court applies the Lemon criteria in almost all Establishment Clause cases. "Since 1971, the Court has decided 31 Establishment Clause cases. In only one

> instance, the decision of *Marsh v. Chambers*…has the Court not rested its decision on the basic principles described in *Lemon*."[82]

Because the Lemon test requires all government action to be secular and free from religious entanglement, religious reason is *a priori* ruled as a violation of the Establishment Clause.

In offering his dissenting opinion in the case *Capitol Square Review Board v. Pinette*, Justice Stevens argued for the enforcement of these secular principles.[83] Stevens argued that "The Establishment Clause should be construed to create a strong presumption against the installation of unattended religious symbols on public property…" and that "the sequence of sectarian displays disclosed by the record in this case illustrates the importance of rebuilding the 'wall of separation between church and State' that Jefferson envisioned."[84] Stevens' "strong presumption of separation" is based on the idea that:

> …when religious symbols are involved, the question of whether the state is "appearing to take a position" is best judged from the standpoint of a "reasonable observer." It is especially important to take account of the perspective of a reasonable observer who may not share the particular religious belief it expresses. A paramount purpose of the Establishment Clause is to protect such a person from being made to feel like an outsider in matters of faith, and a stranger in the political community. If a reasonable person could perceive a government endorsement of religion from a private display, then the State may not allow its property to be used as a forum for that display.[85]

Stevens argues that since it is possible that a reasonable person might perceive private religious items placed on public property as an endorsement by that government, it should be disallowed. He believes allowing the placement of religious items on public property is wrong because a reasonable observer might feel like a "stranger in the political community." Yet, this is exactly the claim being made by many religious groups. A reasonable observer may perceive the disallowing of religious items to be displayed by private parties in the public square as inhibiting their religious activity. This would violate the second prong of the Lemon test, which states that the government's action must not have the primary effect of either advancing or inhibiting religion. Moreover, like the court's "reasonable person," religionists may feel estranged from the political community. Those in the religious communities may perceive themselves as being treated as less than worthy of respect. It may be the case that the courts treat religious ideas as outside of reason and thus they are outside of respect.

There are, however, many examples of religious statements and images connected to the federal and state governments. For example, the United States' dollar bill illustrates God's "eye of providence."[86] All American currency and many federal and state buildings contain the statement "In God We Trust." Moreover, public schools have their students recite the Pledge of Allegiance, which includes the phrase "under God." These symbols and actions have not gone unchallenged.

Atheist Michael Newdow has brought several religion cases before the court. Two of his goals have been to remove the phrase "In God We Trust" from U.S. currency and to forbid the phrase "under God" in the Pledge of Allegiance.[87] So far, Newdow has been unsuccessful. However, this does not mean that the courts have decided these cases based on purely accommodationist attitudes. In *Newdow v. Congress*, the Supreme Court had to overturn the Ninth Circuit Court's decision, which ruled the words "under God" to be unconstitutional.[88] The Supreme Court reasoned that the recitation is secular in purpose. The Court opined:

> The Pledge also has the permissible secular effect of promoting an appreciation of the values and ideals that define our nation. The recitation of the Pledge is designed to evoke feelings of patriotism, pride, and love of country, not of divine fulfillment or spiritual enlightenment. In sum, the students are simply supporting the nation through their Pledge "to the Flag of the United States of America and to the Republic for which it stands." Thus, the Pledge passes Lemon's second prong.[89]

In this case, the Court allowed the words "under God," by stripping them of any theological meaning. Had the Court recognized the theological meaning of the two words "under God," it most likely would have upheld the lower court's decision. With that said, the Court did not allow a breach in the "wall." Instead, the justices maintained their secular position by denying that the words had any religious content.

Just as in *Newdow v. Congress*, U.S. District Judge Frank C. Damrell Jr. rejected Newdow's attempt to remove "In God We Trust" from U.S. currency. Damrell said "the minted words amounted to a secular national slogan..."[90] Again, the words are accommodated, yet they are deprived of their religious meaning. The courts use the notion of a civil religion to accommodate religious language.[91] In this sense, there is accommodation; yet, the courts tolerate the words only inasmuch as they are figures of speech.

Many in the legal community understand the Establishment Clause as enforcing strict separation of religious ideas and state. Because of this, the courts tend to perceive any legislation or political entities that are organically connected to a theological tradition in any way as violating this principle.[92] For example, in 1980 District Court Judge Engels found dual enrollment of students at a Catholic school to be a violation of the Establishment Clause. He did so, even while admitting "abundant proof supports the defendants' claim that the program has been operated smoothly over the years by honest administrators...,"[93] and that there was "not one instance of religious intolerance or strife."[94] Judge Engels justified his opinion by stating:

> Under such circumstances it is particularly difficult for the court to explain to the defendants why such an otherwise worthwhile state of affairs cannot be allowed to continue and why a federal court should feel the need to intervene at all. The short and dispositive answer, of course, is that the program clearly violates the Establishment Clause of the First Amendment as it has been interpreted over the years by the United States Supreme Court. Beyond that, however, is the historical perspective in which the First Amendment was adopted and the role it has played in fostering a robust democratic society in which religious freedom exists to enrich the lives of its citizens.[95]

Judge Engels applied the principle of strict separation even to a case that acted as a counter example to the claim that religious accommodation results in civil strife.

Many religionists do not perceive strict separation as an appropriate answer to issues of church and state. This is because they are tethered to their religious beliefs. People conform to that which they believe; and from this, they influence culture. Hitchcock writes, "…it is precisely the 'culture wars'—the points at which culture affects public policy—that are the locus of the problem."[96] Secularism asks religionists to leave that which informs the most important issues in life at home when acting as citizens. The courts enforced this position in *Ward v. Wilbanks*[97] and *Keeton v. Wiley.*[98] As stated earlier, Ward and Keeton were required to counsel students as though their religious beliefs had no influence on their profession in the public schools.

For citizens to leave all theological justifiers "at home"—if that were possible—would by default mean political defeat for many citizens over the most hotly contested moral debates in the United States. For example, cases concerning abortion, euthanasia, Darwinian evolution, and the nature of marriage are greatly informed by religion. If citizens act according to secular liberal principles, then they may actually act against their religious convictions. This means a good liberal could vote pro-choice, not because she believes abortion to be morally neutral but because she is voting for the liberty of individuals to make moral choices for themselves, free from coercion.[99] Hitchcock argues that:

> Liberalism emphasizes rights so strongly that it overlooks the question of the good that individuals should pursue in their lives, political rights being taken as prior to the good itself. Liberal thought cannot conceive of persons belonging to communities bound by moral ties that are antecedent to choice, an attitude that inevitably sees strong religious groups as dangerous.[100]

Liberalism not only emphasizes individual rights but also prioritizes liberty above all else. Moreover, the liberal position maintains that individuals decide the good for themselves. Rather than the individual being free to choose to act towards that which is good, she perceives herself as free to attribute goodness to her choices.

2.5 Summary

Federal and state judges are not always in agreement, especially over religious issues. They come from different backgrounds and have differing degrees of religious commitment that will color their perceptions of law and policy. However, a case has been made that there is a trend that American judges and legal scholars have followed. This trend is to perceive religion through a schema that places religion in a very negative light. Much of the current legal community describes religious knowledge, religious history, the relationship between church and state, and religious proponents in negative terms.[101]

From this negative perception of religious reasoning, there has emerged the enforcement of secularism in the public square. The courts largely perceive secularism as preventative. This attitude serves to protect civil government from the potential harm they fear religious reasoning brings with it.

As this chapter was merely to show that there is a schema through which many judges and legal scholars perceive religious reasoning, I intend to illustrate further how schemas direct legal scholars and judges to these perceptions of the history of church and state and the original intent of the framers in the following chapter.

Historical Schemas: Original Intent and the Lenses of Separation and Accommodation

Most Americans trust that the American constitutional framers chose the correct form and application of government. Americans' treatment of the country's original documents is almost on par with that of scripture. The correctness of the founders is rarely denied; instead, historians, activists, and judges argue over correct interpretation of the framers' words and how their contemporaries understood them. Those in the discussion often use the framers' predecessors to show a lineage of thought. Interlocutors often cite Roger Williams,[1] John Locke,[2] Thomas Jefferson,[3] James Madison,[4] and the Federalist Papers[5] as the key to unlocking the proper relation between religious ideas and the state. The framers' words are used to justify coercive legislation and as a guide to decide court cases. Because participants in the discussion most often use Thomas Jefferson's writings to justify their claims, I will pay particular attention to how differing scholars have portrayed him.[6]

In this chapter I will continue to further the thesis that schemas allow some beliefs to enter one's noetic structure and filter other beliefs out. Whereas the last chapter focused primarily on how the legal community perceives religious reasoning and practice, this chapter will focus on how schemas affect how different people construe history. To do this, I will contrast a separationist and accommodationist construal of the American framers' intentions concerning the relation and role of religion in the American constitutional experiment. Specifically, I will use two accounts of history that pertain to church and state and original intent.

One such construal of history comes from Isaac Kramnick' and R. Lawrence Moore's book, *The Godless Constitution*.[7] Kramnick and Moore represent a way of reading the framers that is colored by their separationist schema. This work is most certainly a separationist account of how the framers understood the relationship between church and state. The authors write that they intend to lay out the case for "what we call the party of the godless Constitution and of godless politics."[8] To make sure they succeeded in laying out their case, the following was written as a response on the Wallbuilders' website:

> Cornell Professors Isaac Kramnick and Laurence Moore assert that the Founding Fathers were a collective group of atheists, agnostics, and deists who deliberately set out to create a secular government. Unfortunately, this text has become a staple of many universities across the country; and law reviews, courts, and other professors now cite this work as an authoritative source to "prove" the Founding Fathers' alleged lack of religious beliefs.[9]

Kramnick and Moore attribute strong separationist meanings to the words of the framers.[10] Daniel Dreisbach recognizes the authors' schematic history in *The Godless Constitution* and writes:

> The book illustrates what is pejoratively called "law office history." That is, the authors, imbued with the adversary ethic, selectively recount facts, emphasizing data that support their own prepossessions and minimizing significant facts that complicate or conflict with their biases. The professors warn readers of this on the second page when they describe their book as a "polemic" that will "lay out the case for one" side of the debate on the important "role of religion in public and political life."[11]

Because others have recognized the schematic nature of their understanding of the framers, Kramnick and Moore's work will serve as a good foil for an accommodationist construal of history.

In contrast, I will use Garrett Ward Sheldon's book *The Political Philosophy of Thomas Jefferson* to give an accommodationist account of history.[12] Sheldon's text gives a much more congenial account of religious history than Kramnick and Moore's work. Furthermore, to the extent that Sheldon is correct in his assessment of how the framers' writings about church and state were originally understood, Kramnick and Moore are incorrect and vice versa. Before I contrast the two historical schemas, I must give a definition of both separationism and accommodationism.

3.1 Separation vs. Accommodation

3.1a Separation

According to John Witte, separationism is rooted historically "in the writings of eighteenth-century Enlightenment and Evangelical groups."[13] The motivation for separation was to end the rivalries that made use of religious alliances between ecclesiastical and political entities. Separationists argue that religious doctrines or groups should not enjoy any "special aid, support, privilege, or protection...."[14] Moreover, separationists believe that "the state should not predicate its laws on religious premises nor direct them to religious purposes."[15] Strict forms of separationism, which are based on enlightenment principles, are intended to protect the state from religious interference.[16] In line with this thinking, strict separationists tend to perceive any correlation of religion and state as a breach in the wall of separation.[17]

3.1b Accommodation

Accommodationists, on the other hand, "are the modern heirs of eighteenth-century Puritan and Civic Republican groups."[18] Strong versions of accommodationism state that "every polity must support some form of public religion, some common morals and mores to undergird and support the plurality of protected private religions."[19] The modern formulation of accommodationism is much more modest. The current form of accommodation suggests that religious belief may support polity instead of being required to do so. Also, current accommodationism allows for some overlap of ecclesiastical and state entities. The 1952 case *Zorach v. Clauson* is an excellent example of contemporary accommodationism. Justice Douglas wrote:

> We are a religious people whose institutions presuppose a Supreme Being. We guarantee the freedom to worship as one chooses. We make room for as wide a variety of beliefs and creeds as the spiritual needs of man deem necessary. We sponsor an attitude on the part of government that shows no partiality to one group and that lets each group flourish according to the zeal of its adherents and the appeal of its dogma. When the state encourages religious instruction or cooperates with religious authorities by adjusting the schedule of public events to sectarian needs, it follows the best of our traditions. For it then respects the religious nature of our people and accommodates the public service to their spiritual needs.[20]

For the purposes of this book, I will be using the strict version of separationism and the contemporary understanding of accommodationism.

Strict separationists and accommodationists both have the same documents available to them, yet they arrive at different conclusions. This is especially true in cases concerning religion. In light of this, one can draw a line between separationism and accommodationism and observe on which side public policy and court rulings fall.

3.2 Jefferson as a Secularist

Throughout his life and career Thomas Jefferson made several important claims that touch on religion: some of these included the existence of God and the founding of laws on religion;[21] others were on the role of the clergy and their duty to cultivate rational moral citizens;[22] he also spoke of the nature of man;[23] and given the aforementioned, he talked of how man should live within society.[24] There is no debate over what Thomas Jefferson wrote; the debate is over what his original audience understood his writings to communicate. Those who debate such things use Jefferson's influences to support their claims for or against strict separation of church and state. I will discuss two individuals specifically—Roger Williams and John Locke—who influenced the framers' understanding of the religion clauses. In doing so, I am not offering a historical account of these thinkers. I am using the interpretation of Jefferson's, Williams', Locke's, and others' writings to show that it is one's schema that does much of hermeneutical work. It is because of this that I will pay less attention to such thinkers as James Madison and Alexander Hamilton. Instead, I will be discussing how interpretations of their work differ depending on whether one is influenced by a separationist or accommodationist schema. In the following sections I will address how a separationist schema has affected Isaac Kramnick and R. Laurence Moore's reading of Roger Williams, John Locke, and, in turn, Thomas Jefferson.

3.2a Kramnick and Moore's Construal of the Origins of Separation

Contemporary public opinion tends to perceive the American founding fathers as secularists. In their influential book, *The Godless Constitution*,[25] Isaac Kramnick and R. Laurence Moore paint a picture of the history of the United States Constitution as intentionally a secular document.[26] They suggest that secular ideas preceded the Constitution, and it was upon these ideas that the document was based.[27] They rest their argument on a chain of ideas from three thinkers: Roger Williams, John Locke, and Thomas Jefferson.

3.2b Roger Williams

Kramnick and Moore describe Roger Williams as somewhat of a proto-separationist. Though these authors use stronger separationist terms for Williams, they point out that he had a deep mistrust for Catholics, Jews, and Quakers. Williams did not even allow these religious groups into his state.[28] Other scholars recognize this about Williams as well. Philip Hamburger points out that Williams was extremely anti-clerical.[29] Williams believed that those who attended churches under paid clergy were part of the apostate church.[30] Williams' understanding of the clergy was entirely informed by his theology. Yet, Kramnick and Moore almost ignore the religious influence on Williams' push for separation that others include. Instead, Kramnick and Moore focus on Williams' desire for tolerance.[31] In painting the picture of Williams as a separationist hero, the authors describe how they perceive the world in which he lived. Kramnick and Moore write:

> In order to appreciate the shock waves caused by that last complaint of Williams, we must remember that the first English colonists who came to North America had no intention of establishing religious freedom, in the sense that we understand the concept. Most English colonists throughout the seventeenth century and for much of the eighteenth little valued the sort of religious toleration that most of us now take for granted. Rather, they were heirs to the ideal of the Christian commonwealth, an ideal as old as the New Testament and as current as the agenda of today's Christian right.[32]

Kramnick and Moore perceive the world in which Roger Williams lives as an unenlightened world indeed. Keeping with this perception, the authors highlight the fact that the officials of Massachusetts Bay colony forced Williams to leave because he criticized them for their "religious intolerance."[33]

Kramnick and Moore do admit that Williams was a highly religious man, and it was from his love for God that he drew most of his conclusions concerning the relation between the church and state. The authors also state that "the underpinning of his radical views was strictly religious."[34] Like most of his interlocutors, Williams believed in religious truth. Yet, unlike Williams' desire for separation of the clergy from state business, Kramnick and Moore fail to incorporate the importance of his belief in religious knowledge. That is, they accept his religious reasoning as long as it serves to conclude separationism but not if it can inform one about statecraft.

Kramnick and Moore focus on how Williams believed that governments throughout history have been wisely ruled by those who were not Christians. Given that governments do not need a religious leader, Williams argued, it is unnecessary for the state to enforce religion. The authors point to Williams' strong hatred for the Catholic Church, and his belief that if the state were to be wedded to the church, then it would result in pre-reformation type conditions.[35] Kramnick and Moore's depiction of Roger Williams is that of a separationist who viewed the separation of church and state as a necessary shield from the corrupting force of the church.

While Kramnick and Moore do pay tribute to Williams' love for God, they unevenly emphasize his desire for separation. The authors ask and answer three questions for Williams:

> Should civil magistrates necessarily be godly men or religious believers? Second, if it is granted that the state should not support churches financially, should government in other direct or indirect ways promote religion? Third, is religious belief ever relevant to public policy?[36]

For the first two questions, Kramnick and Moore say that Williams would answer in the negative. These authors constructed and answered questions for Roger Williams according to their interpretive schema. This is not to say that Kramnick and Moore are incorrect in their exegesis of Williams' writings. However, their predisposition to perceive the history of church and state as rife with problems more than likely causes them to draw lopsided conclusions. Even if Williams did promote the idea that godliness is not necessary for wise leadership, strict separation does not necessarily follow from the claim. One could grant that the societies lived and thrived under atheist leadership and still maintain that claims consistent with religious reasoning played a part in how these leaders governed and the societies flourished.

As far as Kramnick and Moore's second question concerning financial support of religious entities, the authors merely answer the question for Williams without any reasons for doing so. Hamburger points out that Williams believed that those who take a wage for the spreading of the Gospel were not legitimate servants of the Lord.[37] This is a theological statement about ecclesiology, not a statement about the duties of the government. Here again, a separationist conclusion is allowed in by Kramnick and Moore's schema even though it is based on Williams' theology.

Regarding the third question, asking whether religious belief is relevant to public policy, Kramnick and Moore answered this by stating that "Williams would have accepted the general proposition that religion is private."[38] The authors reinforce the schema of the subjectivity of religious beliefs. Since religious reasoning is outside the purview of the senses, the authors understand it as not being accessible to the public. Regardless of whether they knowingly do so, Kramnick and Moore embrace a doxastic schema of methodological naturalism to separate what they perceive to be opinionated statements of theology from statements of fact, and then they gratuitously place their conclusions on the lips of Roger Williams.[39] Even if Kramnick and Moore were to conclude that Williams was no strict separationist by the twenty-first century's standards, they have still used him to give a schematic history of church and state that influences the perception of the progress towards separation *as* the way things ought to be.

The schema through which Kramnick and Moore perceive Williams causes them to overlook the fact that his reasoning was mostly theological. Williams did not believe that religious knowledge was unavailable; he believed that the anti-christ rose and operated through the established clergy.[40] Williams did not want religion in general separated from the state; he wanted to rid the government of actions that he considered to be damnable. Williams writes, "The provocation of the holy eyes is great in all courts throughout the nation, by millions of legal oaths, which if not redressed, may yet be a fire kindled from his jealousie [sic]; who will not hold him guiltless which taketh his name in vain."[41] Williams believed the anti-christ to be using the state churches to keep citizens away from Christ. He stated:

> The free permitting of the consciences and meetings of conscionable and faithful people throughout the nation, and the free permission of the nation to frequent such assemblies, will be one of the principal meanes [sic] and expedients (as the present state of Christianity stands) for the propagating and spreading of the Gospel of the Son of God.[42]

Williams' motive for separation was to ensure that citizens embraced the true Gospel. Thus, not only was his reasoning theological, but so too was his motive. Though Williams' separation would fail both the religious motive test[43] and as a form of public reason,[44] Kramnick and Moore perceive him as a separationist hero.

3.2c John Locke

Kramnick and Moore describe John Locke's theory as "purely negative."[45] They suggest that for Locke the government's chief task is to "play umpire"[46] for the individual citizens and to protect them during their attempt to gain material wealth and prosperity.

The authors say that Locke's aim of government was not to direct its citizens to virtue; nor was it to propagate religious beliefs for the betterment of society. They see Locke as proposing a form of a socially contracted government that served as an agent of landowning individuals to protect their lives, liberty, and property.[47]

Kramnick and Moore call Thomas Jefferson, Patrick Henry, and Benjamin Franklin "disciples of Locke."[48] It is to Locke's works, specifically *Two Treaties of Government*, that the authors credit the godless constitution.

Whereas there are many differences in Roger Williams and John Locke, the authors arrive at some of the same conclusions from the works of Williams in their exegesis of Locke. One of these conclusions is that Locke perceived religious belief as a matter of conscience. Second, they argue that Locke viewed religious beliefs as private.[49] The third conclusion was that the founders so closely followed Locke that their form of liberalism gave no special place to the church in secular politics.

From this schema one might conclude that the framers so closely followed Locke as to employ all of his views concerning church and state. One might also conclude that since Locke saw religion as a matter of conscience and that government should stay out of such matters, then the framers intentionally tried to form a government that separated itself from religion altogether. Finally, one can draw the conclusion that just as Kramnick and Moore's Locke relegated religious reasoning to the private subjective opinions of autonomous individuals that lacked enough justificatory power to include in reasons concerning civil government, so too did the framers of the godless constitution.

Kramnick and Moore emphasized many correlatives between John Locke and the framers. In their book, the authors used Locke to support their claim that the framers' intention for the United States Constitution was to create a government that was strictly separated from religion. Kramnick and Moore write:

> The framers were writing into America's fundamental law the Lockean liberal ideal. They created a demystified state, stripped of all religious ambition. It would not serve the glory of God; it would merely preside over the commercial republic, an individualistic and competitive America preoccupied with private rights and personal autonomy.[50]

Just like their construal of Roger Williams, Kramnick and Moore overemphasized some of Locke's statements and left out other statements of his altogether. Moreover, in their claim that the framers were disciples of Locke, Kramnick and Moore included only separationist correlatives. The authors pay no attention to areas where the framers and Locke disagreed philosophically or agreed theologically.

The authors' schema does not include Locke's use of religious reasoning to ground his notion of rights. Kramnick and Moore's schema also omits the religious arguments for the origin of rights, whether such a thing as the divine right of kings exists, or whether God has endowed man by nature with rights.[51] Instead,

Kramnick and Moore superimpose a secular social contract theory on the history of Roger Williams, John Locke, and Thomas Jefferson.

3.2d A Separationist Construal of Jefferson's Conclusions

Kramnick and Moore create a construal of Jefferson and his compatriots that sought emancipation from the "strong menace of religious tyranny."[52] The authors perceive the founders as contemplating the notion that "millions of Europeans had died in the two centuries of religious wars between Protestants and Catholics that followed Martin Luther's break from Rome that began in Wittenberg, Germany."[53] Kramnick and Moore go so far as to suggest that the real tyranny referred to in the Declaration of Independence was religious tyranny. The authors write:

> It should be no surprise, then, that behind the godless Constitution crafted by the framers were ideas about church and state borrowed from the mother country. Nowhere is this more evident than in what the founding fathers meant by tyranny.
>
> In the less well-known passages of his Declaration of Independence, Thomas Jefferson offered a long list of "oppressive measures" and "repeated injuries and usurpations" to prove that George III sought the "establishment of an absolute tyranny over these states." "Tyranny" is the key word here. It is a word full of emotive force in American political culture, and at our founding it is the emancipation from the tyranny of George III and his Parliaments that is enshrined in America's basic document. So persuasive is the theme that one is not surprised when visiting the beautiful Jefferson Memorial in Washington today to see emblazoned on its rotunda other memorable words of Thomas Jefferson—"I have sworn upon the altar of God eternal hostility against every form of tyranny over the mind of man."
>
> These words of Jefferson were intended by the memorial's designers in 1943 to convey America's enduring commitment, as a religious people, to oppose vigilantly political oppression and tyranny in all its forms—be it that of George III, German Kaisers, Hitler, or Japanese aggressors. But political tyranny, it turns out, was not what Jefferson intended by those words; it was religious tyranny.[54]

In the letter of which Kramnick and Moore speak, Jefferson was denouncing some in the Episcopal and Congregational churches who desired to have their denominations nationalized. Jefferson writes:

> …The delusion into which the X. Y. Z. plot shewed [sic] it possible to push the people; the successful experiment made under the prevalence of that delusion on the clause of the constitution, which, while it secured the freedom of the press, covered also the freedom of religion, had given to the clergy a very favorite hope of obtaining

an establishment of a particular form of Christianity thro' the U. S.; and as every sect believes its own form the true one, every one perhaps hoped for his own, but especially the Episcopalians & Congregationalists. The returning good sense of our country threatens abortion to their hopes, & they believe that any portion of power confided to me, will be exerted in opposition to their schemes. And they believe rightly; for I have sworn upon the altar of god, eternal hostility against every form of tyranny over the mind of man. But this is all they have to fear from me: & enough too in their opinion, & this is the cause of their printing lying pamphlets against me, forging conversations for me with Mazzei, Bishop Madison, &c., which are absolute falsehoods without a circumstance of truth to rest on; falsehoods, too, of which I acquit Mazzei & Bishop Madison, for they are men of truth.[55]

Even though the Declaration of Independence spells out the "repeated injuries and usurpations" of King George III, which say nothing of religious tyranny, Kramnick and Moore perceive this personal letter as evidence of the unspoken motive for the Declaration of Independence.

Kramnick and Moore emphasized that Jefferson received much negative criticism from religionists for his time in France and philosophical discussions. Much of this criticism was during his candidacy for the presidency. On many occasions Jefferson's religious beliefs were cited by those in opposition as reasons not to vote for him. Kramnick and Moore referred to the comments of his detractors as "a heavy dose of anti-intellectualism";[56] thus, they reinforce the schema of religious reasoning or its adherence as irrational.

3.2e Separationist Construal of Religion

Like their previous conclusion about Williams and Locke, Kramnick and Moore believe that Jefferson perceived religion as solely a private matter. They say "that his views on religious practice were expressions of his radical liberal individualism. Religious belief was purely private concern."[57] Also, like his predecessors, Jefferson is credited with viewing liberal democracies as defenders of personal autonomy. Kramnick and Moore construed Jefferson's words as statements that there ought not to be any connection between religion and the state. This is again consistent with the authors' conclusion concerning Roger Williams and John Locke.

The three major themes that run through Kramnick and Moore's book are: the fusing of church and state results in tyranny; Roger Williams and John Locke were strict separationists, and, therefore, so too were the American founders, especially Jefferson; and Roger Williams, John Locke, and Thomas Jefferson all relegated religion to the private sphere. These themes fit well with three perceptions contained within the schema of the theologico-political problem: first, one concerning the negative impact of religious belief on society; second, the notion that religious belief is merely one's subjective opinion; and third, the need for the separation of church and state.

3.2f Accommodationist Concessions

Though Kramnick and Moore are critical of those with whom they disagree, they do acknowledge certain points of agreement. The authors show that Williams, Locke, and Jefferson all were informed by their religious beliefs. They also showed that the three figures perceived religion as good for the individual. Finally, Kramnick and Moore pointed out that Williams, Locke, and Jefferson agreed that the state can coerce one to act, but not to believe. The state can force one to commit hypocrisy, but it cannot change a man's conscience.

If it is true that schemas do affect how one interprets the words and actions of these historical figures, then it should be no surprise that others differ in their conclusions regarding them. I will use the next section to show that there are competing schemas that allow one to perceive the works of the American founders differently. Specifically, the next section will show that one does not need to perceive strict separation as desired by the American founders. Garrett Ward Sheldon's description of Thomas Jefferson serves as a challenge to Kramnick and Moore's schema.

3.3 Jefferson as an Accommodationist

Garrett Ward Sheldon's *The Political Philosophy of Thomas Jefferson* lays out a portrait of each of Thomas Jefferson's religious claims.[58] Sheldon's hermeneutic of Jefferson's work shows a much different attitude towards religious claims than that of Kramnick and Moore. Specifically, Sheldon's work includes writings by Jefferson that tend to support the view that religion has a place in the public sphere. Whereas Kramnick and Moore use Jefferson to support secularism, Sheldon sees in his "mature political philosophy a coherent blending of liberalism, classicism, moral sense psychology, and Christian ethics."[59]

3.3a Jefferson's Public Religion and Truth

Sheldon writes of Thomas Jefferson's sincere belief in God.[60] The author highlights the perception of Jefferson as one who believed that God existed, and that the claim about His existence is not merely a subjective opinion but instead a reality that all could know.[61] Sheldon points out that Jefferson thought that the universities should maintain the presence of the different denominations so as to cultivate the understanding of the essentials of religious truth. According to the author, Jefferson "assumed" that religious claims are knowable, and that discourse between differing sects would better reveal their truth.[62]

Sheldon's picture of Jefferson is not that of a pluralist. His use of history shows that Jefferson had specific religious beliefs that he believed should be woven into the American fabric. Sheldon further asserts that it was Jefferson's desire to create an environment whereby the differing sects maintaining discourse with each other would better converge upon the true "ethical teachings of Jesus."[63] Jefferson believed that the cultivation of these truths would result in a more virtuous society.[64]

Sheldon's history includes Jefferson's claims about how human nature consisted of man's ability to know ethical truths and the freedom to act towards or away from them. He also underscores Jefferson's belief that man could feel sympathy for his fellow man, and that humans could rejoice in their brethren's wellbeing.[65] From these two abilities, Sheldon provides a lens through which man could understand Jefferson's conception of justice. Through this lens one will perceive Jefferson as defining justice to include one's duty towards others more than to oneself.[66]

3.3b Jefferson's Rejection of the Social Contract

Whereas Kramnick and Moore perceived Jefferson as a disciple of Locke and stressed the two historical figures' similarities, Sheldon draws attention to Jefferson's departure from Locke's ideas. Kramnick and Moore contended that Jeffersonian liberalism was based on a social contract. According to Sheldon's history, Jefferson openly rejected the position that justice is founded on a social contract. In Jefferson's response to the notion that liberal democracy is based on such a thing, he writes:

> He [Destutt de Tracy] adopts the principle of Hobbes, that justice is founded in contract solely. I believe, on the contrary, that is an instinct, and innate, that the moral sense is as much a part of our natural constitution as that of feeling, seeing or hearing; as a wise Creator must have seen to be necessary in an animal destined to live in society.[67]

Jefferson argued that if mankind was created for social intercourse, then mankind requires a sense of justice. From the fact that man is created for social intercourse Jefferson concluded that man was created with a sense of justice.[68]

3.3c Jefferson's Perception of Government as a Guide Towards Virtue

Sheldon's history includes Jefferson's views of political society as culminating from a "natural aristocracy of wisdom and virtue."[69] To this end Jefferson saw public education as a means. He wrote:

> My partiality for that division [education wards] is not founded in views of education solely, but infinitely more as the means of a better administration of our government, and the eternal preservation of its republican principles.[70]

This is in contrast to the current perception of education *as* for the purposes of merely obtaining material success for personal gain. According to Sheldon's history, one would conclude that Jefferson rejected this notion vehemently. Sheldon wrote:

> The moral conduct appropriate to this divinely ordained social nature did not, for Jefferson, consist in a primary concern with individual interests or with the building of a moral philosophy on the basis of human selfishness and greed. Rather, this innate moral quality dictated a concern for the good of others, and the whole community: "the essence of virtue is in doing good to others."[71]

In Jefferson's own words:

> Self-love, therefore, is no part of morality. Indeed, it is exactly its counterpart. It is the sole antagonist of virtue, leading us constantly by our propensities to self-gratification in violation of our moral duties to others.[72]

Sheldon's schema of Jefferson's use of the terms of liberal democracies, such as rights, justice, religion, and happiness, is not consistent with how Kramnick and Moore would have them understood.

Sheldon brought forth that which was unspoken by Kramnick and Moore. Whereas John Locke believed that free and equal people should submit to authority for the sole purpose of protection of themselves and their material preservation,[73] Thomas Jefferson believed that man should submit for the common good. Sheldon contrasts contemporary perceptions of liberal democracy to that of Jefferson's. His belief is that the current perception is that one submits for his own private interests rather than for the societal good.[74]

By contrasting Sheldon's work with Kramnick and Moore's it would seem that there are two versions of Thomas Jefferson, one of them being a strict separationist who sees religious reasoning as detrimental to the rights of citizens and one that believes that religious truth should be sought out and fostered by governments and their citizenry. But why is there such a difference in their understanding of these historical figures? Part of the answer to this lies in how contemporary society perceives the nature of knowledge in general and religious knowledge in particular. One question is whether man is free to change his beliefs by an act of the will. Michael Sandel addresses this issue and how it affects one's understanding of original intent. Presuppositions about religious knowledge remain under the surface and often dictate what one's schema focuses in on. I will use the following chapter to show that presuppositions about one's epistemic abilities have changed, and this understanding has been superimposed on the American founders. If it is true that scholars and judges attribute beliefs to the founders that were in fact not there, then their schema has rendered an inaccurate perception of historical reality. Furthermore, I believe that Kramnick and Moore's schema filters out important facts that, if taken into account, would change their conclusion. In the upcoming chapter I will show how Michael Sandel addresses both the epistemic and historical aspects of this claim.

CHAPTER FOUR

Autonomy, Neutrality, and the Diminishing of Religious Conviction

In the previous chapter, I pointed out that most Americans trust the intentions of the Founding Fathers. Thus, it would seem, the legal culture desires to act in accordance to their intentions. However, as I also pointed out, one's schema can greatly affect how one perceives the historical evidence.[1] Because of this, rather than subjecting the evidence to objective analysis, one's schema amplifies some evidence and filters out other evidence. In this chapter I intend to show that the legal culture uses historical schemas to develop approaches to the relation of church and state. Specifically, I will use Michael Sandel's discussion of the federal courts' treatment of religion. Sandel argues that the courts possess a voluntarist conception of religion, and that this was not how the framers understood it. If this is true, then it follows that the current legal culture may have embraced a strict separationist model of religion and politics where one was never intended.

4.1 Federal Courts, Strict Separationism, and the Autonomous Self

Michael Sandel believes that currently the public perceives religious belief *as* merely a choice between commodities rather than convictions of conscience. Sandel argues that since World War II the courts have used this "inadequate" theory of liberalism to inform constitutional law pertaining to religious liberty.[2] According to Sandel, the contemporary understanding of liberalism perceives the individual *as* an unencumbered self. In contrast to Sheldon's interpretation of the Jeffersonian "natural aristocracy of wisdom and virtue"—the end by which education was the means—current perception is that individuals decide the ends for themselves and education plays little to no part in its development. Sandel believes that the current trend is for individuals to dictate for themselves what the good life is and how to pursue it. From this trend emerges the principle that the government is to remain neutral in cases of determining the good. Sandel argues that the federal courts operate from the belief that autonomy of the individual is prior to the good, and it is one's autonomy that should be protected.

4.2 Federal Courts, Autonomy, and Neutrality

4.2a Protecting the Garden from the Wilderness

Sandel points to two lines of argumentation that justify government neutrality towards religion. Like Kramnick and Moore, advocates of the first line suggest that neutrality is good for both the church and the state.[3] Roger Williams employed a metaphor—common to his day—suggesting that the "wall of separation" is to protect the garden from the wilderness. In this sense, one can perceive the meshing church and state as detrimental to the church. According to Sandel, Williams believed that it was government that possessed the destructive force.

Edward Bean Underhill's account of history describes Williams' motivation as originating from this historical figure's hatred for the Church of England, which he considered to be "anti-Christ."[4] Underhill's history points out that Williams refused to join the congregation in Boston because he believed it to be "a weak and sinful compliance with evil."[5] Williams' reasoning behind this was that the Boston congregation allowed its members to assemble and partake in the sacraments with the corrupted Church of England. He believed that since the king "arbitrarily" controlled the state church by informing the clergy to preach against liberty of conscience that it was too impure with which to commune. Williams alleged that this civil encroachment on church affairs was not endemic to the governments in Europe, but it was also present in the colonies. Because of his fear of government intrusion, Williams found resistance by the Salem civil magistrates to his appointment as pastor at their congregation.[6]

The foregoing construal of history allows one to conclude that Roger Williams' greater concern was not that any theologico-political problem was caused by religion; it was instead that the civil leaders of Williams' day overstepped their authority by dictating matters that take place in the garden. Though this construal of history still lends itself to the separation of church and state, it is a perceptual schema that takes religious reasoning seriously and places the deficiency on the untrained statesmen.

Williams was indignant at the fact that governments had killed to maintain what they saw as pure doctrine. He wrote:

> …it is the will and command of God that (since the coming of his Son the Lord Jesus) a permission of the most paganish, Jewish, Turkish, or antichristian consciences and worships, be granted to all men in all nations and countries; and they are only to be fought against with that sword which is only (in soul matters) able to conquer, to wit, the sword of God's Spirit, the Word of God.[7]

Williams believed that government could not turn hearts to God. If it could, then there would be no martyrs.

The sentiment that government could not create Christians carried up to the Revolutionary War as a mainstream of Baptist thought. In 1773, Isaac Backus wrote, "Religious matters are to be separated from the jurisdiction of the state, not because they are beneath the interests of the state but, quite to the contrary, because they are too high and holy and thus are beyond the competence of the state."[8] Backus believed that the civil authorities lacked the ability to rule accurately in matters of theology. It is on the following point that both Williams and Backus were agreed that by attempting to adjudicate over ecclesiastical matters the state steps outside of its area of expertise.[9] The language of Backus and Williams implies that they took religious reasoning seriously.

4.2b Protecting the Wilderness from the Garden

There is no shortage of scholars who perceive the slightest breach of the wall of separation as a potential cause of various forms of civil strife. They are predisposed to believe that otherwise avoidable problems will arise when religion and government are combined. Many jurists and academicians use their perception of the past events of history as an argument for strict separation of church and state. Their focal points are on wars that have been waged in the name of religion as reasons why the two should not be mingled.

Whereas the argument for separation is not new, the perception of wars that were theologically informed *as* unjust because of the religious element is relatively recent. Pre-revolutionary separationists perceived the misguided and theologically untrained civil government as using religious authority to their own ends, as opposed to submitting to religions' peaceful authority. On the other hand, contemporary scholarship often shapes the perception of religious reasoning as the cause of war instead of the instrument of prevention or guidance of how to conduct war justly. If one perceives religious reasoning as a threat to civil peace, then it follows naturally that one would perceive strict separation as the answer.

While Williams was primarily concerned with the health of the church, almost one hundred years later Justice Hugo Black perceived the wall of separation as protection of the citizenry from religion. Justice Black's writing implies that he held a dim view of religion's impact on the state. When delivering the opinion for *Everson v. The Board of Education*, Justice Black wrote:

> In efforts to force loyalty to whatever religious group happened to be on top and in league with the government of a particular time and place, men and women had been fined, cast in jail, cruelly tortured, and killed. Among the offenses for which these punishments had been inflicted were such things as speaking disrespectfully of the views of ministers of government-established churches, nonattendance at those churches, expressions of nonbelief in their doctrines, and failure to pay taxes and tithes to support them.[10]

Justice Black continued the foregoing line of reasoning by stating "that a union of government and religion tends to destroy government and to degrade religion."[11] He wrote that the founders:

> …knew the anguish, hardship and bitter strife that could come when zealous religious groups struggled with one another to obtain the Government's stamp of approval from each King, Queen, or Protector that came to temporary power. The Constitution was intended to avert a part of this danger by leaving the government of this country in the hands of the people, rather than in the hands of any monarch.[12]

In the same opinion, Justice Black said this about the Founders:

> By the time of the adoption of the Constitution, our history shows that there was a widespread awareness among many Americans of the dangers of a union of Church and State. "These people knew, some of them from bitter personal experience, that one of the greatest dangers to the freedom of the individual to worship in his own way lay in the Government's placing its official stamp of approval upon one particular kind of prayer or one particular form of religious services.[13]

Whether it is perceived as the state corrupting the church or the church using the state to further its ends, the recent answer to the issue has been the attempt at government separating itself from all things religious.[14]

4.2c Adoption of Neutrality

The federal courts adopted the principle of neutrality to create a clean separation. Sandel argues that not only is this principle of neutrality currently firmly engrained in the courts' understanding of religious liberty, but also the courts, only question is whether they have applied it correctly.[15]

Individual freedom is one of the founding principles that drives this new discussion of church and state. This is the voluntarist position, which states that the person is an unencumbered self, and he is free to choose both his ends and the means to them. On this view, government neutrality is merely a tool to aid or promote choices for the religiously autonomous person. Not only is the state a tool for choice, but also it is a safeguard against religious coercion. In *Wallace v. Jaffree*, Justice Stevens opined that "religious beliefs worthy of respect are the product of free and voluntary choice by the faithful."[16]

Sandel believes that the voluntarist position is neither how the founders understood the nature of belief nor adequate to ground answers to issues concerning church and state. He argues that neither the founders nor the courts prior to World War II perceived people as unencumbered selves. People, Sandel argues, are not free to believe whatever they want.[17] Freedom does not come in what to believe, but instead one is free to act in light of his beliefs. For the pre-revolutionary writers as well as the founders, religious beliefs were matters of conscience. These religious beliefs could not be unbelieved at will. Sandel states that "coercion can produce hypocrisy but not conviction."[18] It is because we cannot pick up or drop beliefs at will that they are unalienable. In light of this, Sandel concludes that the founders wrote both the Free Exercise Clause and the Establishment Clause with the protection of personal duties that resulted from matters of conscience in mind.

The proposition that neutrality is good for religion is rarely uttered today in the courtrooms by religionists. The vast majority of cases that include arguments for separation are now presented by those who are anti-theistic. Cases involving prayer, the removal of intelligent design curricula, and financial support of faith-based initiatives are not brought before the courts by theists. These cases are virtually always initiated by atheists.[19]

Sandel states that the courts perceive separation as "not only for the sake of the nonbeliever but also for 'the devout believer who fears the secularization of a creed which becomes too deeply involved with and dependent upon the government.'"[20] Is separation "for the sake of the devout believer?" If the federal courts' intent is to provide the best environment for religion to flourish, then they are not acting from a position of neutrality. That is, if the purpose of separation is "for the good of religion," then that purpose would constitute a violation of the principle of neutrality. This is because the courts' motive of separation is to aid the health of religion. If the mechanism of neutrality is successful, then it would result in the advancement of religion. This would violate the principle of both the neutrality and religious motive test.

4.2d Neutrality to Avoid Civil Strife

Of course, the prior analysis is dependent on whether the federal courts are sincere in their belief that the principle of neutrality is for the sake of the religionist and not merely the pacifying of those who resist religious claims. One can easily construe the goals of neutrality as an attempt to appease anti-religious special interest groups. Yet, many legal scholars and jurists couch the discussion in terms of avoiding "civil strife" that comes from accommodation.[21] This language makes use of the assumption that separation is to protect religious believers from the coercion of other religious sects. As I pointed out in chapter two, federal court judges have maintained that they want to stay out of sectarian conflicts, and that support of religious institutions is detrimental to some if not all of them. They claim that supporting religion results in civil discord and harms the religious beliefs of others.

If the goal of neutrality is to avoid civil strife, then one must ask whether the courts have evenly applied the principle. Sandel says that neutrality has in fact not accomplished the task asked of it.[22] Many Americans still perceive there to be much civil strife in the nation; and much of the debate concerns doxastic practices. Also, if the prevention of civil strife is the true motive for governmental neutrality, then it follows that the government should remain neutral in regards to the other belief-forming practices that cause civil strife. Certain political theories cause much unrest; yet, it is rare—if at all—that the federal courts overturn legislation that results from these debates. On the other hand, the courts often do get involved when religious claims are present.

Federal court judges use language that suggests they are concerned only with religious practices offending other religious practices; however, secular scientific, historical, and moral doxastic practices rarely elicit a response from the courts when these practices clash with religious believers' convictions.

4.3 Autonomy, Choice, and Coercion

Sandel says that the argument for neutrality is motivated by the courts' desire to protect individual autonomy and avoid coercion.[23] Sandel also suggests the principle of autonomy flows from the "liberal conception of the person."[24] Briefly stated, the liberal conception of the person is that individuals are free to decide which religious propositions to believe and which ones to reject.

This theme of doxastic voluntarism is consistent with many current federal court decisions. The courts' motive to stay neutral in matters of religion is an attempt to avoid using the coercive power of the state to dictate that which people believe. This principle comes with some higher-ordered presuppositions: first, coercion by nature is wrong;[25] second, coercion is particularly wrong when religious beliefs are involved; and third, that it is possible to actually coerce one into believing religious propositions against their will.

4.3a Necessity of Coercion and the Presupposition of the Objective Good

The protection from coercion principle is too broad. Governments could not exist without using coercion. If coercion is bad in and of itself, then government by nature would violate this principle. Leo Strauss wrote:

> The meaning of political philosophy and its meaningful character is as evident today as it always has been since the time when political philosophy came to light in Athens. All political action aims at either preservation or change. When desiring to preserve, we wish to prevent a change to the worse; when desiring to change, we wish to bring about something better. All political action is then guided by some thought of better and worse. But thought of better and worse implies thought of the good. The awareness of the good which guides all our actions has the character of opinion: it is no longer questioned but on reflection, it proves to be questionable. The very fact that we can question it directs us towards such a thought is the good as is no longer questionable—towards a thought which is no longer opinion but knowledge. All political action has then in itself a directedness towards knowledge of the good: of the good life, or of the good society.[26]

Laws by nature are coercive. Law presupposes the notion of objective value. For example, law operates from the notion that order is objectively better than chaos.[27] The goal of law is to maintain or direct society and the individual towards that which is good. Many legislators, legal scholars, and judges believe that the basic good is autonomy, and that the good is determined by the individual.[28] Yet, when it comes to an objective notion of the good, coercive law says otherwise. Law presupposes that individuals make bad choices; these choices stray from that which they should be directed.[29] Even though the courts speak as if individuals determine the good for themselves, they make judgments based on overarching principles that limit or require action.

The federal courts operate from the notion that the good is relative to individual choice, but by doing so they affirm an objective and universal notion of the good. Sandel says "that the moral basis for the antiestablishment clause is equal respect."[30] On one hand, the courts reject the notion of an objective good, and on the other hand they presuppose it. Many citizens perceive it as inconsistent for one to speak as though it is an ontological fact that people choose the nature of the good for themselves and then to assert that it is objectively wrong for the government to coerce anyone to act or believe against their personal beliefs. This inconsistency is due to the second-order belief that there is no such thing as statements of value and meaning that are objective facts. If statements about the good are relative to individual beliefs, then so too are statements about badness, evil, and the like.

By enforcing the principle that coercion is wrong by nature, the courts violate the first premise that one chooses the good for himself. The statement entails that it is always wrong to coerce anyone to act, from acting, or believe one way. Yet, to use the force of law to apply this principle requires coercing one to act, not to act, or believe in certain ways. Enforcement of the principle requires some people to act—against their will—as if individuals decide the good for themselves, not to act in ways that are contrary to the notion of personal autonomy, and to believe or act as though they believe the first principle against coercion is true. Yet, many people do not believe that the good is something one chooses for himself; when the state uses the law to force one to adhere to this principle—one chooses the good for himself—it violates the first premise that coercion is wrong. The federal courts do not defend this principle against the notion that it is question begging; the courts merely assume that it is correct and they apply it.

The courts operate as though there is at least one objective, publicly reasoned, universal conception of the good; that conception of the good is autonomy. Thus, the courts justify coercion with a concept of the good; this concept maintains the status quo of individual choice, and it aims to prevent governmental violation of one's choices of belief.

4.3b Doxastic Voluntarism and the Notion of the Good

The claim that individuals chose the good for themselves entails the belief that one is free to choose his beliefs at will. According to Sandel, the federal courts assume doxastic voluntarism, and he quotes Justice Stevens as saying:

> The Court has unambiguously concluded that the individual freedom of conscience protected by the First Amendment embraces the right to select any religious faith or no one at all. The conclusion derives support not only from the interest in respecting

the individual's freedom of conscience, but also from the conviction that religious beliefs worthy of respect are the product of free and voluntary choice by the faithful."[31]

Sandel argues that the courts do not respect religious beliefs; instead they respect religious believers. Sandel construes this respect as conditional; the federal courts respect religious believers inasmuch as they are not promoting their beliefs in the public square. However, the courts do protect religious believers from other competing religious beliefs. This protection is consistent with the court's perception of separationism as a tool to solve inner-sectarian squabbles.

Current cases show that the federal courts have been consistent in opining that religious beliefs may be held privately, but these beliefs may not publically inform liberal society's notion of the good. One the other hand, secular beliefs that legislators use to create coercive legislation are often very antagonistic to religious beliefs; yet, the federal courts do not step in to protect the religious citizen from doxastic coercion from secular reasoning. This is consistent with the courts' perceiving religious reasoning as inferior and unimportant when compared to other doxastic practices.

The courts' application of doxastic voluntarism is almost exclusively applied to religious cases. The courts do not perceive individuals as free to choose beliefs from other sources of justification. The federal courts have never stepped in to protect a student's freedom to choose beliefs concerning principles of arithmetic. Should one respect all answers to the problem 2+2? One can imagine what it would be like if a student gave the answer to 2+2 as 5. The teacher would correct the student by telling him that the correct answer is 4. Now imagine that when doing so the student answers back, "Well, I respect your opinion; but given that there is an infinite number of possible answers to this problem, to suggest that you have the correct one is a bit bold. I again respect your personal opinion, but my personal belief is that the answer is 5." It would be very hard to believe indeed that the federal courts would protect the student's free choice of beliefs from the coercive power of the grade book and standardized tests.

The courts would correctly perceive the aforementioned student's intellectual faculties as not properly functioning if the youngster continued failing to arrive at or recognize the correct answer.[32] Yet, the courts use the same type of reasoning as my fictitious student when it comes to questions concerning religion.

The federal courts' treatment of religious doxastic practices is consistent with their language concerning doxastic practices in general. The federal courts perceive other belief-forming practices as superior to religious justification; therefore, they treat other doxastic practices as superior to religious doxastic practices. Whereas the courts treat math, history, and science as areas of inquiry that converge on truth, they treat religion as merely a collection of subjective opinions. The federal courts perceive math, history, and science as objective aspects of reality that once understood are undeniable. On the other hand, the federal judges' language is indicative that they perceive religious beliefs as chosen; this is in contrast to the treatment of other doxastic practices that discover truths to which people submit just as one submits to the truth of 2+2=4. Sandel says that the liberal conception of the person "ill equips the court to secure religious liberty for those who regard themselves as claimed by religious commitments they have not chosen."[33] If one chooses to pick up religious beliefs at will, then one can choose to put down religious beliefs at will. However, religionists cannot unbelieve religious doctrines and there are clashes with state policies because of it.

4.3c Has Neutrality Delivered Its Promise?

Federal courts have defended strict separation in order to avoid civil strife. Sandel says that separation has failed to fulfill its intended purpose. Sandel argues that separation not only has not solved the problem of civil strife but also has in fact caused much more of it. The difference now is that the conflict is not between the differing Christian sects; instead, the friction is between secularists and religionists. The discord is between those who believe that one can know the truth of religious propositions and those who deny this possibility.

Separating church and state in one sense did end sectarian strife. For example, those who take religious reasoning as a legitimate and reliable source of justification for the truth of their beliefs find themselves united with each other against those who relegate religious reasoning to the realm of emotional speculation and wishful thinking. Whereas separation of church and state diminished strife between religious sects it also created strife between religious believers and the state.

4.4 Religious Conviction and Religious Choice

4.4a Sandel on Conviction, Choice, and Original Intent

Sandel makes the case that Jefferson and Madison understood freedom of conscience as the ability to act within one's beliefs without "suffering civil penalties."[34] He contends that these famous framers did not presuppose that individuals were free to choose their religious beliefs at will. Sandel says that autonomy and choice are nowhere to be found in Jefferson's or Madison's writings. He writes, "The only choice referred to in Jefferson's Bill for Establishing Religious Freedom 'is predicated of God, not man.'"[35] In that same document Jefferson penned, "The opinion and beliefs of men depend not on their own will, but follow involuntarily the evidence proposed to their own minds."[36] Jefferson's language echoes Locke's sentiment put to paper in *A Letter Concerning Toleration* that reads, "It is absurd that things should be enjoined by laws which are not in men's power to perform. And to believe this or that to be true, does not depend upon our will."[37] If what Sandel says is true, then to ask religionists to abstain from using religious reasons to support or reject certain coercive legislation may be asking one to do something outside of his control; thus, to demand one to do such a thing would constitute a violation of his conscience. James Madison in "Memorial and Remonstrance" wrote:

> The Religion then of every man must be left to the conviction and conscience of every man: and it is the right of every man to exercise it as these may dictate. This right is in its nature an unalienable right. It is unalienable, because the opinions of men, depending only on the evidence contemplated by their own minds cannot follow the dictates of other men: it is unalienable also, because what is here a right towards men, is a duty towards the Creator.[38]

Sandel points out that Justice Stevens used Madison's words about one's duty from conscience as support for voluntarism.[39]

Madison was arguing against a bill that would have resulted in a tax that was specifically designed to support Christian teaching. The framer contended that this tax could lead the state of Virginia down a slippery slope from general support of Christianity to the enforcement of particular sects within the religion. Though Madison's language is that of separationism, it is grounded on a hierarchy that places the citizen's obedience to "the governor of the universe" prior to obedience to the civil authorities.[40]

Though Madison rejected the notion of state-funded churches, he did not divorce himself from religious reasoning. Madison's words reiterated Roger Williams' opinion that it is not religious reasoning that lacks merit, but instead it is the non-religiously trained civil magistrates who are deficient in their abilities. His argument was for the defense of one's religious duties to God. If one voluntarily can pick up or put down religious beliefs at will, then Madison's argument would not have worked. This is because one could—in order to comply with the state policy—put down privately held religious beliefs while publically acting in accordance with the tax code and pick them back up when he gets home. As shown in chapter two, the federal courts on more than one occasion demanded that citizens do such a thing.[41] Madison argued that since one's duty to God comes before one's duty to the civil government that man should not be placed in such a situation as to come between man and the will of God.

4.4b Autonomy and the Depreciation of Religious Claims

Though the stated goal of contemporary liberalism is to promote and preserve personal autonomy, Sandel argues that the pursuit of this goal actually depreciates religious claims. This is because those who hold religious beliefs do not do so out of preference or choice, but instead they act on them as one submits himself to reality; yet, the federal courts treat individuals as though they are the creators of their own end and purpose. This treatment of theistic religious beliefs can be likened to the choice of topping one adds to his ice cream; that is, these beliefs are treated as though they are subject to one's desire at best and arbitrary and unimportant at worst. Sandel insists that many religious practitioners' perception of religious beliefs is in fact the opposite of how the courts perceive them; believers search for and discover religious truths, and then they assent to these truths in the form of belief.

One may perceive the federal courts' treatment of theistic claims as mere choices as belittling. This is because religionists do not pick their beliefs to conform to their preferences; if this was the case, the believer would never be in the position to submit his will to any duty. This is because the believer would have handpicked the beliefs that he wants to follow. To choose or create beliefs that one does not like and then follow them as though they are duties is irrational. This is not how religious theists perceive the situation; they operate within a doxastic framework to discover that which God desires, they believe that God wants such and such or forbids such and such, and then they submit their will to His authority even at the expense of personal autonomy. Freedom of choice in this sense is not in the form of choosing one's duty, but instead it is whether one acts in accordance to his duty.

Sandel shows several examples where the federal courts have respected duties as though they were not up to the unencumbered citizen.[42] The court defined religion broadly to include non-theistic beliefs that stemmed from "sincerely held beliefs" in the *United States v. Seeger*. In this case, the Court interpreted §6(J) of the Universal Military Training and Service Act broadly, which interpreted "belief" as "in a relation to a Supreme Being," if a "given belief that is sincere and meaningful occupies a place in the life of its possessor parallel to that filled by the orthodox belief in God of one who clearly qualifies for the exemption."[43] This broad application is, as was said previously, for the sake of including more beliefs for the benefits that the Free Exercise Clause supports. The Supreme Court used the Seeger case as precedent to decide *Welsh v. United States*.[44] Welsh was an atheist, yet he sincerely believed that war was wrong; thus, Welsh's sincerely held belief counted as religion and excuse him from the draft. In both of the foregoing cases, the federal courts did not address whether the claimants were rational in their belief formation; instead, the courts respected the duties that arose from the individuals' conscience without asking them to leave those obligations in the private sphere until they returned home from the war.

4.5 Applying Neutrality

In the mid-1960s the courts started applying the principle of neutrality to religion cases. At that time the principle of neutrality served both accommodationists as well as separationists.[45] The principle simply stated is that government should "neither advance nor inhibit religion."[46] The courts used the principle of neutrality specifically to interpret the Establishment Clause as a safeguard against one ecclesiastical body being forced onto the public by those who resided in power over the state.[47] This application is evident in even Justice Black's discussion of the history of church and state relations.[48] Subsequently, the federal courts started using neutrality to interpret the Establishment Clause as a safeguard from any specific religious idea.[49]

In 1970 Supreme Court solidified the principle of neutrality with the *Lemon test*. The Lemon test's three prongs are: (1) the law must be secular in its purpose, (2) the primary effect neither advances nor inhibits religion, and (3) there is no excessive entanglement of church and state.[50] However, critics have argued that the current construction and application of the principle of neutrality are not neutral. If religious ideas enter into the public square, then they fail the Lemon test and constitute an establishment of religion.

Since 1963, the burden was to prove that there was "sustained or is in immediate danger of sustaining some direct injury as a result of the statute's enforcement and not merely that he suffers in some indefinite way in common with people generally."[51] The courts have since relieved claimants of this burden of proof. Now, challenges to the Establishment Clause do not require proof that the state infringed upon one's free exercise of religion.[52] John Witte points out that a single secular veto can overturn a popular law merely because it is too favorable to religion.[53] Conversely, the religionist shoulders the burden of proving that particular legislation has inflicted injury on his religion. Witte writes "a religious claimant cannot use the Free Exercise Clause to claim an individual exemption from a discretionary regulatory decision that happens to 'virtually destroy' its religion."[54]

4.5a Categorizing the Debates: Public Reason or Sectarian Squabbles

Legislators try to enact bills into coercive laws. The citizens vote for those who will enact legislation that best fits their perception of the best society. Their decisions are informed by many beliefs from many different sources; some of these are religious. As said earlier, the courts have treated theistic religious believers as though they have a choice whether to believe religious propositions about reality. The courts treat religious beliefs as though they are outside the purview of discussion concerning the enactment of public policy. The trend is to treat disagreements over policy concerning issues such as sexual ethics, abortion, euthanasia, and the like as two different discussions: one concerning privately held religious beliefs and the other concerning secular public policy.

4.5a.1 Pro-Life: Theological Debate or Different Answer to the Same Question

Many treat the pro-life position as a religious claim. Inasmuch as the premises or conclusion relies on a dualistic account of humanity and is supported by or supportive of the belief in God the reasoning is religious. Because of this genetic association with theism, the courts perceive the pro-life position as a debate over religious ideas; thus, it is something from which they have determined to remain separate. The federal courts' motive is to use what they consider to be objective reasoning. This is in contrast to their perception of religious beliefs, which many judges and scholars believe to be merely subjective.[55] Because judges perceive pro-life arguments as religious, they have eschewed the evidence as though it is an inner-religious debate between churches.

Justice Blackmun made a distinction between religious conclusions and constitutional law. In doing so he relegated religion to the sphere of emotion and opinion. Justice Blackmun writes:

> We forthwith acknowledge our awareness of the sensitive and emotional nature of the abortion controversy, of the vigorous opposing views, even among physicians, and of the deep and seemingly absolute convictions that the subject inspires. One's philosophy, one's experiences, one's exposure to the raw edges of human existence, one's religious training, one's attitudes toward life and family and their values, and the moral standards one establishes and seeks to observe, are all likely to influence and to color one's thinking and conclusions about abortion.
>
> In addition, population growth, pollution, poverty, and racial overtones tend to complicate and not to simplify the problem.
>
> Our task, of course, is to resolve the issue by constitutional measurement, free of emotion and of predilection.[56]

Justice Blackmun perceives a distinction between the legal task and religious beliefs. For the pro-life advocate—as with pro-choice advocates—the debate is about the reality of rights and the government's obligations to protect them. The pro-life conclusions may be informed by and consistent with religious claims, but they are not specific sectarian doctrines from which the state should remain neutral.

Pro-life citizens do not believe that this is a theological debate. Although there is an organic connection between the belief in God and perceiving the unborn as fully human with all the rights as other humans, the argument does not serve to establish or even affirm theism. Moreover, the pro-life position is not endemic to theism; there are many pro-life atheists. Instead, the argument is over the nature of humanity, rights, and the role of government in protecting those rights. Though the pro-life argument is connected to a religious noetic structure, it is not a different question from secular policy; it is a different answer to the same question concerning the nature of that which resides in a woman's uterus during pregnancy.

Even though the pro-life position is tightly tethered to Christian theism, it does not require it. In fact, there are atheist groups that are committed to ending abortion.[57] Moreover, their arguments are not connected to theistic arguments. Speaking for atheist pro-lifers, Kristine Kruszelnicki writes:

> As a secular pro-lifer I believe my case is scientifically and philosophically sound. Science concedes that human life begins at fertilization, so it follows that abortion is ageism and discrimination against a member of our own species, based on characteristics outside of their control. As I listened to another speaker denounce all pro-lifers as "religious bigots who seek to enslave women and occupy vaginas," it bothered me to see the pro-life position dismissed in its entirety alongside other dogmas of religion.[58]

There are those who believe there to be a rising trend in pro-life atheism. Explaining why many atheists are also pro-life J. Hodgson gives two reasons:

> [First]…Science has caught up to the debate.

> In the ancient days of bell bottoms and disco, the nature of abortion was more mysterious than it is today. When mass abortion arrived in Western culture, the science wasn't developed to the point where we could definitively address the issue of when life begins. The debate, very quickly, became packaged up as a war between religious folks adhering to traditional beliefs about life in the womb and modern beliefs about the rights of female autonomy superseding the rights of a "clump of cells".

> As technology and medical science have evolved, there is no doubt about life beginning at conception.

> [Second]…The debate is now a philosophical one about the value of human life.

> Pro-choicers can no longer win debates regarding abortion. New Wave schooled pro-life activists such as Jojo Ruba and Stephanie Gray routinely wipe the stage with

> pro-choice challengers using logic, and as a result the pro-choice crowds have resorted to simply shouting them down.[59]

The atheists in this case are clearly answering the same question as the theists; is that which is inside the womb the type of entity that has the right to life? The atheist pro-life position shows that this is not a religious argument. This is true even if theism does have something to add to the discussion. It is because many pro-choice advocates perceive the pro-life position as religious and religious arguments as mere matters of personal preference—as Sandel suggests—that they believe the default position should be with a woman's choice. The fact that a political position can be derailed merely by labeling it religious shows that the legal community has little regard for theistic reasoning.

4.5a.2 Marriage and the De Re/De Dicto Distinction

Many in the legal community have treated other debates the same way as the conflict over abortion; the marriage debate is one example of these.[60] All marriages are relationships, yet not all relationships are marriages. Historically, civilizations have used the term marriage to refer to a certain type of relation between a man and a woman. Not all relations involving a male and female are marriages; for example, mothers and sons, brothers and sisters, and so forth are not marriages. The traditional view is that the term refers to a type of relationship designed to procreate. In the *de re* sense, marriage has referred to a relationship between a man and a woman with this end in mind.[61]

Currently many legal scholars do not make the distinction between the term marriage and the object to which it refers. They perceive the pro-traditional stance as a statement about one's subjective religious preference rather than as a statement about reality. The traditionalist takes the prototypical relationship and calls it marriage. On the other hand, currently many scholars treat the term marriage—in the *de dicto* sense—as something malleable to that which the autonomous individual chooses. Ronald E. Long argues that the character of marriage is ever changing.[62] To apply this principle, religionists would apply the word marriage as their privately held beliefs dictate. On the other hand, since the courts do not have a stake in religious arguments, same-sex advocates argue for a distinction between the secular policy and the religious beliefs.

Yet, the traditionalist is not making the claim that his particular sect should be established. Instead, he is giving a different answer to the same question concerning the types of relationships the government should endorse. The traditionalist is making the claim that homosexual relationships are not the same type of relationship as heterosexual relationships. Thus, the term used to refer to these types of relationships should reflect that difference.[63]

Like several other arguments that have been deemed religious, the argument for the immorality of homosexual relations does not necessitate theism. Dr. Kenneth Howell from the University of Illinois at Urbana-Champaign was temporarily suspended for opposing homosexuality grounded on natural moral law. Dr. Howell wrote the following in an email to his class:

> …But the more significant problem has to do with the fact that the consent criterion is not related in any way to the NATURE of the act itself. This is where Natural Moral Law (NML) objects. NML says that Morality must be a response to REALITY. In other words, sexual acts are only appropriate for people who are complementary, not the same. How do we know this? By looking at REALITY. Men and women are complementary in their anatomy, physiology, and psychology. Men and women are not interchangeable. So, a moral sexual act has to be between persons that are fitted for that act. Consent is important but there is more than consent needed.
>
> One example applicable to homosexual acts illustrates the problem. To the best of my knowledge, in a sexual relationship between two men, one of them tends to act as the "woman" while the other acts as the "man." In this scenario, homosexual men have been known to engage in certain types of actions for which their bodies are not fitted. I don't want to be too graphic so I won't go into details but a physician has told me that these acts are deleterious to the health of one or possibly both of the men. Yet, if the morality of the act is judged only by mutual consent, then there are clearly homosexual acts which are injurious to their health but which are consented to. Why are they injurious? Because they violate the meaning, structure, and (sometimes) health of the human body.[64]

Dr. Howell concluded his argument with the following:

> …As a final note, a perceptive reader will have noticed that none of what I have said here or in class depends upon religion. Catholics don't arrive at their moral conclusions based on their religion. They do so based on a thorough understanding of natural reality.[65]

Dr. Howell did not mention God in his email; however, many made the connection to his religious affiliation based on his conclusion. Though this instance never went to court and Dr. Howell was reinstated, his case shows an example of how people view ideas that are organically connected to religion in any way. The complaint that resulted in Dr. Howell's temporary suspension said this:

> …I am in no way a gay rights activist, but allowing this hate speech at a public university is entirely unacceptable. It sickens me to know that hard-working Illinoisans are funding the salary of a man who does nothing but try to indoctrinate students and perpetuate stereotypes. Once again, this is a public university and should thus

have no religious affiliation. Teaching a student about the tenets of a religion is one thing. Declaring that homosexual acts violate the natural laws of man is another. The courses at this institution should be geared to contribute to the public discourse and promote independent thought; not limit one's worldview and ostracize people of a certain sexual orientation.[66]

The student's perception of the incident is consistent with the construal of certain moral conclusions as religious.[67]

Dr. Howell's class was Introduction to Catholicism; his arguments were clearly consistent with Catholic doctrine. The foregoing student was offended that Dr. Howell taught his subject as though its contents are factual. One should ask if the same student is offended when math or science professors teach their subjects as objectively true. The student echoed the current popular understanding of religious and moral knowledge that is present in the legal community's schema when he wrote "…the teacher allowed little room for any opposition to Catholic dogma."[68] The student's schema is consistent with the prevailing perception of religious belief as subjective. Moreover, he also reflects the concept of personal autonomy in moral and religious beliefs. Because of this, the student concluded that public school systems should not use arguments that originate from or are consistent with religion.

In the cases concerning same-sex marriages, many legal scholars are in line with the public understanding of religious reasoning and its role in forming moral beliefs. The student was offended that Dr. Howell declared that morals are objective and not up to the autonomous individual to decide. Like the student, many argue that the courts should apply the principle of autonomy and determine that individuals choose the ends of these devices for themselves. Ultimately, the courts have at times used this reasoning to overturn legislation forbidding widening the usage of the term marriage to include same sex couples.[69]

4.5a.3 Diminishing Religious Conviction

While the pro-life and traditional marriage positions are not exclusively held by religionists, many conclusions regarding these issues are organically connected to religious reasoning. The courts have held firm in their stance that secular policy may be consistent with religious beliefs, but it may not be the result of religious reasoning. Sandel believes that this treatment diminishes religious conviction. As said before, the courts relegate the role of religious reasoning to subjective beliefs. Sandel says that the courts' mission of neutrality:

> …depreciates the claims of those for whom religion is not an expression of autonomy but a matter of conviction unrelated to a choice. Protecting religion as "life-style," as one among the values that an independent self may have, may miss the role that

religion plays in the lives of those for whom the observance of religious duties is a constitutive end, essential to their good and indispensable to their identity. Treating persons as "self-originating sources of valid claims" may thus fail to respect persons bound by duties derived from sources other than themselves.[70]

Sandel and others who rely on religious reasoning do not claim that their favorite policies are the result of their religious personal preferences; they claim that policies should reflect reality. They do not use religious reasoning to construct this reality; instead, they use it to discover it.

Religious reasoning is not the result of choices; instead it results in duties. While many claim that religion is liberating, it is also limiting. Religious beliefs contain restrictions on how one must act and how one must think. Religious reasoning places constraints on one's appetites and subjects the person to another's will. The believer conforms to a lifestyle; he does not create one. If Sandel is correct, the federal courts misunderstand the role of religion in the believer's life, they fail to take religious believers seriously, and they construe religious duties as a made-up set of rules for which there are no eternal consequences when disobeyed.

4.6 Summary

From the analysis of the foregoing interlocutors one may draw several conclusions.

4.6a Equivocal Language

First, those entrenched in the debate interpret the constitutional framers' original intent through the schematic lens of their philosophical presuppositions. These assumptions color the disputants' hermeneutic in such a way as to create a debate that uses equivocal language. This results in the two sides speaking past one another. The end result of this is not an understanding of the argument over which there is disagreement; instead, it is the use of power to enforce one's worldview.

Those from the differing worldviews use the language of the framers—particularly Jefferson—as premises to support their desired conclusions. Both sides of the argument construe themselves to be acting upon the framers' original intent. Both sides use *rights* talk, yet they operate from two different definitions of the term. Many separationists understand rights as stemming from a social contract. Many accommodationists use the term rights to refer to that for which man was designed. This latter understanding is grounded in teleology. Autonomy plays very little role in that which accommodationists refer to as rights. Duties, on the other hand, are a large part of what accommodationists refer to as rights. Whereas separationists often use the term *rights* to refer to the ability to choose to do what one wills—inasmuch as it does not get in the way of another individual's autonomy—without government interference, the accommodationists use it to refer to one's ability and duty to act within one's intended purpose or design. These two positions are clearly discernible, and thus are distinct. The debaters sound like they are speaking the same language when in fact they cannot understand the words that are coming out of each other's mouths.

Another example of the equivocal nature of the debate is seen in the use of the wall of separation metaphor. The metaphor itself is a theological construction referring back to God's casting mankind out of the garden and into the wilderness.[71] God ordered two cherubim to guard the entrance of the Garden of Eden, lest sinful man would enter and partake of the tree of life. The whole metaphor is based on a Biblical reference that serves to protect that which is holy from that which is profane. Jefferson used the theological language consistent with the three major monotheistic religions when invoking the wall metaphor. Many separationists who use the term either do not understand the theological underpinning of the concept, or divorce this meaning from the phrase. For them, the term refers to a legal understanding that religion is a private matter that should not be invoked in the public square. On the other hand, many accommodationists reject the metaphor altogether. After all, Thomas Jefferson used the term in a personal letter, which was not a legal document.[72] Either way, those in the discussion are using the same words, but they are in fact not speaking the same language. These are but two of many examples. I will highlight further uses of equivocation in the upcoming chapters as they appear.

4.6b Points of Agreement

Separationists and accommodationists agree on at least two points. First, both sides agree that the framers used religious language. It would be rationally indefensible for one to argue that the constitutional framers did not make references to God. The sitz im leben of the American colonies was vastly different than that of the current American setting. The framers were far more used to disagreements among the differing sects of Christianity. They did not anticipate that using religious language would one day be construed as a breach of the Establishment Clause. Currently, the United States has many more non-theistic religions and atheists than were present in colonial America. If the framers were present today, would they use secular language to define rights? The federal courts have often been charged with the task of answering for the framers.

Second, both sides seem to be agreed that it is the task of government to "secure" the rights of man. Those who argue for religious freedom do so with the idea that there are such things as rights, and that the courts are the venue to argue for the protection of these things.

The following chapter will address the Rawlsian understanding of rights. From there, I will ask if religious reasoning is appropriate in a liberal democracy where people are not unreasonable in rejecting religious ideas.

CHAPTER FIVE

Rawlsian Liberal Democracy, Religious Reason, and the Disputed View of the Good

In chapter one of this book, I said that I would address the claim that if a religious position becomes part of law it is unjust since it is based on a disputed view of the good life that dissenters are not unreasonable in rejecting. In order to do this, I must first give a brief account of John Rawls' political philosophy, since it is upon his work that many legal scholars and judges stand. Second, I will discuss the legal scholars Stephen Macedo and Ronald Dworkin inasmuch as they use a strict Rawlsian view to suggest the necessity of religious restraint.[1] Along with this, I will draw attention to some of the arguments against these strict Rawlsian principles that require a high level of religious restraint. I will also attend to the dialogue between Robert Audi and Nicholas Wolterstorff. With all of this, I will show that there are scholars who give reasonable arguments for rejecting this Rawlsian argument of religious restraint.

5.1 Rawls and the Natural of Liberal Democracy

As stated earlier, there are scholars who claim that if a religious position becomes law, it is unjust. This is because it is based on a disputed idea of the good. Those who argue this position do so from an understanding of liberal democracy proposed by the political philosopher John Rawls. In order to understand why many judges and legal scholars have followed this attitude towards religious reasoning, one must first understand what Rawls believed about the nature of liberal democracy.

John Rawls' concept of liberal democracy developed over time, and there are certainly different interpretations of his thought. For my purposes here, I will use an understanding of Rawls' liberal democracy that is relatively undisputed and accepted by both those who agree and disagree with his philosophical positions. Rawls argued many of his basic tenets in his 1971 book *A Theory of Justice*;[2] he further developed his thought and in 1993 published *Political Liberalism*.[3] It is on these two texts that scholars rely for tenets of Rawlsian thought. Much of this chapter will draw upon three principles of Rawlsian political theory. Though Rawls' thought is much broader than what will be expressed in these points, judicial decisions and contemporary scholarship concerning matters of church and state commonly express these three principles.

First, Rawls believed that liberal democracies are social contracts. He asserted,

> ...the guiding idea is that the principles of justice for the basic structure of society are the object of the original agreement. They are the principles that free and rational persons concerned to further their own interests would accept in an initial position of equality as defining the fundamental terms of their association. The principles are to regulate all further agreements; they specify the kinds of social cooperation that can be entered into and the forms of government that can be established. This way of regarding the principles of justice I shall call justice as fairness.[4]

This agreement, according to Rawls, is hypothetical. Yet upon reflection, Rawls believed rational citizens who consider justice from the "original position" will agree on certain principles. The rational citizen can build further upon these principles.

This contractualist schema is in contrast to how many others perceive the American constitutional experiment. Unlike John Locke[5] and Thomas Jefferson, Rawls did not describe rights and duties as endowments by the Creator. In his treatment of rights and duties as emerging from the social contract, Rawls writes, "Thus we are to imagine that those who engage in social cooperation choose together, in one joint act, the principles which are to assign basic rights and duties and to determine the division of social benefits."[6] This is not to say that Rawls' position requires atheism; it merely leaves religion out of the discussion. Moreover, on this scheme, the belief in God is not a necessary condition for the belief in rights and duties.

Second, Rawls presumes that beyond a "thin theory of the good" individuals and societies determine what the good is for themselves.[7] Rawls writes:

> Just as each person must decide by rational reflection what constitutes his good, that
> is, the system of ends which it is rational for him to pursue, so a group of persons must
> decide once and for all what is to count among them as just and unjust.[8]

Rawls' theory is different from natural law theorists, who believe that—even beyond a thin theory of the good—a full theory of the good is a fact of reality that one discovers; it is not something upon which societies or individuals decide for themselves.

Rawls stated that the original position "may be viewed as a procedural interpretation of Kant's conception of autonomy and the categorical imperative within the framework of an empirical theory."[9] Rawls asks reasonable people to consider what kind of coercive legislation they would legislate not knowing into what type of situation they would be born. He concluded that reasonable people would try to level the playing field in such a way as to give an advantage only to those who are least well off. Since, according to Rawls, reasonable people would choose this level playing field, citizens should politically operate in liberal democracies in such a way.

First principles of rights and duties emerge from what Rawls called "original position of equality [that] corresponds to the state of nature in the traditional theory of the social contract."[10] Rawls says that the original position is not an actual situation, and one uses it merely to conceptualize justice.[11] From this, Rawls makes use of the concept of the "veil of ignorance." Members in society attempt to construct principles of justice by imagining starting from the original position. In this case, one assumes that he possesses no knowledge about his place in society. Some of the features that one lacks include:

> …his class position or social status, nor does any one [sic] know his fortune in the
> distribution of natural assets and abilities, his intelligence, strength, and the like.…
> the parties do not know their conceptions of the good or their special psychological
> propensities.[12]

One would also have no knowledge of what religion or culture in which he would be brought up.

From this starting point, it is supposed that one should embrace a form of government that affords oneself the best odds of flourishing. In this scenario, citizens would seek to assign rights and duties. Because of the citizenry's lack of knowledge concerning their sitz im leben[13] added to their desire to flourish, it is believed that rights and duties would be evenly distributed. Rawls argues that:

> …given the circumstances of the original position, the symmetry of everyone's rela-
> tions to each other, this initial situation is fair between individuals as moral persons,
> that is, as rational beings with their own ends and…capable of a sense of justice.[14]

According to Rawls, one uses the first principles of justice—arrived at from behind the veil of ignorance—to "regulate all subsequent criticism and reform of institutions."[15] Further, from the conception of justice, members then create a constitution and laws to govern themselves.[16]

All of this is to say that Rawls attempts to construct a means by which a society can assign rights that are just and fair. Rawls writes:

> …[the] idea of the original position is to set up a fair procedure so that any principles
> agreed to will be just. The aim is to use the notion of pure procedural justice as a basis
> of theory. Somehow we must nullify the effects of specific contingencies which put
> men at odds and tempt them to exploit social and natural circumstances to their own
> advantage. Now in order to do this I assume that the parties are situated behind a veil
> of ignorance. They do not know how the various alternatives will affect their own
> particular case and they are obliged to evaluate principles solely on the basis of general
> considerations.[17]

Thus, the veil of ignorance is a thought experiment to reveal to one how he would ensure fair treatment of himself if he could not guarantee the advantages he may actually possess. This fair treatment of oneself also entails the treatment of others as free and equal. This is much like the parent who has the older child split the dessert into two pieces and gives the younger child first choice. Wanting to maximize his dessert eating experience, the older child cuts the dessert as equally as possible.

Third, liberal democracies use public reason to create legislation. Society founds this legislation on the principles of justice as fairness that were determined from the original position. In order to treat others as free and equal, according to Rawls, one must not coerce his fellow citizens to do anything or refrain from anything—by act of law—unless he can first give acceptable justification for doing so. What did Rawls count as "acceptable justification?" Rawls writes:

> Our exercise of political power is fully proper only when it is exercised in accordance
> with a constitution the essentials of which all citizens as free and equal may reasonably
> be expected to endorse in the light of principles and ideals acceptable to their common
> human reason.[18]

That which counts as acceptable justification is referred to as public reason. From this emerges what is known as "justificatory liberalism."[19] It is from this scheme that people decide how to govern their society. Many Rawlsians exclude religious reasoning in the enactment of coercive legislation or constitutional essentials. One reason for this is that one cannot know from behind the veil of ignorance into what religion he will be born or even if he will be religious at all. Thus, it is argued, society should not ground rights and duties on religious reasoning. This is because not every rational citizen would accept religion as a justifiable foundation. On this point, Rawls writes:

> …the guidelines of inquiry of public reason, as well as its principle of legitimacy, have the same basis as the substantive principles of justice. This means in justice as fairness that the parties in the original position, in adopting principles of justice for the basic structure, must also adopt guidelines and criteria of public reason for applying those norms. The argument for those guidelines, and for the principle of legitimacy, is much the same as, and as strong as, the argument for the principles of justice themselves. In securing the interests of the persons they represent, the parties insist that the application of substantive principles be guided by judgment and inference, reasons and evidence that the persons they represent can reasonably be expected to endorse.[20]

Most Rawlsians agree that it is not reasonable to expect everybody to endorse religious claims. Because of this unreasonableness, religious restraint may be necessary for liberal democracies to operate well.[21]

Given that there is a plurality of theistic religions, it is understandable that strict Rawlsians would exclude religious reason of particular religious traditions from public reason. Rawls was familiar with the argument for rights as originating from God. Rawls writes:

> The naturalness of this condition lies in part in the fact that first principles must be capable of serving as a public charter of a well ordered society in perpetuity. Being unconditional, they always hold (under the circumstances of justice), and the knowledge of them must be open to individuals in any generation. Thus, to understand these principles should not require a knowledge of contingent particulars, and surely not a reference to individuals or associations. Traditionally the most obvious test of this condition is the idea that what is right is that which accords with God's will. But in fact this doctrine is normally supported by an argument from general principles. For example, Locke held that the fundamental principle of morals is the following: if one person is created by another (in the theological sense), then that person has a duty to comply with the precepts set to him by his creator. This principle is perfectly general and given the nature of the world on Locke's view, it singles out God as the legitimate moral authority. The generality condition is not violated, although it may appear so at first sight. Next, principles are to be universal in application. They must hold for everyone in virtue of their being moral persons. Thus I assume that each can understand these principles and use them in his deliberations. This imposes an upper bound of sorts on how complex they can be, and on the kinds and number of distinctions they draw.[22]

As it was mentioned earlier, Rawls grounds rights on the social contract. Perhaps this is because rights founded on God turn out to require "contingent particulars." Rawlsians often argue that rights founded on God are not "universal in application," since there are many reasonable people who do not believe in God.

Rawlsians also claim that many are not unreasonable in rejecting certain comprehensive worldviews upon which society may base laws. This is a different claim than saying one is rational in rejecting a particular worldview; it is merely that one is *prima facie* reasonable in rejecting certain views of the good. Moreover, because comprehensive worldviews that include religious doctrines are highly disputed, Rawlsians perceive them as outside of public reason. Those who create laws that are outside of public reason—according to many Rawlsians—do so unjustly. It is upon the definition of public reason that much disagreement takes place.

Based on the foregoing three tenets, many legal scholars and judges claim that religionists should use some level of restraint when operating in the public square. Depending on which scholar or judge one consults, there are different levels of restraint that one should exercise. In many cases, political philosophers and judges argue that religious reasoning should play little to no role in public discourse, much less legislation.[23] These principles most often come to the foreground in literature and court cases dealing with moral legislation and education. The following section will show how two Rawlsian scholars use his principles to mandate a high level of religious restraint on those who would create public policy.

5.2 Rawlsian Principles and Their Detractors

5.2a Stephen Macedo and Public Reason

5.2a.1 Macedo's Schema

Stephen Macedo is a legal scholar who perceives issues of church and state through the schema of the theologico-political problem that I mentioned in chapter one. Like many judges and legal scholars,[24] Macedo believes religious reason to be a cause of civil strife. He also believes that "political liberalism…offers hope of deliverance from both politics as holy war and politics as the embrace of nonjudgmental, unqualified pluralism."[25] As such, Macedo argues for a strict application of public reason based on Rawls' political liberalism. He writes, "Political liberalism is potentially tough-minded—I want to develop that potential here."[26]

His work uses the three Rawlsian tenets that I described earlier. Like Rawls, Macedo is a social contractualist. Because of this, Macedo believes that liberal democracy is as much about forms of justification as it is about "individual rights and limited government."[27] Following a strict Rawlsian scheme, Macedo believes that citizens should introduce coercive legislation only from publically reasoned justification. This reasoning may be acceptable by religious people, but it must not emanate from the religion. Macedo writes:

> Liberal contractualists typically seek justifications that are widely acceptable to reasonable people with a broad range of moral, philosophical, and religious commitments. The aim is reasonable agreement: to be both reasonable and agreeable in a widely pluralistic society. The appropriate means is a process of reasoning that is publicly accessible, but genuinely justificatory.[28]

Macedo rejects religious reasoning as being publically accessible; thus it is not appropriate. He also believes that many religious commitments get in the way of public reason. Expressing this position, Macedo writes:

> The only way that we can achieve a public moral framework while accepting the deep and permanent fact of diversity is by putting aside not only the personal interests and religious beliefs, but also the many philosophical and moral convictions that reasonable citizens will disagree with.[29]

Macedo argues that since reasonable people disagree over religious beliefs, among other things, one should not use these beliefs as justification for the formation of public policy.

Macedo argues further that liberal democracies should not attach political authority to religious reasoning. He writes:

> Do we really want to premise political authority on the contention that critical thinking is the best way to attain religious truth? Perhaps this can be avoided, an alternative approach would be to put aside such matters as religious truth and the ultimate ideals of human perfection and attempt to justify at least the most basic matters of justice on grounds widely acceptable to reasonable people—and not only to those who share our particular view of the whole truth.[30]

This eschewing of the means of religious truth for that which is "widely accepted" is similar to the reasoning in *Kitzmiller v. Dover*. Judge Jones expressed that it was his duty to determine whether intelligent design was religion, not if it was true.[31]

Just like Rawls, Macedo believes that individuals determine the good life for themselves. Like the judgments in the *Keeton* and *Ward* cases, Macedo presupposes doxastic voluntarism and implies that religious citizens can pick up and put down their beliefs about the good life at will. Because he believes that "protestant fundamentalists are hostile…to at least some liberal values,[32] Macedo suggests, "… political liberalism invites us to put some of our (true) beliefs aside when it comes to laying the groundwork for common political institutions."[33] Concerning those who can put their religious beliefs aside, Macedo says that liberals join with them "by respect for their reasonableness."[34] As an example of this Macedo writes:

> As in: "Your Catholicism absurdly defers to the authority of the Bishop of Rome, but I welcome you as a fellow citizen whose public reasonableness is shown by the fact that you do not seek to impose your religious beliefs on me by political means, but instead join with me in acknowledging the political authority of reasons we can share."[35]

According to this, Macedo would define any law that is genetically connected to religious reasoning as outside of public reason and thus off limits. This was the case in both *Kitzmiller v. Dover* and *Varnum v. Brien*.[36] With all of this said, Macedo writes, "our politics does come down to a holy war between religious zealots and proponents of science and public reason."[37]

5.2a.2 Macedo's Religious Restraint Applied

In the book *Natural Law and Public Reason*, edited by Robert P. George and Christopher Wolfe, Macedo uses his allotted chapter to defend a position of Rawlsian liberalism that he believes condemns slavery while still justifying abortion. Macedo argues that his liberalism consists of both the "commitment to broad guarantees of liberty and equality," and "a commitment to a practice of public reasonableness."[38] This second part, he suggests, functions practically to inhibit the "veiled attempts by some group to impose their religious views on others through political means."[39] Macedo puts forth the idea that citizens, legislators, and judges all need to practice public reasonableness, which he believes "characterizes…the best version of the theory and practice of liberal constitutionalism."[40] To do this, Macedo says:

> A fundamental political demand is to convert unthinking habits and practices into reasons, or to revise our practices to accord with reasoned standards, and to seek justification that can be shared by people who disagree reasonably and permanently about their ultimate religious and philosophical ideals.[41]

According to Macedo, for the religious practitioner to participate as a promoter of public policy, legislator, or judge he must conform to the demands of public reason. In order to conform to public reason, the religious practitioner must interpret the Constitution through a Rawlsian-type schema. Further, he must offer reasons for public policy that conform to that schema so that that the only disagreement is over the appropriate interpretations of Rawlsian liberalism. Macedo insists that "the emphasis on public reasonableness and the centrality of public justification to the liberalism [he] wants to defend helps make sense of why and how we can continue to see the idea of a 'social contract'."[42]

If this is true, then citizens, lawmakers, and judges who support, enact, or concur with legislation that is justified by religious reasons have violated liberal reasonableness. To apply Macedo's version of liberalism to federal court cases concerning school funding, ethical issues, and school curriculum will yield consistent results. If evenly applied, the results will always be in favor of those in opposition to certain views that are generally held by traditional religious believers. For instance, the legislative balance will *de facto* tip in favor of the pro-choice and same-sex marriage positions. This is an ace up the political sleeve, for one needs only to pull the religion card to nullify his opponent's legislative agenda.

In chapter two, I gave a few different examples of this type of tactic. In *Kitzmiller v. Dover*, the court recognized the possibility that reasonable students would perceive stickers disclaiming the truth of Darwinism as an endorsement of religion; therefore, the federal court ruled that placing these stickers on biology textbooks is unconstitutional.[43] The court did not want to appear to be endorsing intelligent design, since it includes the possibility that God exists (specifically the God of Abraham, Isaac, and Jacob). Because ID includes the possibility of theism, many in the legal community believe that it is outside of public reason.[44] To be a reasonable citizen, according to strict Rawlsian liberalism, demands that one must reject the notion that religious claims such as ID are knowable while operating in the public square; yet, these same citizens are somehow free to change these beliefs back to conform to their religion of choice when they enter the private sphere.

The claim that one can shed his private religious beliefs before he enters the public sphere and don them again when he gets home leads to an interesting scenario. Imagine a high school biology teacher—who conforms to this understanding of public reason while teaching his course—endorsing the Darwinian account of evolution. Further, being devoted to public reasonableness, the teacher silences religious objectors in his class due to their inability to provide acceptable public justification for their denial of Darwinian evolution. He goes so far to say that even if they offer arguments against the theory that are independent of any religious tenets, reasonable students would see this as an endorsement of a religious theory; thus, their argument fails to meet the standards of public reason. Now imagine one of the silenced students running into this same biology teacher at church teaching a Sunday school class on the first chapter of Genesis. The teacher, to the surprise of the student, is espousing young earth creationism that includes the spontaneous arrival of species. The student then asks his teacher what he *really* believes to be true, evolution or special young earth creation. The teacher then answers the student, "Well, Darwinian evolution is true at school, and it is false outside of school."

This scenario is unreasonable in several ways. First, this teacher fulfills the liberal definition of reasonableness by conforming his justification and beliefs to the liberal position when he is acting on government property and then sheds these beliefs when he leaves his governmental duties. The teacher's beliefs vary by geography, time of day, and whether he is getting paid by the government while he is speaking. My argument is not that theists cannot believe Darwinism to be true. Nor is my argument that those who believe Darwinism to be false are unable to accurately describe the theory. My argument is that it is impossible to pick up and put down one's belief based solely on geography and the time of day, and it is unreasonable to demand one to do so. This type of reasoning is impossible, and if someone found one who actually can fulfill this practice, he would also find someone who has multiple personality disorder. In reality, sane teachers either believe Darwinism to be a true theory or believe it to be a false theory; they do not change their beliefs while punching in and out of work. There are many teachers who do perceive the teaching of Darwinian theory—as though it is true—to be a violation of their religious conscience. For the courts to ask these teachers to shed this belief long enough to fulfill their educational duties is to ask them to perform an impossible task.

The second point is that it is unreasonable for a government to expect its citizens to perform such an impossible task. If Macedo understands that one cannot actually change his beliefs while acting in the public sphere, then he asks that they remain silent about religious topics. On the other hand, if one's job requires the discussion of a topic that is in disagreement with his religious views—such as the teaching of Darwinian evolution—then that employee is required by public reason to refrain from giving any argument that may endorse his religion. The two counseling students (Keeton and Ward) who were discussed in chapter two found themselves in this position. Their training required them to talk about a subject that was informed by their religious beliefs. Yet, they were expected to act in accordance with public reason even if it meant violating their religious consciences.

Third, banning the teaching of ID because it is perceived as inherently religious commits the genetic fallacy. One can expect the banning of theories that are false or not widely accepted. However, the alleged religious origin of ID neither falsifies the theory nor indicates to what degree it is accepted. This is not to say that ID should be taught in public schools. It is to say that to prohibit the teaching of it merely because it is organically connected to religion lacks sufficient reason.

Finally, Macedo's construction of liberalism creates a situation where religious citizens are compelled to act disingenuously. By saying that religiously motivated laws violate the Constitution, the court has forced legislators to pretend as if they don't have religious motives. This problem exists with the courts' treatment of legislation as well.[45] According to this strict form of public justification, laws that are enacted from religious beliefs—whatever the purpose may be—are unconstitutional. Francis Beckwith has pointed out that "both the United States Supreme Court and other federal courts have rejected the constitutionality of [certain] laws and policies on the grounds that they have an exclusively religious purpose."[46] Beckwith argues that the courts have conflated the terms purpose and motive.[47] He shows that purposes and motives are conceptually distinct. According to Beckwith, two individuals can support the same legislative purpose yet have two distinct motives for doing so.[48] On the one hand, one person may have a religious motive for supporting a piece of legislation, whereas, on the other hand, another person may be motivated to support the same piece of legislation from secular reasoning. Beckwith points out that the courts' judgment of the legislation's constitutionality depends on who introduces the bill. If the citizen motivated by secular reasoning introduces the bill, then the bill is constitutional. Yet, if the religiously motivated citizen introduces bill, then the bill is unconstitutional. Beckwith's observation shows that legislation may be guilty by merely being associated with religious reasoning.

Regardless of whether Macedo's religious restraint is placed upon citizens in general or legislators in specific, the result is that religionists are often on unequal footing with their secular counterparts, which is something that Rawlsian democracies attempt to cure. Just as Macedo's requirement of religious restraint compels religious citizens to act disingenuous while in the public square, so too do the courts compel religious legislators to act disingenuous when enacting legislation.

Macedo's Rawlsian conclusions come with a heavy price tag for the religionist, for if the religious citizen adheres to the rules set out before him, he commits himself to cognitive dissonance. He must believe something to be unjustified that he believes to be justified. That is, unless he recognizes the distinction between public justification and private justification, in which he is called to make a decision to act on what he believes to be true or to conform to the requirements of democratic liberalism. Where there are controversial notions of the good, the religionist is asked to be a good liberal rather than to be obedient to his God. Governments historically have used strong forms of coercion to get people to act in ways that are inconsistent with their religion. Other than governmental enforcement, I do not see how a religionist would accept the Rawlsian arguments as stated by Macedo.

5.2b George and Wolfe on Macedo's Public Reason Criteria

Robert P. George and Christopher Wolfe have responded to Macedo's claims concerning public reason in a liberal democracy. Specifically, in their edited book *Natural Law and Public Reason* the two take exception to Macedo's criteria for public reason. George and Wolfe focus on Macedo's criteria for public reason as given in his book *Liberal Virtues*.[49]

Stephen Macedo describes acceptable public reason as having three elements:

(1) Publicly stated,
(2) Openly debated, and
(3) Widely accepted.[50]

Macedo believes that religious arguments fail this because they are:

(1) Private,
(2) Too complex to be widely understood, and
(3) Otherwise incapable of being widely appreciated by reasonable people.[51]

George and Wolfe disagree with Macedo on these criteria. They argue that there is no commonsense understanding of what these notions mean. The answer to what is widely appreciated by reasonable people will vary from person to person. What seems complex to one person may seem elementary to another person. They further argue that "people's disagreements about what is or is not 'too complex' or 'publicly accessible' will almost certainly replicate their substantive moral disagreement regarding the underlying matters in dispute."[52]

According to George and Wolfe, what it means to fulfill this criteria is almost impossible to ascertain. The two scholars ask for an explanation of what it means to be "simple." How many people relative to society have to understand the argument to fulfill the simplicity criteria? George and Wolfe point out that "it is difficult to imagine many serious arguments on difficult issues of basic justice that all (or even virtually all) citizens would understand."[53]

George and Wolfe reject Macedo's requirement that an argument must be "widely accepted." They argue that this:

> …would make any conventional view ipso facto publicly accessible, irrespective of how irrational it truly was, and any unpopular or unconventional view ipso facto not publicly accessible, irrespective of how rational it truly was, which would make reform and improvement of public views excessively difficult."[54]

It is very difficult to see how abolitionist arguments in the pro-slavery south could have passed for public reason prior to a majority of the population holding to abolitionist sentiments. It seems that public justification must include unpopular conclusions in order to ensure justice.

George and Wolfe also reject Macedo's criteria of public reason on the grounds that it is self-referentially defeating. They make it clear that the "publicly accessible" criterion is itself not accessible to the public.[55] George and Wolfe suggest that this is true of many Rawlsian-type doctrines. For example, the claim that public reasons should not be complex or controversial is itself a complex and controversial claim. The average citizen—and arguably many scholars—does not understand the complexities of Rawls' formulation of public reason. Furthermore, many of those who do understand what Rawlsians mean by public reason reject it. Rawlsian-type public reason is both too complex for the majority to understand, and too controversial for many to accept; thus, it fails to bear its own weight.

George and Wolfe respond to Macedo's argument against natural law[56] as being outside of public reason.[57] In doing so they argue that liberals have placed natural law theorists in a "Catch-22."[58] For example, if the natural law theorist argues that a certain piece of legislation ought to be passed because the majority of society recognizes it as good, then liberals may argue that this violates public reason because it is merely based on societal prejudices. On the other hand, if in light of this criticism the natural law theorist offers up a more sophisticated argument, then liberals can argue that it is too complex for public reason. George and Wolfe argue that liberal concepts about sexuality and moral issues fall prey to the same criticism. If one supports same-sex marriage on the grounds that in the public eye it is a morally legitimate lifestyle, then another can claim that this is based on mere prejudice. On the other hand, if the same-sex proponent develops and articulates a sophisticated defense, then the opponent may retort that it is just too complex for reasonable people to accept as public reason.[59]

Besides presenting the problems with Macedo's criteria for public reason, George and Wolfe maintain that the courts and intellectual elites have defined religious reasoning outside of public reason. They argue that "since *Everson*…'separation of church and state' has been gradually, but radically, redefined to view public acknowledgement of God as a violation of fundamental constitutional principles."[60] They further argue that:

> This has primarily been the work of intellectuals and their allies in the "knowledge class." Whose religious beliefs and practices, it should be noted, are in most cases dramatically out of line with the beliefs and practices of their fellow citizens.[61]

Prior to *Everson*, the courts perceived religious reasoning as part of the American framework. Remnants of this remained in *Zorach v. Clauson*, in which Justice Douglas writes, "We are a religious people whose institutions presuppose a Supreme Being."[62]

According to George and Wolfe, much of the intellectual criticism of religious reason is based on the presupposition that it is not publically accessible. They point out that though many citizens cannot articulate their reasons for believing in God, as well as say a college professor might articulate his atheism, it does not follow that their belief is outside of public reason. George and Wolfe make a distinction between "inarticulate knowledge and more fully developed knowledge."[63] Being able to articulate what it means for God to exist and having knowledge that God exists are two different things. George and Wolfe argue that they, "like virtually all of the founders of the American government,"[64] think that the statement God exists "…is defensible at the bar of public reason," in virtue of it being true.[65]

5.3 Ronald Dworkin and Justificatory Liberalism

Along with the general principle of public reason, there is a specific principle that many strict Rawlsians share. This is the principle of justificatory liberalism (JL), which states that governments must justify the enactment of coercive legislation to the citizens it serves. With this, if a citizen is not unreasonable in rejecting certain legislation, then there remains liberty. Francis Beckwith defines JL thusly: "Supporters of Justificatory Liberalism maintain that the state may not coerce its citizens on matters of constitutional essentials unless it can provide public justification that the coerced citizens would be unreasonable in rejecting."[66] Applying this principle to laws forbidding same sex marriage, opponents often argue that the legislation originates from a religious position[67] that they are not unreasonable in rejecting; thus, the state should grant liberty for them to marry.[68] Many legal scholars have endorsed JL,[69] and several court rulings have subsequently enforced it.[70]

The Rawlsian principle that individuals decide what the good life is for themselves is implicit in JL. Ronald Dworkin echoes this in his discussion over whether the government is right in forbidding homosexual sodomy. Dworkin writes:

> The principle of personal responsibility distinguishes between these two kinds of judgmental justifications because it insists only that people have responsibility for their own ethical values, that is, their own convictions about why their life has intrinsic importance and what kind of life would best realize that value for them.[71]

From this, it should follow that governmental action forbidding homosexual practice is a violation of JL. If it is true that ethical decisions are decided by the individual, then homosexuals are not unreasonable in rejecting the constraints of those who believe that homosexual conduct is immoral.

However, if the courts are to be neutral in regards to public reason, then it seems that they should make sure that government neither advances nor inhibits personal moral choices. This is similar to how the courts attempt to apply governmental neutrality towards religion.

Dworkin believes that ethical choices regarding abortion and sexual orientation are analogous to religious convictions. This means that they are part of one's personal comprehensive doctrine. Concerning the courts' treatment of these two subjects, Dworkin writes:

> Orthodox religious convictions are plainly in that category, and so are people's convictions about the role and direction of love, intimacy, and sexuality in their lives. These beliefs and commitments fix the meaning and tone of the most important associations people form; they are drawn from and feed back into their more general philosophical beliefs about the character and value of human life.[72]

If beliefs about abortion and sexual orientation are part of a comprehensive doctrine, then—like theological beliefs—they ought to be treated as such. This means, like the courts do with religious beliefs, beliefs and commitments regarding sexual orientation should be relegated to the private sphere. However, this is not the case. Recent state governments have started mandating the teaching of history that celebrates gay, lesbian, and transgendered citizens. California Senate Bill 48 (SB 48) amended the state's instructional requirements to include highlighting the sexual orientation of contributors to American history. SB 48 reads:

> Existing law prohibits instruction or school sponsored activities that reflect adversely upon persons because of their race, sex, color, creed, handicap, national origin, or ancestry. Existing law prohibits the State Board of Education and the governing board of any school district from adopting textbooks or other instructional materials that contain any matter that reflects adversely upon persons because of their race, sex, color, creed, handicap, national origin, or ancestry.[73]

This legislation requires that teachers abstain from publically teaching anything that may challenge the moral status of homosexual behavior. Moreover, it requires teachers to paint the acceptance of homosexual behavior in a positive light. This legislation requires not only public schools but also private schools to adhere to it. SB 48 reads further:

> This bill would state the intent of the Legislature that alternative and charter schools take notice of the provisions of this bill in light of provisions of existing law that prohibit discrimination in any aspect of their operation. This bill also would make other technical, nonsubstantive [sic] changes.[74]

SB 48 seems to require that private religious institutions adhere to its mandates. Thus, under this law, parochial schools are required to abstain from ethical judgments concerning sexual orientation. That is, the mandate stands unless they are teaching about homosexuals' positive contributions to society.

If Dworkin is correct, that ethical convictions over sexual orientation are on par with theological beliefs, then public reason demands that the government remain neutral on such discussions. Yet, this is not what the state of California has done. Instead, California has endorsed part of a comprehensive worldview that celebrates a view of the good life that others are not unreasonable in rejecting. If the state required teachers to include the religious beliefs of historical figures and to exclusively do so in a positive light, one would be correct to assume that secularists would claim that the Establishment Clause was violated. And, as a matter of fact, this is exactly what has happened in Texas.

Legislators in Texas have been debating about the content of social science textbooks. Conservatives want the social science curriculum to reflect the religious beliefs of the contributors to the founding of the United States.[75] So far, the debate is divided along party lines. Democrat legislators believe that the inclusion of the founders' religious worldviews in history textbooks is another attempt to inject religion into the curriculum. On the other hand, Republican legislators believe that the textbook authors have intentionally omitted the religious motivations of the American founders, and that they have cast religious believers in a bad light.[76] The final decision over such matters will ultimately climb up to the federal courts.

Many liberals argue that courts should disallow the founders' religious motivations to be taught in the social sciences[77] just as many conservatives argue that the courts should disallow the teaching about historical figures' sexual orientation.[78] Again, if Dworkin is correct that ethical views on sexual relationships are part of a comprehensive worldview, then the requirements of SB 48 fail to meet the criteria for public reason. Just as liberals argue that governments should not enforce the celebration of private religious positions, governments should also not enforce the celebration of private ethical positions regarding sexual orientation.

State legislatures are not the only ones to use the power of the state to endorse the lesbian, gay, biSexual, and transgendered (LGBT) worldview concerning sexual orientation. Presidents Bill Clinton[79] and Barack Obama[80] have proclaimed June to be Lesbian, Gay, Bisexual, and Transgender Pride Month. In chapter two, I showed that the courts perceive an endorsement of religion as an act of coercion. For example, the courts ruled against school prayer and disclaimers of Darwinism on biology textbooks because they believed that prayers would alienate some students,[81] and that by disclaiming Darwinism the government backed a particular religious doctrine.[82] Just as the court perceives endorsed public praying as coercive to the non-religious students, it can equally be argued that the endorsed celebration of a gay pride month entails the coercion of religious students. Just as judges can imagine hostility to those who will not pray, it can also be imagined that there will be hostility to those who will not acquiesce to celebrating Lesbian, Gay, Bisexual, and Transgender Pride Month.

The bottom line is that JL mandates that liberal democracies should not create coercive legislation that citizens are not unreasonable in rejecting. Dworkin has equated the ethical reasoning of sexual behavior with that of religious reasoning. Just as with religious reasoning, detractors are not unreasonable in rejecting the moral conclusions of the LGBT population. Thus, the courts should protect its citizens from legislation that is based on such a controversial view of the good life.

Beckwith argues that the consequences of same-sex marriage include "coercion, punishment, and marginalization of citizens who cannot in good conscience accept SSM as real marriage because their reasonable comprehensive doctrines require them to reject SSM."[83] One example of how the enactment of SSM would unjustly coerce citizens is in the case of adoption. Beckwith points out that Catholic Charities has already exited the business of adoption because Massachusetts law forbids it from excluding same-sex couples. If Catholic Charities wants to provide adoption services, it must acquiesce to the power of the state and treat homosexual couples as though they are morally equal to heterosexual couples. Yet, this is something that the Catholic cannot approve of in clear conscience.[84] This is similar to the *Keeton* and *Ward* cases that I discussed earlier in this chapter and in chapter two. If the young ladies wished to receive their degrees, they would have had to violate their consciences by violating that which they were not unreasonable in believing.

Beckwith also argues that SSM legislation will result in punishing those who are not unreasonable in believing homosexuality to be immoral. Beckwith gives three examples of how this has already happened. First, he shows that foster care families in the United Kingdom have been deemed unfit to foster children due to their religious convictions concerning homosexuality. He writes:

> The Johns were denied foster children because they believe that human sexuality has a certain intrinsic purpose that may only be consummated by one man and one woman within the confines of matrimony, and that it is their responsibility to properly instruct the children in their care of this truth.[85]

Second, Beckwith shows that religious business owners who do not make public accommodations to homosexuals fall prey to anti-discrimination laws. The case *Willock v. Elane Photography* is an example of this. According to Beckwith,

Albuquerque photographer Elaine Huguenin "had to pay more than $6,600 in legal fees for declining to photograph the same-sex commitment ceremony of Vanessa Willock and her partner."[86] Judge Garcia delivered the following opinion of the New Mexico Court of Appeals:

> This appeal arose from the refusal of Elane Photography, LLC (Elane Photography), to photograph the commitment ceremony of Vanessa Willock (Willock) and her same-sex partner (Partner). Elane Photography denied Willock's request to photograph the ceremony based upon its policy of refusing to photograph images that convey the message that marriage can be defined to include combinations of people other than the union of one man and one woman. Elane Photography's owners are Christians who believe that marriage is a sacred union of one man and one woman. They also believe that photography is an artistically expressive form of communication and photographing a same-sex commitment ceremony would disobey God and the teachings of the Bible by communicating a message contrary to their religious and personal beliefs. We conclude that Elane Photography's refusal to photograph Willock's ceremony constitutes a violation of NMSA 1978, Section 28-1-7(F) (2004) of the New Mexico Human Rights Act (NMHRA). As a result, we affirm the decision of the district court in favor of Willock.[87]

Because Elane Photography did not want to communicate that homosexual acts are morally acceptable, the court ruled that it violated the New Mexico Human Rights Act. Thus, the court perceived the owner's refusal to act against her conscience as a violation of homosexuals' human rights.

Finally, Beckwith argues that legislation from SSM results in the marginalization of religious citizens. He argues that:

> …parents have complained that the schools were instructing their children in ways that are inconsistent with the lessons they were given at both home and church. Instead of suggesting that citizens from different perspectives hold contrary, though reasonable, views on matters of sexual morality and family life, the public schools (at least, in these cases) are teaching that negative moral judgments of homosexual conduct or same-sex marriage constitute an irrational prejudice. Thus, the schools are not portraying the parents' point of view as one entitled to respectful consideration and serious reflection, but rather, as an irrational view that no enlightened person would ever entertain.[88]

Beckwith is referencing an article concerning the case *Parker v. Hurley*,[89] in which two sets of parents sued a Massachusetts school district for not giving them prior notice before reading aloud the book *King and King*.[90] One can reason that if the doctrine of JL were evenly applied, the courts would recognize that people are not unreasonable in rejecting SSM legislation; and thus, the courts should determine that this type of legislation is just as unconstitutional as the moments of silence were in *Wallace v. Jaffree*.[91]

Just as with pro-traditional marriage advocates, it can be argued that advocates of SSM are not unreasonable in rejecting legislation that forbids them from receiving marriage licenses. JL fails to solve the problem of SSM legislation in that it is unable to fairly adjudicate between competing views of which neither one of the advocates are not unreasonable in holding. SSM legislation fails the JL criteria whether it is enacted or rejected. In cases such as SSM, the courts are faced with which side the government will endorse. Even if the courts "choose not to decide, they still have made a choice."[92]

5.4 Robert Audi and Nicholas Wolterstorff

5.4a Robert Audi

Stephen Macedo and Ronald Dworkin perceive religion in a dim light. They also hold to a very strict form of Rawlsian liberal democracy. Robert Audi, on the other hand, shows that one does not need to epistemically perceive religious reasoning so dimly to endorse a Rawlsian schema.

Robert Audi has at least three views of liberal democracy in common with the Rawlsian position.[93] First, he agrees that liberal democracy requires one to treat others as free and equal citizens. Second, Audi believes that one should use public reason to promote coercive legislation.[94] Finally, Audi agrees that there should be some form of restraint on the reasons for legislation, particularly on religious reasons. For example, Audi gives his account of secular reasons as those that are:

> …simply evidentially independent of religion in a certain way. Specifically, a secular reason for an action (such as a consideration of public safety on the highway) is roughly one whose status as a justifier of action (or belief) does not evidentially depend on—but also does not deny—the existence of God; nor does it depend on theological considerations, or on the pronouncements of a person or institution as a religious authority.[95]

The goal for Audi is epistemic neutrality regarding coercive legislation, not epistemic superiority.

Audi deviates from Macedo and Dworkin on some points. He believes that religious reasoning can play a justificatory role in determining one's position on certain legislation. Audi does believe, however, that the religionist has a *prima facie* obligation to both possess and be willing to offer up secular justifications for enacting coercive legislation.[96] Audi states that if God is omnipotent, omniscient, benevolent, and so forth, then He will also provide secular reasons that rational-well-informed citizens would understand and to which they would agree. For example, in the case of supporting legislation for universal health care, one may ground his belief in religious reasoning.

According to Audi, to recognize other citizens as free and equal one must possess and be willing to express his beliefs with secular reasons.[97] The reasons could be according to several different secular sources. One such source is utilitarianism. The advocate can, along with his religious foundation, suggest, accept, and expect other rational citizens to understand that universal health care promotes the greater good of society. This particular piece of legislation, of course, is debatable. However, the point I am trying to make is that for Audi such secular reasoning is available for the religious believer to use. Given the principle of treating citizens freely and equally and the availability of secular reason to religionists, Audi maintains that the advocate must recognize and offer up such reasons for promoting coercive legislation.

Audi believes not only that one should exercise restraint in order to recognize citizens as free and equal or because secular reasons are available for use, but also that there are certain problems that arise when using exclusively religious reasons in the public square. Audi refers to the religious wars that tore Western Europe apart throughout history. The exclusive use of religious reasoning risks the possibility of the rise of sectarian violence. This is because the differing sects would not accept the opposing reasons as valid sources of justification for legislation and would unwaveringly resist such laws to the point of violence. Audi wrote, "if religious considerations are not appropriately balanced with secular ones in matters of coercion, there is a special problem: a clash of Gods vying for social control."[98]

Another problem that Audi envisages is that non-religious citizens would become frustrated with legislation that has no public rationale. Individuals or minority groups would be subject to laws that they feel they have no reasons to believe are rational.[99] Thus, they would feel alienated from the greater society. On top of that, when a group is unreasonably subjugated and silenced, they are more likely to resort to violence. This potential violence comes from alienation and frustration along with not being treated as free and equal citizens.

With the foregoing said, I want to point out that Audi takes a much weaker position on religious restraint than Macedo and Dworkin. For example, these aforementioned scholars believe that religious reasons have no place in public discourse. Audi's reasoning is similar to theirs in that he perceives the use of religious reasoning as potentially dangerous, which may lead to oppression;[100] however, he differs from Macedo and Dworkin in that he does not see religious reasoning as irrational.[101] Audi believes that one can use religious reasons to draw conclusions regarding public policy; however, religious reasoning cannot be the sole justifier, and one needs also to bring secular reasons with it.[102] Unlike Macedo and Dworkin, this restraint is merely a moral duty and it should not be a legal duty.[103]

5.4b Nicolas Wolterstorff

Nicolas Wolterstorff's thought, like the other detractors in this chapter, has little in common with Rawlsian thought. This is not to say there is no point of agreement between Wolterstorff's thought and Rawls' followers. It is clear that they all operate from the same basic motivation. That is, all of them desire to maximize liberty. For Rawls and Audi, religious restraint is not an attempt at suppression, but instead it is a means by which one treats his fellow citizen as free and equal. It is an attempt to keep from placing an unreasonable burden on others who do not share your reasoning.

With the foregoing said, Wolterstorff agrees with Rawlsians on this principle, yet he disagrees with them in practice. First, Wolterstorff disagrees that there is such a thing as public reason. Instead, he believes that there are "public reasons."[104] That is, interlocutors are very seldom univocal in social discourse.[105] This is especially true when it comes to coercive legislation. Going along with the example of universal health care given earlier in this chapter, Wolterstorff would agree that these are unique reasons; and, though citizens may draw the same conclusions, they do so for reasons that are foreign to others. His argument is that since there really is no such thing as one secular public reason, there is no reason to restrain religious reasoning in the public square.[106]

Second, Wolterstorff believes that not all free and equal citizens are well informed and rational. Some citizens are uninformed and irrational.[107] Many people not only do not know the facts about debated legislation, but also lack the rational ability to access or understand the proponents' arguments. For this reason, among others, Wolterstorff rejects the idea of a shared public reason. There is one qualification that could be made. One could ask himself what a citizen would agree to if he were well informed and rational. This could work; however, I could conclude that if others were well informed and rational, they would all agree with me. Then I would go out and endorse my favorite law. Then I would coerce not the imaginary well-informed and rational citizens that I conjured up, but instead, real citizens with whom I disagree. Wolterstorff rejects this qualifier on the grounds that it allows the use of imagined people to coerce real people.[108]

Third, Wolterstorff believes that to require restraint on religious reasoning—moral or otherwise—violates the nature of liberal democracy. He suggests that religious freedom is an essential part of a liberal democracy, and to require restraint on forms of reasoning violates a necessary condition for a liberal democracy to exist.[109] In dialogue with Audi, Wolterstorff writes "The liberal position—restraint on religious reason—appears to be in flagrant conflict with the idea of liberal democracy."[110]

Given that Wolterstorff holds to a Reformed position on epistemology, he believes that religious knowledge can be properly basic. He agrees with William Alston[111] and Alvin Plantinga[112] that one can have religious knowledge apart from positive justification. In this case, one is *prima facie* justified in holding certain religious propositions to be true. It is the skeptic's duty, in cases such as this, to show that the belief is in fact false. I believe that this is important to Wolterstorff's position since religious restraint rules out the use of religious beliefs that are properly basic as a source of justification for the enactment of coercive laws. Following from the traditional position that the goal of epistemology is to gain truth and avoid falsehood, Wolterstorff may say that one has an epistemic duty to offer up that which he knows to discussions concerning coercive laws rather than withholding.

Wolterstorff argues that advocates of many laws that protect citizens' rights do so from their religious beliefs.[113] Moreover, these beliefs, he suggests, are independent of secular reasoning.[114] While Rawlsians suggest that rights emerged from a social contract out from behind a "veil of ignorance," many scholars do not hold that view. In fact, without grounding rights on God's endowment, many citizens would reject the concept of rights at all. The notion that one "ought" to treat others as free and equal citizens, to many, is not adequately founded apart from God's injunction to "do onto other as you would have done to yourself." Thus, to exercise religious restraint would, for many, cut off the legs on which liberal democracy stands.

5.4c Agreement Between Robert Audi and Nicolas Wolterstorff

Robert Audi and Nicolas Wolterstorff both agree that religious liberty is a good that pluralistic democracies ought to preserve. Given that Audi fits well into the Rawlsian camp, it should be no surprise that there are several points of difference between his and Wolterstorff's view of religious reasoning and public discourse over coercive legislation. However, they do agree that religious reasoning need not be left out of the individual's decision making over such important issues of church and state. This is probably due to the fact that both Audi and Wolterstorff come from the Christian tradition. Thus, their views on how one is to reason in the public arena are informed by their experiences and background beliefs.

In addition, Audi is very sympathetic to Wolterstorff's reformed position of epistemology. Audi believes that there is "no cogent reason to deny the possibility of religious knowledge."[115] Audi most likely agrees with Wolterstorff *et al.* that there are some properly basic beliefs about God.[116] It is probably the case, also, that Audi and Wolterstorff agree on much coercive legislation that is motivated by their Christian beliefs. However, regardless of whether that is true, the two of them do differ on the doctrine of religious restraint.

5.4d Disagreement Between Robert Audi and Nicolas Wolterstorff

As I said before, Audi believes that one is *prima facie* morally required to possess as well as be willing to communicate secular reasons for any coercive law that he wishes to enact.[117] This comes even with his congeniality towards reformed epistemology. Audi agrees that there may be some properly basic beliefs about God and His will. He also believes like William Alston that one can be *prima facie* justified in beliefs from religious experience. However, Audi believes that though one can be justified in believing that God is just, loving, omnipotent, and so forth through religious experience, one cannot know whether one should raise taxes to cut the federal deficit.[118] This requires further evidence that is not generally available during religious experiences.

Audi suggests that one can be sufficiently motivated by religious reasoning; he can even have to some degree sufficient evidence from religious experience to ground advocacy of a certain piece of coercive legislation. Regarding his definition of public reason, Audi writes:

> This characterization is theologically neutral but in no way atheistic and, more important for political philosophy, allows for the possibility that religious reasons bearing on political life are both evidentially adequate and, from an ethical point of view, permissible or even desirable as *motivating grounds* for action.[119]

However, to treat people as free and equal citizens while in the public square, Audi requires that one be able and prepared to give reasons that are acceptable to those who do not share the same religious justification. Audi writes, "What it (public reason) precludes is a kind of evidential dependence of the reasons in question; it does not require reasons, such as those deriving from scripture, clerical authority, or religious experience."[120] This is a distinction between being justified and justifying one's belief. Audi admits that one may be religiously justified; however, the religious citizen must secularly justify his position to others. Again, Audi does not see this as disingenuous. He believes that God has so ordered things that if one believes that a coercive law is in line with God's will, there will also be sufficient secular justification for it.

Audi endorses the doctrine of separation. He believes that there may not be laws created *to* advance religion. However, he does believe that there may be laws *that* advance religion.[121] Audi writes, "I cannot say too emphatically, however, that this (religious neutrality) does not require abstaining from adopting policies that have the effect of advancing religion."[122] For example, many religionists desire the enactment of legislation that provides vouchers for students to attend private schools. According to Audi, the legislation has adequate secular reasons in that it provides higher-quality education for poor-inner-city students who otherwise would not be able to afford to attend a private institution. It may even be the case that religious institutions benefit and are able to teach their doctrines to the new students. However, the secular reasoning is what is important to Audi. If the voucher system's sole purpose was to advance religion, then Audi would suggest that the advocate is not "exhibiting civic virtue."[123] However, since secular reasoning accompanies the legislation, Audi accepts the fact that religion benefits from it.

Audi also believes, in contrast to Wolterstorff, that unrestrained religious reasoning will bring about groups and individuals who are rigid and unyielding in their beliefs.[124] That is, religious reasoning will come with pronouncements of condemnation and threats to undermine the system. By allowing only those beliefs upon which are publically agreed these problems are minimized.

Wolterstorff believes that Audi is wrong on several of his points, some of which are epistemological, while others are pragmatic. Frist, Wolterstorff disagrees that there should be a restraint on religious beliefs that are properly basic and to allow only beliefs that are based on secular reason. I mentioned before that the notion of rights for some is religiously justified. Wolterstorff believes that the requirement of religious restraint would render many religionists speechless when it comes to discussions over human rights.[125]

Second, where Audi believes that religious reasoning will result in religious hardheadedness, Wolterstorff has a much more confident view. Wolterstorff believes that by offering religious reasons in the public square, one has given something from which others would not have benefitted. A paradigmatic example is Martin Luther King's speech "I Have a Dream."[126] Much of King's reasoning is religious by nature. Yet, there are many out there who have found it to be rich with meaning and sufficient to justify equal treatment legislation.[127] This religiously reasoned speech was so powerful that non-Christian and non-theistic groups still use it as a jumping off point for their own causes. For example, gay rights groups have used this speech to demand the right to equal treatment laws regarding marriage.[128] Many of these advocates are neither religious in general nor Christian in specific.

Third, Wolterstorff disagrees with Audi that religious reasoning will result in religious wars. He believes that in the specific pluralistic climate—particularly in America—that freedom of religion is a good that is recognized to be preserved. More than that, Wolterstorff argues that religious reasoning leads people to believe that they ought to treat others with kindness no matter what their religious belief is. According to Wolterstorff, religious reasoning provides a basis for tolerance.

Wolterstorff believes that liberal democracy does not need to restrain certain types of reasoning in order to flourish. To treat other citizens as free and equal means to be able to tolerate—within reason—losing to the majority over an election or particular piece of legislation.[129] Liberal democracies flourish inasmuch as the losers are willing to live with their loss and not try to upset the system.[130]

Finally, Wolterstorff uses Audi's example of the non-religionists being frustrated in their alienation. He believes that the same is true for those who wish to use religious reasons. By requiring people to restrain their religious reasoning, religious groups will feel marginalized.[131] Religionists will eventually become bitter; and as a result, they will be alienated and resent their community.

According to some versions of justificatory liberalism, religious reasoning is acceptable to use as justification for enacting coercive public policy; however, all legislation must be justified to the general public through public reasons. Yet, religious reasoning that requires the presence of public reasoning is neither necessary nor sufficient to enact public moral policy. If the religionist is—or can be—motivated by other than religious justifiers, then his religious beliefs are irrelevant. If the religionist cannot be motivated by anything other than his religious convictions, then his reasons are not publically sufficient to enact coercive legislation. Either way, religious belief plays no robust part in the public policy.

5.5 Summary

At the beginning of this chapter I stated that I would address the claim that if a religious position becomes part of law it is unjust since it is based on a disputed view of the good life that dissenters are not unreasonable in rejecting. In doing so I discussed the legal scholars Stephen Macedo and Ronald Dworkin inasmuch as they use a strict Rawlsian view to suggest the necessity of religious restraint. Finally, I analyzed the dialogue between Robert Audi and Nicholas Wolterstorff concerning the place of religious reason in the public square. This analysis highlighted several problems that arise from justificatory liberalism.

First, JL asks too much from religious citizens. The requirement of religious restraint—that JL imposes on citizens—often forces religious people to choose between their understanding of the will of God and the mandates of government. JL requires that religious citizens deny that God's will has anything to do with statecraft, if they are to operate in the public arena. The alternative is for the religious citizen to refrain from taking part in certain practices of citizenship.

Second, JL fails to fulfill its own criteria. The different proponents of JL give similar criteria for what public reason entails. The need for an independent source, simplicity and being uncontroversial, and being publically accessible are some of the criteria of JL given by Rawlsian scholars. JL as a theory of public reason fails each one of these criteria. One such failure is that there is no one source that all reasonable citizens agree upon that citizens accept without question. Wolterstorff made this point clear when he asserted that there are several public reasons that are brought to the legislative table. Another example is that Rawlsian forms of JL are not at all simple. Rawls was a complex writer, and the average graduate student does not always understand his theories, much less the average American citizen who possesses much less education. Further, JL is highly controversial. Many argue that JL serves the political left, and alienates religious citizens from the public square. On top of all of this, JL is no more publically accessible than any religious tenet that it rules out. Reasons for legislation are often vague and even sometimes unavailable to the public for scrutiny. The public often lacks access to the resources that motivate certain laws, and they have to trust in the authority of the legislator who writes and enacts legislation.

Finally, JL fails to accomplish the purpose set out before it. First, JL as part of a larger Rawlsian scheme is supposed to result in the fair treatment of all citizens within the liberal democracy. However, in applying JL, the courts have shown that this treatment is not symmetrical. For example, on the one hand, the courts protect non-religious citizens from the slightest bit of religious coercion, and on the other hand, allow for high levels of coercion of religious individuals. Another example is that JL tends to rule out only the rationality of religious beliefs and leaves all other sources of justification untouched. Thus, the non-religious citizen can bring to the table any reasons she wants to enact legislation, whereas the religionist is told to hold back that which is often the most important reasons he has for voting.

JL also fails to bring about the civic peace that it promises. One of the motivations to seek out a form of public reason with which all reasonable citizens can agree is to prevent political division. However, because JL is controversial, it may fail to prevent division. It can also be argued that JL may have caused many of the current political divisions. As I said before, JL tends to stack the deck in favor of those who prefer certain laws. Because of this, detractors not only perceive those laws as unjust, but also take issue with JL, which governed the accepted types of justification that were used to enact such laws. For example, not only do many citizens disagree with pro-choice legislation, but also they reject the fact that JL *de facto* rules out pro-life arguments in the public square. This division concerns not only the law itself but also the principle of JL that was supposed to bridge the divide.

My intention for this chapter was to investigate whether a strict Rawlsian schema could justify the restraint of religious reasons for the enactment of coercive legislation. What I have attempted to show is that Rawlsian liberalism is not the obvious deliverance of reason its advocates claim it to be. Many scholars disagree with Rawlsian principles that constrain public reason. Moreover, to employ Rawlsian language, neither the Rawlsian detractors nor their arguments appeared to be unreasonable. Thus, in the end it appears that JL turns out to be a principle that citizens are not unreasonable in rejecting. Because of this, JL cannot justify itself, much less command citizens to acquiesce to its principles.

Whether JL has delivered on its promises is not as important as how it might influence how one perceives the interaction of religion and politics. The following chapter will give an account of how the separation of church and state has morphed into the separation of religious beliefs and politics. Whereas the separation of church and state refers to governing bodies, the separation of religious ideas and politics suggests something much more restrictive.

CHAPTER SIX

Intellectual Revolutions

I ended the last chapter by stating that a problem with the current state of American jurisprudence is that the separation of church and state has morphed into the separation of religion from politics and public policy. How did this happen? I intend to use this chapter to show that revolutions take place in intellectual traditions within the framework of politics. I will further show that features of an intellectual revolution are present in the current debates concerning the place of religious reasoning in a liberal democracy.

6.1 The Structure of Intellectual Revolutions

In 1962 Thomas Kuhn published the book *The Structure of Scientific Revolutions*, in which he compared the history of science to that of political revolutions. In describing the parallelism that justified his metaphor, Kuhn gave a threefold answer. First, Kuhn pointed out that "political revolutions are inaugurated by a growing sense, often restricted to a segment of the political community, that existing institutions have ceased adequately to meet the problems posed by an environment that they have in part created."[1] In the case of scientific paradigms, Kuhn suggested that these cease to be effective for that which they were created.

Perhaps the paradigm no longer yields predictive power or fails to explain certain phenomena adequately.[2]

Second, Kuhn writes, "Political revolutions aim to change political institutions in ways that those institutions themselves prohibit."[3] One example would be a democratic vote taking place in a monarchy. This parallel is also present in other intellectual traditions. An example of this from astronomy is the case of the prohibition of accepting heliocentric theories for the retrograde motion of planets from a geocentric model of the solar system.

Third, the revolutionary act of change occurs. Kuhn writes:

> …as the crisis deepens, many of these individuals commit themselves to some concrete proposal for the reconstruction of society in a new institutional framework. At that point the society is divided into competing camps or parties, one seeking to defend the old institutional constellation, the others seeking to institute some new one. And, once that polarization has occurred, political recourse fails. Because they differ about the institutional matrix within which political change is to be achieved and evaluated, because they acknowledge no supra-institutional framework for the adjudication of revolutionary difference, the parties to a revolutionary conflict must finally resort to the techniques of mass persuasion, often including force.[4]

Kuhn gives different examples of how parties within science have divided into camps defending each of their own paradigms. Eventually, a gestalt-like shift takes place and the old paradigm is no longer considered as adequate for the practice of normal science. Kuhn writes "The normal-scientific tradition that emerges from a scientific revolution is not only incompatible but often actually incommensurable with that which has gone before."[5]

Kuhn's description of scientific revolutions by use of the political revolution metaphor is apropos to the discussion of the structure of liberal democracy. I suggest this for two reasons. First, it appears that there are differing camps that embrace different paradigms concerning the nature of "normal" liberal democracy. Second, Kuhn's description of paradigm shifts in science is important to illuminate issues concerning church and state. This can be seen in the debate in the courts over what counts as real science and what counts as pseudoscience.[6] The argument over what can be taught as science in the public schools depends largely on what a liberal democracy may allow. That which liberal democracy can allow, in this case, depends on which paradigm one uses.

Kuhn's critique of the development of science reveals two things: first, those who operate in a particular paradigm are often unable to be persuaded to believe a part of a competing paradigm without embracing the whole paradigm from which it comes; and second, persuasion often comes in the form of force. This is true not only in scientific theory and large-scale revolutions in government but also for particular political theories within a governmental framework. In this case, elements of a Kuhnian type revolution are present in the current debate over American liberal democracy.

6.2 Paradigms Within the American Liberal Democracy

There are several paradigms within the American liberal democratic framework. For the purposes of this book I will focus on two particular paradigms. The first paradigm is what I will call traditionalism. The second paradigm I will call the new intellectualism.[7] These two competing paradigms fit, in many ways, the description of an intellectual revolution. Each of these paradigms is based on one's weltanschauung,[8] which largely determines the parameters of liberal democracy. Second, each one is distinct from one another in an incommensurable way. Finally, each paradigm can be used as a pedagogical tool to answer questions that arise in a liberal democracy.

6.2a Traditionalism

The traditionalist paradigm includes three principles:

1) God exists
2) Man has been endowed with rights, and
3) Religious reasoning plays a vital role in liberal democracy.

The traditionalist paradigm includes the recognition of America's religious history. For example, Michael Novak suggests that the American liberal democracy is largely based on a Jewish metaphysical and ethical system.[9] According to Novak, the early form of liberal democracy that America practiced was based on the Torah. Novak quotes the 1799 Thanksgiving sermon by Abiel Abbot, which reads:

> It has been often remarked that the people of the United States come nearer to a parallel with Ancient Israel, than any other nation upon the globe. Hence OUR AMERICAN ISREAL is a term frequently used; and common consent allows it apt and proper.[10]

Traditional accounts of the American liberal democracy not only recognize the religious language present in the founders' speeches and written work, but also take it seriously. Thus the traditionalist takes seriously John Adams' words when he says:

> We have not a government armed with power of contending with human passions unbridled by morality and religion. Avarice, ambition, revenge, or gallantry, would break the strongest cords of our Constitution as a whale goes through a net. Our Constitution is made only for a moral and religious people. It is wholly inadequate to the government of any other.[11]

Novak argues that even Jefferson was genuine in his religious beliefs. He points out that "Jefferson suggested 'a representation of the children of Israel in the wilderness, led by a cloud by day and a pillar of fire by night'" to be used for the seal of the United States.[12]

The traditional paradigm of liberal democracy contains the belief that man's rights are an endowment by God. Rights on this view are part of man's nature; and thus, they are unalienable. This is why, according to Jefferson's words, "to secure these rights, governments are instituted among men."[13] For the traditionalist, rights transcend government and law. On this view, rights exist regardless of whether society recognizes them as such; and governments can either protect them or violate them, but they cannot create them.

The foregoing understanding of rights is consistent with certain controversial philosophical principles. First, the discussion of natural rights endowed by God implies that He exists. This is a view that not all share in the current American milieu. Second, if one takes the words of Thomas Jefferson seriously, then one can know oneself to be reasonable in asserting certain religious claims as true. If one takes religious truth claims seriously, then there is no reason to leave religious influence outside the realm of public policy.

Traditionalists understand the American founders to have held a religious worldview. Furthermore, they see their religiosity as inseparable from the American form of liberal democracy. Also, traditionalists tend to perceive the religious underpinnings of the American framework as relevant today as it was at the founding of the nation.

The relevance of traditionalism finds its way into specific legislation concerning several moral issues. However, even with the religious pedigree, the traditionalist does not see this as a violation of the Establishment Clause. Contained in this paradigm is a different interpretation of the now controversial Establishment Clause.

The traditionalist interprets the Establishment Clause in light of the wording of the First Amendment that reads, "Congress shall make no law respecting an establishment of religion, or prohibiting the free exercise thereof..." Most traditionalists understand this clause to be directed to the legislative body of the federal government. Novak believes that the First Amendment has been piecemealed in such a way as to change its original intent. Novak writes:

> The authors of the Constitution, as the constitution debate and the sequence of drafts demonstrate, wished to protect the free exercise of religion in the states, including the establishment of religion in some states. To that purpose, they insisted that the federal government could neither establish one religion nor abolish the establishments existing in some states. The purpose of most of the founders was far removed from wishing to ban religion from public life altogether; it was almost directly the opposite.[14]

In this case, the term "respecting" is interpreted to mean that the federal legislature should not create laws concerning establishments of religion. That is, Congress should neither create a new national church nor destroy existing state churches. Stephen L. Carter writes:

> This history is consistent with a proposition vigorously argued by the legal scholar Steven Smith—that the original understanding, if there was one, on the separation of church and state was only to separate the *institutions* we call church and state. It was, says Smith, the church, not the people of the church, that was banned from holding power over government. And it was arguments by the institutional church, not religious arguments by ordinary citizens, that the founding generation puzzled over how to control.[15]

Whether the traditionalist desires state-endorsed churches is not the point. The point is that traditionalists tend to perceive the meaning of the amendment as a broad protection of religious liberty rather than protection from religion.

Donald Drakeman offers another example of a traditionalist understanding of the American founding. Drakeman points out that both the Establishment Clause and state-endorsed churches existed contemporaneously. Further, Drakeman asserts that the federal government paid little to no attention to this fact. It is from the sound of silence that Drakeman claims that the establishment of religion was not controversial. Drakeman uses Arthur Conan Doyle's Sherlock Holmes to illustrate his point.

> "Is there any other point which you would wish to draw to my attention?"
>
> "To the curious incident of the dog in the night-time."
>
> "The dog did nothing in the night-time."
>
> "That was a curious incident," remarked Sherlock Holmes.[16]

Drakeman refers to this as "The Clause That Didn't Bark in the Night."[17] It is because there was no controversy over the endorsement of religion the original intent was not that of the radical separation that we experience today.

Traditionalists most often interpret the Establishment Clause as merely forbidding the establishment of one particular ecclesiastical entity over all of the others, not forbidding the interaction of religion and politics altogether. Phillip Hamburger makes this point when he discusses the historical context from which the religion clauses were born. Hamburger writes:

> Yet, even as dissenting Protestants objected to the "adulterous union" of church and state and attempted to "sever" any "unnatural alliance," they did not thereby clearly endorse a separation of these institutions. On the contrary, their attacks on a union or alliance left open the possibility of other, nonestablishment connection. There were many potential connections, ranging from the cooperative to the merely moral and sociological, that came nowhere near a formal "alliance" or establishment, let alone a genuine union of church and state.[18]

This distinction between the separation of church and state and religion and politics is the result of the gestalt shift from the traditionalist paradigm to the new intellectual paradigm.

6.2b The New Intellectualism

The new intellectual paradigm is in many ways a rejection of the philosophical foundations of traditionalism. First, the new intellectuals reject the Jewish metaphysic that Novak argues for. This is not to say that new intellectuals are atheists. However, they tend to eschew the metaphysical grounding of rights. This Rawlsian approach to metaphysics also includes the rejection of religious reasoning as legitimate for public policy on matters touching fundamental rights. Because of this, the new intellectuals define rights as emerging from man and not from God.

The new intellectual paradigm interprets history differently from the traditionalists in that it perceives liberal democracy as liberating individuals from the religious superstitions of the past. According to Novak:

> Those who confine themselves to the modern outlook find it hard to believe that the founders could have been serious in using faith to lift their project off the ground. Many today imagine that the founders, being men of the Enlightenment, could not really have taken faith seriously. And if they did, well, that part of their inheritance is no longer valid or credible, but belongs in the attic with knee britches and powdered wigs. What remains valid from the founding is only what meets the test of reason: a few principles from Locke, the secular philosophy of natural rights detached from Judaism and Christianity. That is the way most historians and political philosophers seem to present the founding.[19]

As I pointed out in chapter three, Kramnick and Moore fit Novak's description in their treatment of the U.S. Constitution and the framers' original intent.[20]

Novak traces the change in paradigms back to the late nineteenth century. He argues that American academicians started looking to "Germany and other European centers to emulate."[21] According to Novak these academic elites believed America to be ideologically backwards compared to Europe. Subsequently, secular liberals from the academy, law, and media began an assault on the traditional paradigm.[22] The year 1948 ushered in one Supreme Court case after another, spurred on by the likes of Leo Pfeffer,[23] Protestants and Other Americans for the Separation of Church and State,[24] and the American Civil Liberties Union.[25] Each of these groups argued for a secular morality. According to Novak,

> …the traditional morality was relentlessly mocked and marginalized. The unmistakable subtext of the morality plays produced by the new artistic class was that a new morality is "blowing in the wind," and that the dying of the old ways should be celebrated as liberation. In the wake of this cultural cyclone, roaring in behind it, radical feminism, the celebration of homosexual life, and the relentless logic of "non-judgmentalism" raced forward unchecked.[26]

Novak argues that the reason this shift happen so quickly after 1945 was that historians and philosophers had long since dismissed the need for religious truth—specifically God—for the existence of rights.[27]

Whereas the traditionalists perceive the separation of church and state as forbidding the federal institutionalization of an ecclesiastical body, the new intellectuals see it as the complete separation of religion and politics. As shown in earlier chapters, this paradigm has become deeply entrenched in both legal scholarship and the courts.

If Kuhn is correct, the legal and political community is in what he called "the interim phase." That is, the American liberal democracy is divided into two camps, the old traditionalists and the new intellectuals. If Kuhn is correct, the next phase is a paradigm shift that will occur through coercion and force.[28] It is understandable that competing camps (on this model) would resort to coercion and force given the inability to convince the other side through reason. This is because the two paradigms are incommensurate, as Kuhn suggested. Given that the courts are presented with the task of adjudicating between the two sides, it is unfortunate that they are not immune to the shift in paradigms. If I am correct, then not only are those within the legal community not immune from this, but also the majority of them have taken sides. At this point, if Kuhn is correct, these legal scholars and jurists are unable to reason from outside their own paradigm.

The inability to reason with the competing paradigm is seen in the fact that the two sides are using equivocal language. Rights to the traditionalists mean one thing and another to the new intellectuals. For example, the traditionalists define rights in relation to the creation and one's τελος (telos).[29] On the other hand, the new intellectuals define rights as posited legal rights.[30] Even discussions concerning moral issues result in the two sides speaking about two different subjects. This is especially true in the case of abortion. Pro-lifers are speaking about the right to life of the unborn, whereas pro-choicers speak about the pregnant woman. Their arguments fall on deaf ears. Given this breakdown in communication, it is understandable that the two sides might resort to stronger forms of coercion that appear unethical to the other.

6.3 Is Kuhn Correct?

Is Kuhn's model correct? Perhaps it is correct in a descriptive sense. However, his model might not be correct in a prescriptive sense. The fact that paradigm shifts in science and other fields of inquiry have taken place does not suggest that they ought to have taken place. And just as new ideas have challenged a particular paradigm it does not follow that the paradigm will eventually be abandoned. It is my contention that though the current debate has similar features to a Kuhnian type revolution, the two paradigms are not necessarily incommensurable, and that it may be possible to reason across the current divide.

As I stated in chapter one, I believe the problem is perceptual. Because our schemas allow us to focus on one aspect of the debate while filtering out other features we are unable to reason properly. I contend that the problem lies in the fact that many on the two sides of the debate lack the ability to objectively recognize and assess the strengths and weaknesses of their own paradigms. To do such a thing, the legal community would do well to understand the philosophical foundations of their political positions. Alvin Plantinga argues that conflicts of reason between disciplines such as science and religion occur because of this lack of understanding.[31] Beckwith argues a similar point in discussing Christianity. He suggests that like secular positions, religious positions are tied together with a variety of supporting beliefs. Beckwith writes, "the Christian faith is a philosophical tapestry of interdependent ideas, principles, and metaphysical claims…"[32] I believe that focusing on these supporting beliefs is where much progress can be made.

The discussion of these second-order philosophical positions is where there may be a neutral meeting ground to adjudicate between competing paradigms of liberal democracy. By attending to one's epistemological presuppositions he may understand why he believes the other side to be unreasonable. The following chapter will focus on the epistemic features that justify the belief in one particular theory over another. I will specifically apply these features to the religious paradigm of liberal democracy and ask how it holds up compared to a secular paradigm.

CHAPTER SEVEN

Analysis of Two Competing Schemas

If what I have described in the first five chapters is accurate, the legal culture since *Everson v. the Board of Education* has operated as though the American constitutional experiment is by and large in line with the new intellectuals' paradigm that I mentioned in chapter six. This shift in paradigms can be seen in the many court decisions that correlate with the perception of the American framers as embracing certain Rawlsian principles.[1] For example, I pointed out in the previous chapters that the federal courts have expressed their perception of religion as outside of public reason and a catalyst for civil strife. Moreover, legal scholars, educators, and the wider culture reinforce these ideas. Regardless of whether one agrees with this understanding of the nature of liberal democracy, the fact remains that this is the current American political state of affairs.

I used the previous chapter to suggest that there is a divide between two competing paradigms of liberal democracy. The legal culture uses these paradigms as standards by which they govern their political ideas This chapter will ask if it is possible to perceive issues of church and state differently than that which has become entrenched in the legal culture's collective schema.

To accomplish this task I will use this chapter to critically assess the predominant paradigm that has found its way into the American federal court decision-making process. In doing so, I will compare and contrast two schemas: the federal courts' version of liberal democracy inasmuch as it pertains to church and state and religious reason in the formation of coercive legislation with an account of liberal democracy that allows, if not invites, minimalistic commitments to theistic reasoning. My intention is to show that a liberal democracy that enjoys a minimalistic amount of theism may more adequately accomplish the tasks of liberal democracy than that of its new intellectual detractors. If this is true, then it would not be unreasonable to ask for a legal system that was more open to religious reason for the enactment of coercive legislation.

7.1 The Schema of the Federal Courts

From the beginning of this book, I argued that schemas affect how one perceives answers to the fundamental questions. I stated that what one allows to count as appropriate justification for belief is often affected by one's schema. It is also the case that schemas affect one's approach to metaphysics. In the same way, whether one accepts the notion that aspects of reality are non-physical, non-existent, or unknowable is affected by this schema. From these first principles of philosophy, we approach other areas of inquiry, such as ethics, philosophical anthropology, philosophy of religion, philosophy of science, philosophy of law, and political theory. I also showed that schemas affect the interpretation of history, and I gave different accounts of the American founding that exemplified this. Finally, I showed that the federal courts have operated with a particular historical interpretation of the founding of America, an understanding of political philosophy inasmuch as it pertains to liberal democracy, and a set of philosophical assumptions regarding knowledge, reality, and morals. It is from all of this that the federal courts make decisions regarding matters of church and state.

7.2 The Legal Culture's Version of Liberal Democracy

As I said in chapter two, the federal court judges are not univocal; however, there are trends that have emerged in their decisions and language that reveal much about the dominant schema through which the courts as a whole perceive issues of church and state.[2] First, the courts tend to perceive knowledge permitted for legislation and use in the public square as limited to that which is empirically verifiable.[3] Second, the federal courts have enforced the position of methodological naturalism; this is especially true in cases concerning the definition and boundaries of scientific inquiry.[4] Third, the federal courts have accepted and espoused a version of history that ignores and at times denies the religious reasons that grounded the American constitutional experiment.[5] Fourth, because of their perception of religion as irrational, divisive, and dangerous, the courts have relegated religious reasoning to the realm of the private sphere.[6] Fifth, and finally, the legal culture by and large has used the idea of separation of church and state as an umbrella to shield the state from all religious input.

7.3 Religious Reasoning as Irrational?

This section is intended to show that religious reasoning is minimally not inferior to secular public reason; and that it may in some instances be better suited for the demands of liberal democracy. I will make much use of what J.P. Moreland refers to as the "epistemic virtues"[7] to show several points where I believe theistic reasoning is arguably superior to that which entrenched is in the legal culture. In other words, theistic schemas fulfill epistemic virtues, and they often do so better than secular schemas.

7.3a Theistic Reasoning Is Wider in Scope

My first point is to show that the new intellectual schema that has largely been embraced by legal scholars and the federal courts is narrower in scope than that of a theistic schema. As I said earlier, the courts largely embrace empiricism as a form of public reason and reject theistic reasoning. By doing this the courts narrow the amount of possible types of questions, evidence, and answers that can be brought to the table to create just laws or to recognize unjust laws. For example, the moral grounds on which the abolitionist movement stood was largely religious and not able to be empirically verified. Moral claims are not within the purview of science. Stephen Carter argued this when he writes:

> The abolitionist preachers did not think it possible to confine their vision of justice to a narrow, walled-off region called "church"; they considered action in the world not only justified but imperative. Ezra Gannett explained that the survival of the institution of slavery "is not purely a political question." Why not? Because "it has its moral side, and religion and Christianity are entitled to examine it as entering within their domain."[8]

One can verify shackles, whip marks, and slave deeds, but the moral wrongness of treating humans as beasts of burden is not something that can be taken in by means of sense perception. It was theistic arguments that informed the debate over the nature of the black race and their endowment with rights.[9]

Theistic reasoning along with empirical facts can inform moral hypotheses. The facts that were established through the senses were judged in light of a philosophical anthropology that was informed by theism; the independent physical facts did not by themselves justify a moral judgment. It was the use of theistic premises in conjunction with empirical evidence that resulted in the moral conclusion. This epistemic principle is true not only in science but also for all overlapping sources of justification. Irvin Copi writes the following concerning science and hypothesis:

> The point is that, where hypotheses of a fairly high level of abstractness or generality are involved, no observable or directly testable prediction can be deduced from just a single one of them. A whole group of hypotheses must be used as premises…[10]

Limiting knowledge to the deliverances of the hard sciences unreasonably excludes other possible ways of knowing, such as what may be derived from religious reasoning.[11]

7.3b Theistic Schemas Solve Internal Conceptual Problems

One of the signs of a good theory—in any academic discipline—is that it possesses minimal amounts of internal conceptual problems. This is true in science, history, theology, and the like. Internal conceptual problems are logical inconsistencies between the differing aspects of a theory. It is my contention that the traditional theistic account of American liberal democracy has fewer internal conceptual problems than the non-theistic account of the new intellectualism practiced in the federal courts.

One internal conceptual problem that the new intellectuals face in their construal of liberal democracy comes from the founders' use of religious language and claims about original intent. As I showed earlier, federal courts decisions have largely followed a Rawlsian schema of liberal democracy. Promoters of a strict form of Rawlsian liberal democracy often use language that is contrary to that of Thomas Jefferson. Rawlsians assert that rights arise from a social contract, whereas Jefferson wrote that God endowed man with them. If the new intellectuals want to claim that Jefferson's form of liberal democracy is a social contract in the likes of Hobbes and Rawls, then they must explain why Jefferson would use such religious language. Moreover, their explanation needs to account for why Jefferson specifically rejected the notion of a social contract in his personal letter to John Adams.[12]

Another internal conceptual problem that emerges from the current construal of liberal democracy is its inability to symmetrically apply its own principles. I have used the prior chapters to show that the federal courts have provided what would appear to be universal principles to create unbiased decisions; and yet, they have not universally applied these principles. For example, the courts have enforced the notion of doxastic voluntarism when it comes to religious belief and then dropped the principle when applying it to other doxastic practices.[13] This shows that this principle violates other parts of the larger legal theory from which the courts make their decisions.

A theory of democracy that includes theism solves these internal conceptual problems. For example, the religious language used by the framers is consistent with the notion that rights exist and that governments are established to secure them. Whereas a Rawlsian account of the American constitutional experiment has to either explain away or ignore theological language, a theistic account requires neither explanation nor ignorance.

Though simplicity is an epistemic virtue in its own right, internal conceptual problems in a theory often violate the virtue due to the need to explain away emerging problems. A theistic theory of American liberal democracy is simpler than a Rawlsian model. Given that the Rawlsian model is a fairly recent addition to the American courts' schema, it has been placed on top of the existing schema of American liberal democracy. The result of this has been the need to explain conflicting language and concepts in light of this new schema to those who maintained the prior model. Rather than simplifying the theory of liberal democracy, the Rawlsian schema has to give new reasons for both the existence of rights and explanations for how this was the framers' actual original intent.

Further, because Rawlsian liberal democracy eschews metaphysics, it surrenders itself to circular reasoning. While, alone, certain Rawlsian schemas may possess consistency, this is not the case within the current American political climate. The current state in which the courts operate contains two opposing schemas. The result is confusion of both the terms of liberal democracy and principles of liberal democracy. This is because both schemas include the same terms, but they have radically different definitions at times.

A theistic account reduces this equivocal language inasmuch as it is used in American liberal democracy. Under the current schema, terms such as "rights," "justice," "reason," "knowledge," and so forth vary in definition depending on who is using the terms. The superimposition of Rawlsian liberalism over the prior understanding of these terms creates incoherent conversations between detractors. Pro-life groups use the term rights in a way that is consistent with the language of endowment and natural law, whereas pro-choice advocates use the language of positive law and constitutional rights.[14] As I pointed out earlier and in earlier chapters, those who are engaging in legal debates are using the same terms; yet they are speaking about different things.

By operating within a theistic construal of the American liberal democracy interlocutors will be forced to use the same terms in the same way, and they will be forced to use different terms to tag different concepts. By doing this, the theory of liberal democracy is less vague, and thus, internally more coherent.

Operating under the theistic construal of liberal democracy does not entail the acceptance of its premises or conclusions. It is merely perception of the American constitutional history that includes the theistic framework of the founders. This construal does not mean that one must accept that God exists and has endowed man with rights. On the contrary, it invites disagreement. However, because of the theistic construal, that which is debatable becomes much clearer. One could now say, "I see that Jefferson believed that God endowed man with rights, but I disagree with him." He could then suggest that he still wants to enjoy performing certain acts without government interference, but he would use different terms—other than rights that entail endowment—to articulate what he means.[15]

The placing of a Rawlsian schema over that of the prior language of liberal democracy has created a complex, internally inconsistent, and at times incoherent political theory. Both theories independently of each other show more internal coherence than they do when they are combined. Rather than trying to force fit the square peg of Rawlsian liberal democracy into the round hole of theistic language, one might be wise to merely reject the original language as false, and argue for a different form of liberalism that is more consistent with one's own language.

7.3c Theistic Schemas Solve External Conceptual Problems

Certain conceptual problems arise when a theory or fact that is external to the current theory acts as a defeater for that theory. J.P. Moreland articulates how other disciplines such as philosophy can create external conceptual problems for certain scientific theories. Moreland writes:

> Conceptual problems may arise from a discipline outside of science but still be legitimately a part of science.
>
> For instance, Ptolemy's system of astronomy conflicted with general contemporary metaphysical views (which were rational beliefs at the time) that celestial motion should be perfect, that is, perfectly circular at constant speed. Leibniz and Berkeley raised conceptual problems with the meaning and intelligibility of absolute space, absolute motion, attractive and cohesive forces, and so on.[16]

Theistic accounts of American liberal democracy act as external defeaters to the current Rawlsian theory of American liberal democracy. First, theistic accounts of liberal democracy include metaphysical claims that if true, falsify aspects of Rawlsian liberalism. Contained in the theistic account is the claim that God exists and has endowed man with unalienable rights. These rights are tied up in human nature. If this claim is true, it falsifies the claim that rights are merely quid pro quos of a social contract.

Second, the Rawlsian theory understands man as an unencumbered self, and that the government should recognize and protect individuals' rights to choose the good for themselves. The theistic theory denies that man is an unencumbered self.[17] The theistic account recognizes the teleological language in the Declaration of Independence. Rather than an action or moral position being good because one believes it to be such, one believes an action or moral position to be good because it actually is good. Notice the moral property in this latter sense is contained in that which is perceived rather than the perception. This is the affirmation that proper living requires adherence to a designed plan that leads to the good that has been predetermined by something other than the individual or society. If it is true that the nature of the good life is not up to individuals, then the Rawlsian construal of man as an unencumbered self is false.

Third, external conceptual problems have been solved by giving in to the theistic account of public reason and rights. Theistic reasoning guided much of the civil rights movement. Reverend Martin Luther King Jr. preached from the pulpit, incorporated religious premises into his arguments, juxtaposed scripture with talk of rights, and referenced Christian hymns in his demand for equal treatment of the black race. If the religious motive test were applied to the reverend's arguments, he would have been silenced. However, since it has arguably been shown that his reasoning, which is outside of the Rawlsian definition of public reason, is justified and was rightfully permitted, it falsifies part of strict Rawlsian liberal democracy.[18]

7.3d Theistic Schemas Possess More Explanatory Power

Another epistemic virtue that a good theory possesses is explanatory power. A good theory should be able to identify and answer for the relevant phenomena contained within its scope. In the case of liberal democracies, the phenomena of reason, rights, and duties require explanation. Strict Rawlsian language concerning these phenomena—if consistently applied—is tautological. For instance, a reasonable person is one who uses public reason; and one who uses public reason is one who agrees with the outcome of the original position. Further, that which compels one to agree with the original position is that he is a reasonable person. The whole structure is self-referentially supporting. This is a coherentist application of truth. One could literally operate logically within the system without ever having to ostensively refer to external reality. According to this view, the only way one could be wrong is to use language differently from a source outside liberal linguistic structure. From a strict Rawlsian position, to enter into the political discussion requires that one must first divorce himself from comprehensive worldviews and metaphysical positions. To do such a thing leaves the terms concerning the abstract phenomena of reason, rights, and duties without ontological objects. On the other hand, theistic accounts of the American liberal democracy bring metaphysical commitments to the discussion. These include the belief in the existence of objective rights and duties, and the belief that reason can discover them. Theism, in this case, provides explanatory power as to why there is language of rights in the first place. It is because the language communicates some non-physical aspect of humanity to others that demands certain types of treatment.

7.3d.1 Grounding Human Rights in the Imago Dei

Theism grounds human rights in the *imago dei*.[19] The imago dei provides the grounds for intrinsic dignity and equality that the strict Rawlsian account of autonomy cannot. Francis Beckwith writes:

> …if bioethics commits itself to the idea that "human dignity" is essential to its practice, as the President's Council suggests, it follows that bioethics must embrace a philosophy of the human person, a philosophical anthropology, if you will, that can provide substantive content to the notion of "human dignity." But such a suggestion seems to run counter to two ideas that are dominant in the secular academy: (1) Enlightenment Liberalism, and (2) Scientific Materialism.[20]

Enlightenment liberalism (EL) runs counter to this because it is committed to the Rawlsian notion of justice as fairness. This notion requires that liberal democracies refrain from creating coercive legislation based on controversial notions of the good that others are not unreasonable in rejecting. In a sense, any conclusions in bioethics drawn by enlightenment should be neither contested nor controversial. Yet, EL has defined itself out of the conversation because conversations concerning human dignity require discussing the controversial subject of philosophical anthropology.

On the other hand, scientific materialism (SM) runs counter to human dignity because it cannot physically account for it. According to Beckwith, SM is committed to the claim that

> …science is the best or only way of knowing, and that science is committed to methodological naturalism (that science must proceed under the assumption that non-natural entities cannot be items of knowledge that may count against the deliverances of the hard sciences). Therefore, philosophies of the human person that affirm non-material

properties like "human dignity" are not items of real knowledge. Thus, such philosophies of the human person, though they may be privately embraced and practiced by individual citizens in accordance with their own religious sensibilities or believed on the basis of utility, none of these philosophical anthropologies may ever serve as the basis on which a society may regulate research and practices of bioethical controversy, such as embryonic stem-cell research, physician-assisted suicide, abortion, or reproductive technologies.[21]

If SM cannot account for human dignity, then there must be another account of it or it does not exist. This is the type of claim that Steven Pinker makes; and it is this claim that Beckwith is critiquing. According to Pinker, dignity is subjective. Pinker writes:

> One doesn't have to be a scientific or moral relativist to notice that ascriptions of dignity vary radically with the time, place, and beholder. In olden days, a glimpse of stocking was looked on as something shocking. We chuckle at the photographs of Victorians in starched collars and wool suits hiking in the woods on a sweltering day, or at the Brahmins and patriarchs of countless societies who consider it beneath their dignity to pick up a dish or play with a child. Thorstein Veblen wrote of a French king who considered it beneath his dignity to move his throne back from the fireplace, and one night roasted to death when his attendant failed to show up. [Leon] Kass finds other people licking an ice-cream cone to be shamefully undignified; I have no problem with it.[22]

Beckwith gives three refutations to Pinker's claim: (1) it is a non sequitur, (2) it is self-refuting, and (3) it is equivocal. Pinker's claim is a non sequitur because, as Beckwith states:

> It does not follow from the fact that there are differing understandings of human dignity that there is no such thing as intrinsic human dignity or that no one has authentic or even approximate knowledge of it. The fact that Mother Teresa and Margaret Sanger, for example, had different conceptions of human dignity does not mean that neither one was right. The premise—"people disagree on what constitutes human dignity"—is not sufficient to support the conclusion, "therefore, intrinsic human dignity is either not known or non-existent."[23]

Beckwith also points out that Pinker's claim is self-refuting because if it is true, then it falsifies itself. Beckwith writes:

> …according to Pinker's own principle, disagreement over the question of human dignity means that one ought to believe that there is no truth on the matter. Thus, Pinker himself ought to abandon his own position about human dignity's relativity as the truth on the matter, since some of us, after all, disagree with it.[24]

Finally Pinker's claim is equivocal because he is confusing accidental social conventions of behavior with the intrinsic property of dignity that grounds human value. Beckwith states:

> Conceptually, Pinker is confusing the "dignity" we often associate with social practices and what they may or may not mean to the community with the idea of dignity as a philosophical or theological concept that refers to an intrinsic property had by human persons from the moment they come into being. The former, no one doubts, is in a sense relative. But as many have pointed out, these social practices are often relative to that which is non-relative. That is, the sorts of practices offered by Pinker as evidence of dignity's relativity typically acquire their meaning and justification because of their power to actualize and protect deeper and apparently unchanging truths.[25]

Beckwith points out that the conclusion of subjectivity is the result of trying to give an empirical account of human dignity, which he finds akin to "looking for love in all the wrong places."[26]

Pinker also believes that human dignity is not necessary for bioethics, and that autonomy accomplishes the task adequately. He writes:

> Ruth Macklin…[has] argued that bioethics has done just fine with the principle of personal autonomy—the idea that, because all humans have the same minimum capacity to suffer, prosper, reason, and choose, no human has the right to impinge on the life, body, or freedom of another. This is why informed consent serves as the bedrock of ethical research and practice, and it clearly rules out the kinds of abuses that led to the birth of bioethics in the first place, such as Mengele's sadistic pseudo-experiments in Nazi Germany and the withholding of treatment to indigent black patients in the infamous Tuskegee syphilis study. Once you recognize the principle of autonomy, Macklin argued, "dignity" adds nothing.[27]

Beckwith, however, gives four points as to why Pinker is wrong on this: (1) autonomy is not identical to dignity, (2) dignity has greater explanatory power than does autonomy, (3) non-autonomous beings can have their dignity violated, and (4) Pinker's view has problems accounting for autonomy as a power had by a rational agent.

Beckwith argues his first point—autonomy is not identical to dignity—by showing that since one's autonomy "can be exercised inconsistently" with one's dignity, the two are not identical. Beckwith's second point argues that dignity has better explanatory power for the grounding of ethical research than autonomy. This is because autonomy cannot adequately rule out evil acts that take place in bioethical research. Beckwith writes:

...suppose we discovered that half of the Nazis's victims had come to believe Adolph Hitler's rhetoric and concluded that they were in fact to blame for all that was wrong with Germany. And imagine that some of them willingly became Mengele's guinea pigs and the remaining went to the gas chambers because of their love for the Fatherland. These courses of action would be entirely voluntary, an exercise of the principle of autonomy. Yet, the reason why these people were gassed was precisely the same reason why the non-voluntary victims were gassed. A bad reason to do evil does not become less of a bad reason simply because the victim voluntarily participates in his own unjustified homicide.[28]

The principle at work is not autonomy; it is human dignity. Without human dignity, autonomy fails to adequately access the morality of some acts. Beckwith points out that it is in fact autonomy that is unnecessary and not human dignity when he states, "it is the idea that human beings have intrinsic dignity that best accounts for our understanding of the wrongness of the Nazi atrocities."[29]

Beckwith's third argument shows that a human's dignity can be violated, even if he is not autonomous. Beckwith writes:

Not only can the principle of autonomy not fully account for the wrongness of the Nazi atrocities, it also cannot account for the wrongness of intentionally creating non-autonomous human beings for apparently noble purposes. And it seems that only intrinsic human dignity can do that.[30]

Beckwith suggests that if it is "prima facie wrong to destroy the physical structure necessary for the realization of a human being's basic, natural capacity for the exercisability of a function that is a perfection of its nature"[31] then two problems surface. First, autonomy is completely absent from the argument and has failed to do the work asked of it.[32] Second, this entails that humans have certain "ends that are perfection of their nature."[33] This latter point does not mesh with SM or EL, but it is at home in a theistic account of human dignity.

Beckwith's fourth point is that Pinker's account of autonomy had by rational agents has problems. Pinker believes that all of our rational faculties are the result of evolutionary chance. Pinker writes:

Our organs of computation are a product of natural selection. The biologist Richard Dawkins called natural selection the Blind Watchmaker; in the case of the mind, we can call it the Blind Programmer. Our mental programs work as well as they do because they were shaped by selection to allow our ancestors to master rocks, tools, plants, animals, and each other, ultimate in the service of survival and reproduction. Natural selection is not the cause of evolutionary change. Organisms also change over the eons because of statistical accidents in who lives and who dies, environmental catastrophes that wipe out whole families of creatures, and the unavoidable by-products of changes that are the product of selection. But natural selection is the only evolutionary force that acts like an engineer, "designing" organs that accomplish improbable adaptive outcomes (a point that has been made forcefully by the biologist George Williams and by Dawkins).[34]

Yet, if this is true, Beckwith pointed out, this means that our mental faculties cannot be trusted to be reliable. Here Beckwith was using Alvin Plantinga's evolutionary argument against naturalism. This argument states that one's faculties are geared towards survival and not necessarily true belief. Thus, to ground autonomy on rationality is futile, that is unless rationality is the result not of chance but of design. Teleology is the best explanation for autonomy, and this is best explained by theism.

7.3d.2 More Qualitative and Quantitative Explanations

Theistic accounts of reason provide both more quantitative and qualitative explanations of political phenomena within the purview of liberal democracies. Because of the metaphysical and epistemological limits placed on citizens by Rawlsian liberalism, explanations of rights and duties are limited to that which has been decided by the definition of public reason. Whereas strict Rawlsian liberals necessarily have to provide a non-religious explanation of liberal concepts, theists are at liberty to provide both non-religious and religious explanations. For example, theists can accept a social contract theory and explain that it is necessary for the greater good of mankind. The theist can further explain the nature of the greater good for mankind on theistic grounds. According to theism, the greater good is not subjectively arrived at by individuals; people discover and adhere to it. Theism explains not only objective accounts of the good but also the origin of objective duties.

According to Rawlsian liberalism, one could reason that the social contract that emerges from behind the veil of ignorance can be explained further by one's biological imperative to survive; however, it seems to me that this is as far as one can go. A biological imperative to survive and procreate does nothing to explain one's duty to survive at all or to even sincerely adhere to Rawlsian principles of fairness. A social contract that is explained by teleology does, however, objectively ground one's duty to survive and to help others do the same. Without the use of intrinsic purpose to objectively ground the proper ends of human existence, one could just as easily conclude that humans are, as William Lane Craig says, "an accidental by-product of nature, on an infinitesimal speck of dust called planet earth, which are doomed to perish individually and collectively in a relatively short amount of time."[35]

This is not assuming that all Rawlsians are naturalists. However, Rawlsian liberalism, which disallows religious or metaphysical reasoning in the public square, leaves only naturalistic explanatory options. If one does not agree with naturalism or Darwinism, then while operating in the public square he has the option of remaining silent when it comes to explaining why one would or should adhere to the social contract. The fact that acceptable public reason often requires citizens to restrain the expression of certain types of reason shows that Rawlsian liberalism has limits to what it can or is willing to explain.

For the theist, duties of fairness and civility can be explained from God's commands that are grounded in His nature. The citizen's duties can be explained by more than a behavioral aversion to harm and a chemical reaction in the brain that leads one to spawn. Theism explains why it is sometimes one's duty to put oneself in harm's way for the sake of others or to restrain oneself from certain acts. Accounts from what is acceptable public reason—that construe the individual as an unencumbered self—objectively provide no higher-ordered explanations as to why any citizen should ever commit acts of altruism or sexual restraint, or feel a moral duty to act with civility.

According to Rawlsian liberalism, to enact coercive legislation one should be able to justify the reasons for doing so in terms to which reasonable individuals would agree. Rawls knew that not all reasonable citizens would agree on coercive policy. He simply wanted to provide a framework of justification that would maximize liberty. Yet, the Rawlsian framework results in a doxastic practice that lacks the quantity of explanatory power that theism provides; and along with this, citizens are limited to explanations of political phenomena that may be qualitatively inferior to other explanations that are publically off limits.

Strict Rawlsians—who deny the existence of such metaphysical entities— could argue against the foregoing by suggesting that public reason that uses naturalism is adequate to explain objective rights and duties. Their argument may include the claim that a reasonable person who starts from the original position from behind the veil of ignorance grounds the abstract terms of Rawlsian democracy and commands acquiescence. If Rawlsian language is tautological as I have argued, then one's reasonableness means nothing more than agreement within the Rawlsian schema. This, however, is question begging, and it explains nothing except how one might apply a set number of terms when encountering another set of terms. The problem is that Rawlsian language that is uninformed by external metaphysical objects reduces to nothing more than linguistic behaviorism.

7.4 Does Religious Reasoning Lead to Civil Strife?

I stated in chapter one that issues of church and state by and large have been perceived as problematic. This perceptual starting point has driven much of the debate over religious reason in the public square. Does religious reason have a place in a liberal democracy? This question depends on the goals this form of government is expected to accomplish. For Rawlsians, autonomy is of vital importance. One's duties in this form of government stem from civility, which requires that one not violate another's autonomy unless one is justified in doing so.

I showed earlier that the prevailing legal culture's language describes religion as irrational, divisive, and dangerous. Because of this understanding, the federal courts have relegated religious reasoning to the realm of the private sphere.[36] I intend to use the following section to show that the current legal culture operates with an incomplete perceptual schema, and that one does not have to perceive religious reason as divisive and potentially dangerous.

7.4a Religious Reason as Unifying

I pointed out that many scholars and federal court judges enter into the discussion of church-state relations from the schema of the theologico-political problem. One of the problems that federal courts assume is that religion is divisive. Divisiveness is not unique to religious reason; thus, unless restraint is placed on all divisive sources of justification, to do so only in religious cases may be unreasonable. I do not intend to deny that divisions do arise with religious reasoning. I do intend, however, to show that historically religion also has shown the ability to unify people; and when this is taken into account, it has a mitigating effect. I am making the modest claim that religious reason does not necessarily entail division or danger. To show this modest claim requires only one counter-example; however, I shall endeavor to provide more than that.

History lessons are replete with examples of religious wars, inquisitions, and witch hunts.[37] However, history is replete with examples of brotherhood and charity that have been the result of religious reasoning and practice. By focusing on one aspect that is correlated with religious thought, the courts ignore the greater picture of theologico-political relations.

On the evening of December 24, 1914, British troops heard singing from the trenches on the opposing side of the battlefield of the western front. Though the lyrics were in German, the British soldiers recognized the song as "Silent Night". British soldiers joined in with their enemies from across the battlefield; thus, the *Christmas Truce* had begun. One of the British troops described the onset of the peace thusly:

They finished their carol and we thought that we ought to retaliate in some way, so we sang 'The first Noël', and when we finished that they all began clapping; and then they struck up another favorite of theirs, 'O *Tannenbaum*'. And so it went on. First the Germans would sing one of their carols and then we would sing one of ours, until when we started up "O Come All Ye Faithful" the Germans immediately joined in singing the same hymn to the Latin words *"Adeste Fidéles"*. And I thought, well, this was really a most extraordinary thing—two nations both singing the same carol in the middle of a war.[38]

The following morning a German soldier delivered a Christmas tree to the center of the battlefield known as "No Man's Land." Before long an impromptu armistice broke out in celebration of the holiday. This peace came in the face of charges of treason of those who participated in it. One German soldier who participated in this treasonous act of peace said, "It was a day of peace in war…It is only a pity that it was not a decisive peace."[39]

During the short time of peace, the two sides took the time to bury the dead that littered No Man's Land. Single graves were shared by British and German soldiers while chaplains from both sides shared in the duty of providing religious rights for the dead.[40] The enemy combatants celebrated a religious holiday together, sang songs of praise together, and mourned and prayed together. The celebrations also included playing soccer, exchanging gifts, and sharing meals. On the British line's eastern flank Muslim allies fired at Germans while they celebrated. Once they learned about that which was happening in their enemies' trenches, they showed due respect to those celebrating.

On September 11, 2001, four airliners were hijacked and used to attack American civilian and military targets. These terrorists were motivated by their religious beliefs. The hijackers' actions strengthened many people's perception of religion as a divisive and dangerous practice. This is what the prevailing schema allowed into their perceptual framework. What religious critics did not perceive for the most part has gone unspoken.

Later that evening, both houses of Congress bowed their heads for a moment of silence. One of the members, who stood in the front row, could be seen making the sign of the cross. This moment of silence by one of the three branches of government was never denounced as a misuse of governmental authority that might have a coercive effect on those who watched it. Nor did anyone cry out that the practice of religion was what caused the act of terrorism, and thus, Congress should restrain themselves lest they resort to the same terroristic-type actions. Instead, it was described as "an act of unity."[41] Immediately following this moment of silence, the two bipartisan houses began to sing "God Bless America." Whether Congress planned to do this or whether it was reaction to the trauma that arguably the most diverse city on the planet had just experienced, Americans as well as people of other nations were unified in calling out for God's blessing. Both houses were univocal in believing that something terribly evil had just been committed, and even the atheists among them respected their public display of religiosity.

The Christmas truce and the national appeal to God on 9/11 are not the only examples of unity that religion may bring. Religion unifies cultures to cultures and individuals to individuals. When American law permitted practice of slavery in the Southern states, many Catholic churches made no distinction between slave and master. Though in civil society the black man was perceived as inferior to the white man, while at mass, there was no segregation between the two races. According to the church, all were perceived as equal in the sight of God.[42] Many Catholic churches were unified with other denominations of Christianity in the abolitionist movement. Their reasoning was unequivocally religious.

There was disagreement between congregations and the pro-slavery Southerners who often used religious arguments; even many Catholics resisted the Church's official teachings[43] concerning the practice.[44] However, as time passed, the churches became more and more decidedly abolitionist.[45] As a result of their reasoning, the religionists became more unified in their belief about the nature of humanity and the moral nature of the practice of slavery. Catholics in both the North and South were unified in their denial of the scientific theory of polygenesis. This was the belief that the black man was not merely another race but instead a completely other species. John McGreevy wrote:

> One Mississippi bishop specifically urged local Jesuits to criticize the "abominable idea of the plurality of races," and Savannah's Bishop Augustin Verot, a staunch defender of slavery, later urged the world's bishops to denounce theories positing a spurious "white humanity" and "Negro humanity."[46]

It goes without saying that a large portion of the discussions over slavery included religious reasoning.

The debate over God's will and slavery was not the only consideration that colored the argument. The Southern economy was bound up by the practice of slavery. Moreover, the immediate emancipation of millions of slaves would flood the South with unemployed and uneducated citizens. Religious reasoning was arguing against the strong secular force of economic necessity. George Marsden writes:

> Therefore, by the end of the eighteenth century, with changing views of the rights of individuals reinforced by revolutionary ideology, many Americans began to question the anomaly of slavery. After the Revolution, some churches in both the North and the South took stands condemning slavery and slave owning. However, such stands prevailed only in areas where the economic and social reasons for perpetuating slavery were not strong. Hence, slavery was gradually eliminated in the North after the Revolution. In the upper South, however, where antislavery sentiment was strong for a time, both churches and politicians soon found they would lose their constituencies

if they took a strong stance. In the Deep South, more economically dependent on the slavery system, abolitionism never had a chance.[47]

When the economic variable was taken out of the picture, the prophetic voice of religious reasoning was less likely to be ignored or relegated to the private sphere.[48] The North and South's perceptual experience of religious reasoning concerning the practice of slavery became clearer and more univocal as the economic lens was lifted. While racism still exists in the United States, the predominant religious and political voices are in unison on the subject of slavery, that it was immoral and a stain on American history.

7.4b Morality and Justice

As I discussed in the previous chapters, scholars and federal court judges describe the history of church and state in ways that imply that the inclusion of religious reasoning with state policy leads to injustice and atrocities. Though Robert Audi is congenial to religious reason, he believes that due to religious wars it is best that religionists apply restraint when it comes to voting on coercive policy. I mention Robert Audi specifically because he is a Christian, and that he perceives issues of church and state largely through the same schema as many secularists. I intend to suggest that a schema that broadly paints religious reasoning as a risk factor for war is quite possibly a misrepresentation of reality.

First, correlation does not entail causation. In chapter four, I cited Kramnick and Moore as referencing the "millions" of people killed in all the religious wars of Europe.[49] It is true, there were wars in Europe. However, to refer to the wars that took place throughout the Middle Ages as "religious wars" is perhaps a misnomer. Because of the high level of integration of religion and society prior to the Reformation, it would have been hard to make a distinction between church and state. The church was the center of societal life. It provided not only a place of worship but also the hub of the social intercourse.[50] It does not necessarily follow that because state-endorsed religion correlated with state military action the former caused the latter. Each military action would have to be addressed independently to determine what role religious reasoning played in choosing to engage an enemy nation. This is especially true of one of the paradigm cases of religious wars, the Crusades.

With the foregoing said, it should be noted that the history of European conflict is one of nations fighting nations and empires fighting empires. The Crusades are not one war. Each Crusade has to be judged on its own merit. Paul F. Crawford lists four myths about the Crusades, one of which was "The Crusades represented an unprovoked attack by Western Christians on the Muslim world."[51]

In A.D. 638 Jerusalem had been taken over, and the Byzantine Empire was in constant defense of its territories. By A.D. 732 Christian territories were under threat of invasion by Muslim expansion. The original motivation for the Western Christian Empire's engagement with the Muslim Empire was not religious; it was instead defensive in nature. This defensive war would have been fought by any secular government without any religious motivation. However, given that there was such a close link to the religions of Islam and Christianity to their respective homelands, it was hard to make a distinction between the bureaucratic acts of government and the theocratic identities of the people. To this day, many Muslims associate western countries with Christianity despite attempts to separate religion from politics.[52]

Regarding wars stemming from the Protestant Reformation, the religious motivations may have been overstated. William T. Cavanaugh writes:

> For the main instigators of the carnage, doctrinal loyalties were at best secondary to their stake in the rise or defeat of the centralized State. Both Huguenot and Catholic noble factions plotted for control of the monarchy. The Queen Mother Catherine de Medici, for her part, attempted to bring both factions under the sway of the crown. At the Colloquy of Poissy in 1561, Catherine proposed bringing Calvinist and Catholic together under a State-controlled Church modeled on Elizabeth's Church of England. Catherine had no particular theological scruples and was therefore stunned to find that both Catholic and Calvinist ecclesiologies prevented such an arrangement. Eventually Catherine decided that statecraft was more satisfying than theology, and, convinced that the Huguenot nobility were gaining too much influence over the king, she unleashed the infamous 1572 St. Bartholomew's Day massacre of thousands of Protestants. After years of playing Protestant and Catholic factions off one another, Catherine finally threw in her lot with the Catholic Guises. She would attempt to wipe out the Huguenot leadership and thereby quash the Huguenot nobility's influence over king and country.
>
> The St. Bartholomew's Day massacre was the last time it was easy to sort out the Catholics from the Protestants in the French civil wars.[53]

At least in this case, it seems that secular interests played a role in causing strife.

7.4c Secular Reasoning and War

Has secular reasoning minimized the problems of strife and injustice that comes with religious reasoning? The answer is no, it has not. There have been several wars that have been waged on exclusively secular grounds. The short essay "The Communist Manifesto" encouraged revolutions that resulted in the loss of millions of lives. Georg von Rauch wrote the following regarding the great communist purge of Russia:

> The upheavals were set off by the murder of a prominent Party member, the Leningrad Party Secretary, Sergei Mironovich Kirov. The murder, which occurred on December 1, 1934, started a chain reaction of arrests, interrogations and executions which found its climax in the great purge, the *Chistka* of 1937–1938. According to conservative estimates about 7 to 8 million people—according to others, 23 million—became victims of this purge.[54]

While much of the purge had to do with political enemies, the Soviets targeted the church as well. The communist government killed twenty-eight archbishops and bishops and 6,775 priests. They also confiscated church land, treasures, and sacred objects. The Soviets arrested the patriarch and almost all of the surviving ecclesiastical dignitaries.[55]

Sixty-seven million Germans embraced Hitler's vision to rebuild Germany on the back of a master race. Hitler's propaganda tactic was not religious or intellectual, it was emotional. Hitler did not want to deliver complex speeches that could be understood only by the educated. He believed that offering both sides of an argument would result in the ambivalence of the crowd. According to Randall Bytwerk:

> He [Hitler] thought that the average person is uninterested in complex arguments, being ruled more by emotion than intellect. Nazi rhetoric therefore avoided presenting detailed solution to complex problems. The effective leader, Hitler thought, made things seem simple, and could "make even adversaries far removed from one another seem to belong to a single category." A speaker who attempts to persuade an audience by a complicated, developed argument, or by attacking multiple enemies, is doomed to fail.
>
> A speaker should aim at the lowest common denominator, speaking so that everyone in the audience could understand. "Among a thousand speakers there is perhaps only a single one who can manage to speak to locksmiths and university professors at the same time, in a form which not only is suitable to the receptivity of both parties, but also influences both parties with equal effect of actually lashes them into a wild storm of applause."[56]

Yet, while Hitler's propaganda tactic was emotional, he used a form of reason that was common to the general public. Hitler's public reasoning was in line with social Darwinism. In his book *From Darwin to Hitler*, Richard Weikart pointed out that while "Darwin was a typical English liberal, supporting laissez-faire economics and opposing slavery,"[57] the political demagogue Hitler made use of Darwin*ism* to convince his citizens that killing millions of people was justified.[58]

Beyond justifying acts against public enemies with Darwinian ideas, Hitler:

> …removed some of his [religious] opposition by falsely accusing churchmen of treason, theft, or sexual malpractices. Goebbels, the propaganda minister, insisted that those trials be published in detail in newspapers, thus parading lurid details about known ministers, priests, and nuns. Priests who warned parents against letting their children become a part of the Hitler Youth were subject to blackmail. Thus Catholic priests, nuns, and church leaders were arrested on trumped-up charges, and religious publications were suppressed.[59]

Hitler believed that one was a German first and a Christian second.[60]

I used the examples from communism and German fascism for three reasons. The first reason is that both of the foregoing wars were undergirded by philosophical assumptions that would pass as secular reasoning in the eyes of the United States federal courts.[61] The second reason I used these two examples is that they both shared a commitment to the silencing of the religious voice in matters that conflicted with state policy. Third, by widening one's perceptual scheme one can see that theistic reason does not necessitate war and that it may even be necessary for justice.

7.5 Summary

I intended to use this chapter to illustrate three things. First, I showed that religious reasoning in many cases fulfills certain epistemic virtues. Given this, theists can rest assured that they are justified in their beliefs; and further, they are not irrational as many scholars, judges, and those in the public square perceive them to be. Moreover, because religious reasoning often fulfills such criteria, one is not irrational in asserting the truth of his claims inasmuch as they are epistemically sound.

Second, I gave a sample of positive historical events that were correlated with theism. This was to illustrate that the history of religion is not necessarily one of violence and injustice. I left out long discussions of charity work for the homeless, substance abusers, women's shelters, and advocacy for civil rights. My point was to show that if one changes his focus, he can perceive theologico-political issues differently. This is not to say that I wanted to portray the history of church and state in only a positive light; instead, it is merely to show that discussions that include only negative encounters with religion are too narrow in scope to have a complete perception of the relationship of church and state.

Third, I wanted to contrast the positive accounts of religious reason and practice with accounts of moral failures based on secular reasoning. My intention was to show that war, strife, and injustice are not endemic to religious reasoning. Wars happen regardless of whether religion informs the combatant; there is another variable that causes these types of problems. I also endeavored to show that religious reason can prevent war or provide just grounds to go to war. Moreover, once in war, religious reasoning provides a moral framework to act justly in war.[62] Given this, if the real purpose of restraint on religious reasoning in the public square is to avoid civil strife and war and it turns out that the problem is not with religious reason *per se*, then we would do well to focus on that which is the real problem, whatever that may be.

CHAPTER EIGHT

Conclusion

8.1 Summary of Goals

At the beginning of this book I said that I would assess whether the legal culture has accurately perceived the subject of church and state. In doing so, one can also determine if the relationship between church and state is the most reasonable or even historically accurate. To achieve this goal I analyzed both well-known and more obscure court cases. I also surveyed different accounts of the American founding. From there I discussed a popular conception of liberal democracy as introduced by John Rawls. I contrasted the ideas of Rawlsian scholars with the ideas of natural law theorists to understand how one might answer the Rawlsian critique. After that, I discussed the nature of intellectual revolutions. The goal of doing so was to determine the prevailing legal culture's perception of issues concerning church and state. Finally, I challenged some of the secularist perceptions concerning religious reasoning and its place in the public square.

8.2 Findings

8.2a Legal Culture's Perception of Religious Reason

In chapter two I analyzed the federal and state courts' treatment of religious reasoning and practice. I found that the courts by and large have a negative perception of religion. There are several cases where federal and state judges revealed that they have low regard for religious reasoning and practice. Judges have used pejorative language when discussing the subject matter of their cases. Furthermore, they have dismissed and ruled against parties merely on the grounds that these parties were or are organically connected to religion in some way or another.

The courts also, by and large, perceive religious practice as divisive and dangerous. Just as federal and state judges asserted that religion is irrational, they also have issued warnings about the dangers of mixing religion and politics. Judges have reminded citizens about the religious wars that occurred when religion and politics merged. They have attributed the deaths of millions of people to the connection of church and state. The courts use this perception of religion to serve as a warning to those who desire certain accommodations to be made for their religious beliefs or practices.

The courts also perceive religious reason to be coercive and a threat to citizens' autonomy. Several cases show that judges perceive religious reasoning as indoctrination. It can surely be argued that judges perceive their duty to protect the public square from religious reasoning. This has been made clear in the many court cases that condemn religious ideas and practices for their apparently coercive nature. This perceived duty is especially evident in cases concerning class instruction and school prayer. The courts seem to fear that exposure to religious ideas might sway students away from the secular topics taught in the schools. The implication of this being that public schools represent "reason," whereas religious institutions represent something "subrational."

Although the courts have insisted that their motive is to protect the private religious beliefs from the coercive nature of the state, they instead have protected the teaching of secular concepts that belittle or reject religious ideas. The cases I surveyed revealed that the courts perceive themselves as protecting religious ideas from other religious ideas, and they are not concerned about protecting religious ideas from secular and even atheistic viewpoints.

The courts have claimed to use the principle of neutrality to try to fairly adjudicate cases concerning religion and politics. I found, however, the principle they employ is in fact not neutral. In the cases I observed, it almost always served the interests of those who rejected religious reasoning. I found that the courts tended to protect secularists at the expense of religious citizens. This was especially true in cases of school prayer and moments of silence. The courts also failed to protect religious students from the strong coercive force of state-funded schools. Judges have affirmed the rights of public universities to drop students from their programs if those students were unwilling to act against their religious consciences. What is presented as a "principle of neutrality" has resulted in the asymmetrical treatment of religious and non-religious citizens.

Because of the perception of religion as irrational, divisive and dangerous, and coercive, many judges have insisted that religion should be relegated to the private sphere. Justice Scalia recognized the Court's trend to insist that religious beliefs remain private. He went so far as to suggest that "The Court apparently thinks it [religion] to be some purely personal avocation that can be indulged in secret, like pornography in the privacy of one's room. For most believers it is not and never has been."[1] Because of this perception, there is no shortage of decisions that favor complete separation of religion and politics. The courts have incorporated Jefferson's wall of separation metaphor as though religion is an invading horde from which the secular world needs protection.

8.2b Differing Historical Schemas

In chapter three I compared and contrasted differing historical schemas. I showed that there are different ways in which one may interpret the history of the American founding and the framers' original intent regarding church and state issues.

8.2b.1 Separationist Schema

I examined Kramnick and Moore's interpretation of constitutional history. These two scholars, like the courts, incorporate the perception of religion as irrational, dangerous, and divisive. It is through this lens that they give their analysis of American history. Kramnick and Moore place much emphasis on the negative aspects of religion in colonial life. Their work leaves out any positive effects of religion on society. Like the lens through which the courts perceive issues of church and state, the authors' lens filters out the positive effects of religion and leaves only the negative correlatives. This is true even with very religious individuals to which they appeal to support their case.

Kramnick and Moore, for example, paint a very liberal picture of Roger Williams. Their work gives the impression that Williams would have rejected any religious reasoning in the public square. Moreover, one gets the sense that Williams had a disdain for the sacred being made public. This is problematic because Williams was largely motivated by religious truth.[2] While Kramnick and

Moore acknowledge his religious beliefs, they filter out his religious motivation for his political ideology. The authors' schema emphasizes Williams' separationist tendencies while blurring his value for the Christian life.

Williams, himself, would have perceived issues of church and state through his own schema. The context in which he worked was largely ignored by Kramnick and Moore. For example, the vast majority of colonial America was Christian; it was not a secular state. Disputes concerning church and state were not squabbles about religion versus secularism. Kramnick and Moore leave one with the impression that twenty-first-century attitudes concerning church and state were present in the seventeenth century.

Kramnick and Moore did give some attention to Williams' religiosity. In doing so they emphasized his departure from it. They construed Williams' secular tendencies as acts of progress in the right direction. Kramnick and Moore implied in their treatment of Williams that separation is a good, and that he is a hero of the cause.

Kramnick and Moore's description of Thomas Jefferson is very similar to their treatment of Roger Williams. They portray Jefferson as a hero to the cause of separation. The authors emphasize the fact that his political opponents called his belief in God into question. The authors failed to account for Jefferson's rebuttal of this accusation. Further, they overlooked Jefferson's own faith that may be considered by some as very sincere and deep. Kramnick and Moore perpetuated the myth that Jefferson's religious beliefs were that of a twenty-first-century secularist.

These authors emphasize Jefferson's use of the wall of separation metaphor. They bring forward the notion that Jefferson thought it should be "high and impregnable." Unfortunately, Kramnick and Moore allow this statement to stand without context. The Danbury Baptists were worried about the Congregationalists becoming the established church of the land.[3] What was a personal statement about the federal government establishing a particular denomination of Christianity has been interpreted as an official edict outlawing any involvement of religion and politics.

8.2b.2 Accommodationist Schema

As I noted in chapter three, Garrett Ward Sheldon does not overtly call for accommodation. However, his depiction of the political philosophy of Thomas Jefferson is one of congeniality. Sheldon's description of Jefferson includes the fact that Jefferson was a regular attendee of a church in which he held membership.[4] His account reveals that Jefferson had a journal with all of his favorite passages of scripture. This would later become known as Jefferson's Bible.

Sheldon also discusses Jefferson's belief that there was a "true Christianity."[5] Unlike the courts' subjective construal of religious belief, Jefferson believed there to be objective religious truth. Furthermore, I noted in chapter three that Sheldon brings to his readers' attention that Jefferson endorsed the religious instruction at all of the schools and universities. He believed that by allowing dialogue, we could converge on the true Christianity. This is certainly in contrast to the picture painted by the courts and Kramnick and Moore.

Finally, Sheldon emphasizes Jefferson's desire for the government's role in creating virtuous citizens. Sheldon's schema allows for the idea that individuals do not choose the good for themselves, and that government has a role in directing its citizens towards that end. Not only does Sheldon not ignore Jefferson's religious attitude, but also he emphasizes it.[6]

Others have noticed a lopsided treatment of history, particularly with the attention that is given to or withheld from some of the constitutional framers. Michael Novak writes:

> To celebrate James Madison's 250th birthday, the Library of Congress hosted a symposium attended by the country's most distinguished Madison scholars; the probing of Madison's religious views played a significant role. Afterward, one noted scholar told me that since he was himself a secular man, "The more secular Madison's position turns out, the more I cheer." For him, I suppose, "secular means good, progressive, forward-looking. So, yes, the fitting response is hurrah. "Religion" may be linked to intolerant, divisive, backward, dying, passé. That suggests at least a quiet boo.

> In this vein, the concentration of historians and political theorists on the least religious of the founders makes perfect sense. Why highlight what is least relevant to the future? The three figures of the founding era most studied nowadays are the figures regarded as the least religious: Jefferson, Madison, and Franklin. That there is such a concentration is not in dispute; it characterizes some Straussians on the right as well as mainline academics on the left.

> By contrast, Madison's two companions in writing The Federalist, John Jay and Alexander Hamilton, are relatively little studied. Even though John Adams was the man most admired of the age as the Father of Independence, the preeminent parliamentarian, and the leading jurist of constitutional law and history, he has today been almost forgotten. About John Dickinson, George Mason, Benjamin Rush, James Wilson, Sam Adams, John Witherspoon and other first-class minds we have been taught very little. For most of these important leaders, worthy biographies are not available, and their writings go relatively unstudied.[7]

Once a particular understanding of the framers' original intent becomes imbedded, it influences the legal culture. Cases that touch on a historical understanding of church and state are determined by the schema that the judges tend to embrace.

8.2c Sandel and Original Intent

I used chapter four to show Sandel's argument that the courts have embraced a particular stance about church and state. He strongly suggested that the courts perceive individuals as unencumbered selves. In this sense, his portrayal of the courts shows that they have embraced a schema closer to that of Kramnick and Moore's than that of Sheldon's.

Sandel's history draws different conclusions than Kramnick and Moore's. His portrayal of Roger Williams supports the use of religious reason in the public square, whereas Kramnick and Moore's portrayal supports the privatization of religious beliefs. Williams, according to Sandel, perceived government as the threat rather than religion. Sandel points out that the wall metaphor distinguished the garden from the wilderness.[8] It was the state that represented the wilderness while the church represented the garden. This point is absent in Kramnick and Moore's history and not mentioned in the many court cases I surveyed.[9]

Sandel also discusses the courts' understanding of history in its application to issues concerning church and state. The courts adopted the principle of neutrality in response to their perception of the civil strife that religion causes. The principle of neutrality tends to favor strict separation. The courts' negative perception of religion is consistent with the schema presented by Kramnick and Moore. Because of this, the courts strive to maintain government neutrality in religious matters to protect society from the perceived ills that religion brings with it.

Sandel shows that the principle of neutrality has failed in its attempt to solve the problem of civil strife. He argues that the courts do not take matters of conscience seriously because they perceive religious belief as though it is merely one's personal preference. This is evident, as I note in chapter two, by the courts' demands that religionists leave their convictions at home.

Because they have trivialized religious belief as personal preferences, some jurists have also treated controversial moral positions as though they also are statements about one's subjective opinion. For example, some jurists have used this understanding to treat the opposing positions on abortion as though they were two different answers to two different questions rather than two different answers to the same question.[10] Admittedly, for the religionist, the pro-life position is about an aspect of reality that is in most cases shaped and informed by his religious beliefs. Because much of the legal culture perceives religious claims to be irrational, any moral claims tethered to them are perceived as *de facto* irrational.

8.2d Rawlsian Unreasonableness

In chapter five I challenged the notion that one should show religious restraint when it comes to creating coercive laws.[11] I surveyed both a more radical application of Rawls' principles and a more moderate application. In both cases, I found there to be little reason to accept that coercive public policy organically connected to religion is somehow unjust merely because of its genesis.

I concluded that a strict Rawlsian schema fails to adequately justify religious restraint. The strict Rawlsian mandate fails because it cannot bear the weight of its own scrutiny. The mandate is not part of public reason. Rawlsian principles are not available to the average rational citizen. The Rawlsian schema is also based on a controversial view of the good life that others are not irrational in rejecting. Many, in fact, are rational in rejecting the Rawlsian principles upon which the doctrine of religious restraint stands. Furthermore, strict Rawlsianism fails to solve the problems it was created to solve. The search for the independent source promises to find a source of justification that is acceptable—for the creation of coercive legislation—to all rational citizens. Instead, this search marginalizes and effectively silences a whole class of rational citizens on many issues. One might argue that people who use religious reasoning are not being treated as free and equal citizens. It can be pointed out that this treatment is unfair, and thus unjust, which is exactly what the Rawlsian is trying to avoid.

8.2e Power and Reason

In chapter six I explored the Kuhnian model of intellectual revolutions. I then applied its concepts to the debate over the nature of American liberal democracy. It strengthened my claim that there are two competing schemas, each of which focuses on certain aspects of the relation between religious belief and government. Because of this, the different parties tend to speak past each other. Often, the dialogue is filled with equivocal language. Terms such as rights, justice, and reason mean different things to different people. The result is that a line has been drawn between those who hold to a religious account of American liberalism and those who reject the religious principles contained within the founders' language.

I also showed in this chapter that Kuhn argued that because competing paradigms are incommensurable, persuasion takes place through coercion. This is the situation in which the American liberal democracy finds itself. There are two sides that disagree about the history, intent, and reality of the American constitutional experiment. They also disagree vehemently over America's religious heritage and religion's place in public policy making. Unfortunately, the courts, which have the responsibility to fairly adjudicate such disputes, have largely taken a side. The courts, for the most part, have embraced the schema of the new intellectuals. As a result, the courts have helped facilitate and legitimatize the new intellectualism to the general public, something requiring coercion. This can be seen in the fact—as I showed in chapter two—that religionists have to hide their religious motives and operate from a secular paradigm while arguing before the court.

8.2f Confronting the Myths

In chapter seven I challenged the prevailing schema concerning church and state. I specifically challenged the perception of religious reasoning as irrational. The legal culture has accepted the schema of religious reason as *prima facie* unreasonable. However, upon investigation I found that religious reasoning—specifically theism—adequately fulfills many epistemic virtues even better than a secular account of American liberal democracy. I found that theists often fulfill a higher epistemic bar of rationality than do their secular counterparts.

I challenged another aspect of the legal culture's schema. I questioned the notion that religious reason is necessarily divisive and dangerous. Yet, one can just as easily perceive the peaceful unifying effects of religious reasoning as they can the negative effects. The secular schema allows the legal culture to overlook the good deeds that have come from religious reasoning. Moreover, I concluded that secular reasoning falls prey to the same criticism of divisiveness that religious reasoning does. History is full of atrocities that apparently resulted from secular reasoning. Some of these atrocities faced the lone voice of religious reason. Thus, one does not prevent division and civil strife by ridding the public square of religious reasoning. Finally, I found that religious reasoning has historically led to acts of charity, peace, and tolerance.

8.3 Implications: Two Liberal Democracies in One

One of the implications of this current legal culture is that there are two forms of liberal democracy competing for power in America. One form is understood to be founded upon principles consistent with theistic reason. The other form is founded on a secular social contract. Both of these communities use the same language of the American Constitution, but they possess two constitutions in meaning. The result of this is political power plays that leave one of the parties marginalized and increasingly voiceless.

Another implication is that if this paradigmatic struggle is unable to be solved through rational debate, then the parties involved will resort to stronger forms of coercive behavior. This is not to say that there will be a bloody revolution over the privatization of religious reasoning. However, if hardheadedness prevails, it is possible that interlocutors may forego any attempt at public reason and resort to mere public manipulation for their favorite legislation.

Finally, this book implies that the current American situation is not the best liberal democracy it can possibly be. While no liberal democracy will be without disagreement, one where its citizens agree on the rules of the game is much better than one where two games are being played. For America to flourish, especially with religious freedom, its citizens need to stand united under the same form of liberal democracy.

8.4 Suggestion

If one of the problems with the issues of church and state is the result of two competing conceptions of liberal democracy, then how should this be resolved? The available options seem to be to abandon one conception for the other or to somehow meet somewhere in the middle in some way as to appease both sides. Meeting in the middle allows for some religious accommodations; thus, for the strict separationist, this is not an option. On the other hand, to do nothing is to remain divided and leave the traditionalist in the hands of a court system that denies the rationality of its religious citizens; this is unacceptable.

One of the problems with this dilemma is that each side perceives it to be an all or nothing argument. Accepting the possibility that religion can be an adequate source of justification for legislation is not the acceptance of all religious propositions as true. Just because not all religious beliefs are rationally justifiable, it does not follow that no religious beliefs are rationally justifiable. Rationally defensible arguments are made for God's existence,[12] His will through the natural law,[13] and His action in history.[14] If the American liberal democracy is to overcome the divide, it might do well to stop bracketing arguments based on their sources. If each argument is judged on its own merit as to its truth value, then the sources of justification perhaps may become irrelevant. This means that many religious arguments will fail. Yet, this does not de facto rule out all religious arguments. What this does require is the tolerance of reasons about whose truth we are not convinced. It is also a call to religious citizens to continue to be able to articulate their legal positions rationally.

Though the foregoing dilemma is perceived as an all or nothing game, victory for a religiously justified piece of legislation does not entail an all-out theocracy. The same is true for a certain degree of separation. That is to say, separation of church and state does not entail an establishment of all-out secularism. As long as legislation aims to protect citizens' consciences, secular laws appear to be allowable.[15] Tolerance requires that we are at times willing to allow that with which we disagree to exist. Without disagreement, there is no tolerance. Thus, like earlier, not all citizens will agree with every piece of legislation; this is true in the current legal setting. Tolerance does not demand that all of its citizens agree with laws or principles upon which those laws stand; but instead, it demands that individuals respect the law inasmuch as that respect does not entail the violation of one's conscience.

What I am suggesting is that, for legal purposes, a broad scope of public reason that includes religious reasoning be accepted on a case-by-case basis. As I said earlier, this may be unacceptable to the new intellectuals. However, given that democracy demands tolerance of legislation that is enacted for the people and by the people, it seems fitting that if the people enact certain legislation, then the government ought to show the same tolerance it demands of the people.

Notes

Chapter One: Introduction

1. Pierre Manent, *An Intellectual History of Liberalism*, translated by Rebecca Balinski (Princeton, Princeton University Press, 1995), 114.
2. John Lennon, "Imagine," *Imagine* (Capitol Records, 1971).
3. See John Rawls, *Political Liberalism*, rev. ed. (New York, Columbia University Press, 1996).
4. Francis Beckwith, "Rawls's Dangerous Idea?," *Journal of Law and Religion*, Vol. 20, No. 2 (2004–2005): 433.
5. See Richard Weikart, *From Darwin to Hitler: Evolutionary Ethics, Eugenics, and Racism in Germany* (New York, Palgrave Macmillan, 2004).
6. It goes without saying that there are those who desire the removal of Darwinism from the public schools. However, the motive for its removal is that it is controversial; it is not because it is science.
7. This is a statement about beliefs as rational, not individuals. Individuals may be rational in their belief-forming practices, yet they still may be wrong. Conversely, individuals may be irrational in their belief-forming practices, and yet they might somehow form true beliefs.
8. See Isaac Kramnick and R. Laurence Moore, *The Godless Constitution: The Case Against Religious Correctness* (New York, W.W Norton & Company, 1997).
9. See Garrett Ward Sheldon, *The Political Philosophy of Thomas Jefferson* (Baltimore, Johns Hopkins University Press, 1991).

10. See Michael Sandel, "Freedom of Conscience or Freedom of Choice," *Articles of Faith, Articles of Peace: The Religious Liberty Clauses and the American Public Philosophy*, ed. James Davison Hunter, Os Guinness (Washington D.C., The Brookings Institution, 1990).

11. See Hadley Arkes, *First Things: An Inquiry into the First Principles of Morals and Justice* (Princeton, Princeton University Press, 1986).

12. Daniel L. Dreisbach, "'Sowing Useful Truths and Principles': The Danbury Baptists, Thomas Jefferson, and the 'Wall of Separation.'" *Journal of Church and State* 39 (Summer 1997).

Chapter Two: The Courts' Perception of Religion

1. To refer to *the courts* as an entity is vague. By suggesting that the courts do so and so or believe such and such lacks precision. Courts do not do, believe, or say anything. People do, believe, and say things. Those who operate in the courts are not univocal. Thus, to say that the courts say, believe, or do anything is less than accurate. Dissenting opinions in Supreme Court cases and the overturning of lower court decisions exemplify this fact. However, there are trends that judges follow from which patterns emerge. Therefore, when I use the term the *courts* I will not be using it as though the judges are univocal; but instead, I will use the term inasmuch as there appears to be a trend that emerges in court case reasoning and decision making.

2. Daniel L. Dreisbach, "'Sowing Useful Truths and Principles': The Danbury Baptists, Thomas Jefferson, and the 'Wall of Separation.'" *Journal of Church and State* 39 (Summer 1997). 456.

3. James Hitchcock, *The Supreme Court and Religion in American Life, Volume II: From "Higher Law" to "Sectarian Scruples"* (Princeton, Princeton University Press 2004), 70.

4. Hitchcock, Vol. 2, 71.

5. Kedroff v. Saint Nicholas Cathedral, 344 U.S. 94 (1952).

6. Hitchcock, Vol. 2, 70.

7. Serbian Orthodox Diocese v. Milivojevich, 426 U.S. 696 (1976), 714–715.

8. Hitchcock, Vol. 2, 71.

9. Ibid. 71.

10. Ibid. 65. See also Wolman v. Walter, 433 U.S. 229, 1977.

11. I will make the case that this has in fact happened later in this book.

12. Francis Beckwith, "Must Theology Always Sit in the Back of the Secular Bus?: The Federal Courts' View of Religion and Its Status as Knowledge." *Journal of Law and Religion* 24, No. 2 (2008–2009).

13. Ibid. 547–548.

14. Ibid.

15. U.S. v. Ballard, 322 U.S. 78 (1944).

16. Beckwith, "Must Theology," 554.

17. Ibid. 557. Beckwith gives Ludwig Wittgenstein, H.L.A. Hart, and John Rawls as examples of legal scholars whose theories are no more rational than those of certain theological claims.

18. Ibid.
19. Ibid.
20. Lee v. Weisman 505 US 577, 599–608.
21. Hitchcock, vol. 2, 48.
22. Ibid. 49.
23. West Virginia State Bd. of Educ. v. Barnette, 319 U.S. 624 (1943), 653.
24. Prince v. Massachusetts, 321 U.S. 158 (1944), 175–176.
25. Hitchcock, vol. 2, 49.
26. Everson v. Board of Education of Ewing TP., 330 U.S. 1 (1947), 5–6.
27. Ibid. 6.
28. I will address the courts' understanding of church and state history along with their perceptions of the framers' original intent for the First Amendment in the following chapter.
29. McCollum v. Board of Education, 333 U.S. 203 (1948).
30. Ibid.
31. See Abington v. Schemmp, 374, U.S. 203. In this case, the issue of Bible reading in public schools was argued. The plaintiffs who were Unitarians were joined by the atheist activist Madalyn Murray O'Hare and her son in arguing against such an activity. Hitchcock stated that Justice Clark perceived Bible reading as coercive, and that "today's trickle may become a raging torrent." See also Engel v. Vitale, 320, U.S. 421.
32. James Hitchcock, *The Supreme Court and Religion in American Life: Vol.1, The Odyssey of the Religion Clauses* (Princeton, Princeton University Press, 2004), 100.
33. Stone v. Graham (449 US 39). See also Hitchcock, *Supreme Court in American Life*, 101.
34. Santa Fe Independent School District, Petitioners, v. Jane Doe, (530 US 290), 306–308.
35. Ibid., 309–310.
36. Wallace v. Jaffree, 472 U.S. 38 (1985). Jaffree did not charge anyone with the alleged abuse his children endured. Thus, Jaffree was never shouldered with the burden to prove such allegations.
37. http://ffrf.org/outreach/awards/freethinker-of-the-year-award/ishmael-jaffree/.
38. Lee v. Weisman, 505, U.S. 577 (1991).
39. Ibid.
40. Allegheny v. American Civil Liberties Union, 492 U.S. 573.
41. Ward v. Wilbanks, No. 09-CV-11237, 2010.
42. Ibid.
43. Ward v. Polite et al., Nos. 10-2100/2145.
44. Ibid.
45. Ibid. 15. Judge Sutton wrote the following:
    None of this means that Ward should win as a matter of law with respect to her free-speech and free-exercise claims. In view of the university's claim that a no-referral policy existed for the practicum class, supported by the testimony of several professors and administrators, and in view of the reality that the purported policy arises in the context of a university's curriculum and its counseling services, the district court properly rejected Ward's cross-motion for summary judgment. Construing the evidence in the university's favor, a jury might credit the university's claim that such a policy existed and conclude that practicum students were subject to a general ban on referrals, making it difficult for Ward to demonstrate that

she was expelled on pretextual grounds as opposed to the ground that she refused to adhere to a general and reasonable curricular requirement. Just as the inferences favor Ward in the one setting, they favor the university defendants in the other. At this stage of the case and on this record, neither side deserves to win as a matter of law.

46. Often cases settle to mitigate the risk of losing. That is, both plaintiff and defendant recognize that they might lose and settle the case to minimize the damage or to maximize the reward. If this case went to trial, Ward could have been awarded a larger sum of money than what she settled for. However, the fact that this case settled shows that her counsel recognized the risk of losing.

47. See "EMU Student Achieves Final Victory After Court Rules 'Tolerance Is a Two-Way Street'," http://www.alliancedefendingfreedom.org/News/PRDetail/141. This is in contrast to another article concerning the same case, "Appellate Court Sends Ward v. Wilbanks Back to District Court," http://ct.counseling.org/2012/02/appellate-court-sends-ward-v-wil banks-back-to-district-court/. Whereas one source perceives Ward as obtaining a victory, the other perceives merely a legal procedure that resulted in a settlement.

48. Keeton v. Anderson-Whiley, No. 10-13925, 2011.

49. Ibid. 7

50. Ibid. 9. There is much to speculate about the remedial plan that was never followed. It is conceivable that Keeton could have attended the workshops, read the peer reviewed articles, increased her interaction with the homosexual community, and written all of the reflection papers detailing what she learned, and still be removed from the program. Though nowhere in the remedial plan does it stipulate that her findings must support the moral neutrality of homosexuality, one could hardly expect that her professors expected no less than that.

51. Ward v. Polite, 20. See also Keeton v. ASU, 5.

52. Ward v. Polite.

53. This is not to say that a court will not in the future find in Keeton's favor.

54. Sherbert v. Verner, 374 U.S. 398, (1963).

55. Hitchcock, *Supreme Court*, vol. 2, 69.

56. United States v. Seeger, 380 U.S. 163 (1965).

57. See Universal Military Training and Service Act, §6(j), (1948).

58. Ibid.

59. United States v. Seeger.

60. Ibid.

61. Welsh v. United States, 398 U.S. 333 (1970).

62. Ibid.

63. U.S. v. Seeger, Welsh v. U.S.

64. See McGowan v. Maryland, 366 U.S. 420 (1961). This case centered on the protection from the enforcement of Sunday closing laws.

65. Hitchcock, *Supreme Court*, vol. 2, 161.

66. Robert P. George, "A Clash of Orthodoxies," *First Things*, August, 1999.

67. Lemon v. Kurtzman, 403 U.S. 602, 1971.

68. Ibid.

69. Ibid.

70. Ibid.

71. Ibid.

72. Ibid.

73. Ibid.

74. John Witte, *Religion and the American Constitutional Experiment: Essential Rights and Liberties* (Boulder, Westview Press, 2000), 137.

75. See Jones v. Wolf, 443 U.S. 595 (1979). In 1976, Servian v. Milivojevich established that the state would not interfere with inner church squabbles. This one-hundred year stance was broken with Jones v. Wolf in 1979.

76. Ibid.

77. Serbian Orthodox Diocese v. Milivojevich (1976).

78. Witte, *Religion*, 137.

79. Goldman v. Weinberger, 475 U.S. 506 (1986).

80. Lee v. Weisman, 505 U.S. 577 (1992), 609–31.

81. Ibid.

82. Doe v. Tangipahoa Parish Sch. Bd, United States District Court for the Eastern District of Louisiana, 2005 U.S. Dist. LEXIS 3329, footnote 2. See also Lee v. Weisman, 505 U.S. 577, 603, 112 S. Ct. 2649, 120 L. Ed. 2d 467 (1992).

83. Capitol Square Review and Advisory Board v. Pinette, 515 U.S. 753, (1995).

84. Ibid.

85. Ibid.

86. See Derek H. Davis, *Religion and the Continental Congress 1774–1789: Contributions to Original Intent* (Oxford University Press, 2000), 143.

87. See Elk Grove Unified School District v. Newdow, 542 U.S. 961 (2004).

88. Newdow v. Congress 292 F. 3d 597 (9th Cir. 2002).

89. Newdow v. Congress 540 U.S. 962 (2003).

90. "Court Rejects Atheist's Challenge to 'In God We Trust,'" Associated Press, Wire Report (Tuesday, June 13, 2006).

91. See Robert Bella, "Civil Religion in America," *Daedalus, Journal of the American Academy of Arts and Sciences* 96, no. 1 (Winter, 1967).

92. Americans United for Separation of Church & State v. Porter, 485 F. Supp. 432; 1980 U.S. Dist. LEXIS 11719.

93. Ibid.

94. Ibid.

95. Ibid.

96. Hitchcock, *Supreme Court*, vol. 2, 161.

97. Ward v. Wilbanks, No. 09-CV-11237, 2010.

98. Keeton v. Anderson-Whiley, No. 10–13925, 2011.

99. See Ronald Dworkin, *Life's Dominion: An Argument About Abortion, Euthanasia, and Individual Freedom* (New York, Vintage Books, 1994), 154. Dworkin argues that one should be free to make moral choices free from religious coercion. As such, moral decisions about abortion, euthanasia, and so forth are always up to the individual.

100. Hitchcock, *Supreme Court*, vol. 2, 162. See also Michael J. Sandel, "The Procedural Republic and the Unencumbered Self" *Political Theory*, Vol. 12, No. 1. (Feb., 1984), 81–96. Sandel

states that what liberalism "presupposes is a certain picture of the person, of the way we must be if we are beings for whom justice is the first virtue. This is the picture of the unencumbered self, a self-understood as prior to and independent of purposes and ends."

101. I quoted a few judges in this chapter. The following is a list of some of the terms that were used to describe religion: incomprehensible, hostile, threatening, persecuting, intolerant, oppressive, bondage, obnoxious, indoctrinating, and evil.

Chapter Three: Historical Schemas: Original Intent and the Lenses of Separation and Accommodation

1. See *The Complete Writings of Roger Williams*, vol. 7, ed. Perry Miller (New York, Russell & Russell, Inc., 1963)

2. See John Locke, *Two Treatises of Government* (New York, Cambridge University Press, 1988). Locke writes:

The state of nature has a law of nature to govern it, which obliges every one: and reason, which is that law, teaches all mankind, who will but consult it, that being all equal and independent, no one ought to harm another his life, health, liberty, or possessions: for men being all the workmanship of one omnipotent, and infinitely wise maker; all the servants of one sovereign master, sent into the world by his order, and about his business; they are his property, whose workmanship they are, made to last during his, not one another's pleasure: and being furnished with like faculties, sharing all in one community of nature, there cannot be supposed any such subordination among us, that may authorize us to destroy one another, as if we were made for one another's uses, as the inferior ranks of creatures are for ours. 8–9.

See also "A Letter Concerning Toleration," http://www.constitution.org/jl/tolerati.htm.

3. See "The Declaration of Independence" (1776), http://www.constitution.org/jl/tolerati. htm; See also Jefferson's "Letter to the Danbury Baptists" (1802), http://www.loc.gov/loc/lcib/9806/danpre.html.

4. See James Madison, "Memorial and Remonstrance" (1784), http://www.loc.gov/loc/lcib/9806/danpre.html.

5. See Alexander Hamilton, "The Real Character of the Executive," Federalist No. 69, where it is written:

He (the British King) can confer titles of nobility at pleasure; and has the disposal of an immense number of church preferments[sic]. There is evidently a great inferiority in the power of the President, in this particular, to that of the British king; nor is it equal to that of the governor of New York, if we are to interpret the meaning of the constitution of the State by the practice which has obtained under it.

And, "The one (the U.S. President) has no particle of spiritual jurisdiction; the other (the British King) is the supreme head and governor of the national church!"; see also "The Duration in Office of the Executive," Federalist No. 71, which states:

…if they have been able, in one instance, to abolish both the royalty and the aristocracy, and to overturn all the ancient establishments, as well in the Church as State; if they have been able, on a recent occasion, to make the monarch tremble at the prospect of an innovation attempted by them, what would be to be feared from an elective magistrate of four years' duration, with the confined authorities of a President of the United States? What, but that he might be unequal to the task which the Constitution assigns him? I shall only add, that if his duration be such as to leave a doubt of his firmness, that doubt is inconsistent with a jealousy of his encroachments.

6. Some believe that the founders' statements have been misused, specifically Jefferson's "wall of separation" metaphor. John W. Whitehead writes, "the ['wall of separation'] phrase has often been used as a bludgeon by various interest groups to suppress an entire class of citizens—religious people from rightly exercising their basic freedoms." John W. Whitehead, *The Truth About the Wall of Separation* (Charlottesville, VA, The Rutherford Institute, 1997).
7. Isaac Kramnick and R. Laurence Moore, *The Godless Constitution: The Case Against Religious Correctness* (New York, W.W. Norton & Company, 1997).
8. Ibid., 12. See also R. Lawrence Moore, *Selling God: American Religion in the Marketplace of Culture* (New York, Oxford University Press, 1994) 67. Moore writes:

Brief reflections about European history leave us dazed by the various patterns of conflict and accommodation that have marked the interaction between those who have ruled churches and those who have ruled states. The one thing that these historical figures have rarely done, although the formula has been prescribed often enough, is to leave one another alone. The United States was supposed to have learned something from the turmoil of the European past and to have written a Constitution that took politics out of religion and religion out of politics. That sundering proved impossible in the young republic. What emerged were new patterns of church/state interaction that subsequently baffled just about everyone, not least the members of the nation's Supreme Court. Although the First Amendment to the Constitution banned a national establishment of religion, although Thomas Jefferson recommended a wall between church and state long before the Constitution's proscription was formally applied to them in the 1940s, religion and politics in America have remained closely related.

9. http://www.wallbuilders.com/libissuesarticles.asp?id=100766. While the Wallbuilders' description of *The Godless Constitution* may seem harsh, Kramnick and Moore use the same hyperbolic language. The authors use war metaphors when discussing accommodationists. For example, they suggest "their crusade is an old one," and that their (Christians of the

"religious right") "prime target is abortion clinics." They ask the question "should we be worried?" regarding religionists, and answer "yes." 12.

10. A separationist understanding of the framers language is common. Former dean of the Harvard Law School General Erwin N. Griswold remarked:

> Jefferson is often cited as the author of views leading to the absolutist approach. His "wall of separation" is the shibboleth of those who feel that all traces of religion must be barred from any part of public activity. This phrase comes from Jefferson's reply to the Danbury Baptist Association, dated 1 January 1802. It is clear that he wrote it deliberately, and with planned effect, as, before issuing it, he sent it to the Attorney General for comment … . What Jefferson wrote was a powerful way of summarizing the effect of the First Amendment. But it was dearly neither a complete statement nor a substitute for the words of the Amendment itself. Moreover, the absolute effect which some have sought to give to these words is belied by Jefferson's own subsequent acts and writings.
>
> Erwin N. Griswold, "Absolute Is in the Dark—A Discussion of the Approach of the Supreme Court to Constitutional Questions," *Utah Law Review* 8 (1963): 174.

11. Daniel Dreisbach, "A Godless Constitution?: A Response to Kramnick and Moore." http://www.wallbuilders.com/libissuesarticles.asp?id=84.

12. Garrett Ward Sheldon, *The Political Philosophy of Thomas Jefferson* (Baltimore: John Hopkins University Press, 1991).

13. John Witte, *Religion and the American Constitutional Experiment: Essential Rights and Liberties* (Boulder, Emory University Press, 2000), 152.

14. Ibid. 153.

15. Ibid.

16. Ibid.

17. Though Everson v. Board of Education is understood to be where the "wall of separation" became solidified, Lemon v. Kurtzman introduced the Lemon test, which banned all public entities from being excessively entangled with religion. See Everson v. Board of Education, 330 U.S. 203 (1948), and Lemon v. Kurtzman, 403 U.S. 602 (1971).

18. Witte, *Religion*, 154.

19. Ibid. 155.

20. Zorach v. Clauson, 343 U.S. 306 (1952).

21. See "The Declaration of Independence," http://www.archives.gov/exhibits/charters/declaration_transcript.html. Jefferson wrote:

> When in the Course of human events, it becomes necessary for one people to dissolve the political bands which have connected them with another, and to assume among the powers of the earth, the separate and equal station to which the Laws of Nature and of Nature's God entitle them, a decent respect to the opinions of mankind requires that they should declare the causes which impel them to the separation.

22. See Thomas Jefferson to Thomas Law, June 13, 1814, *The Complete Jefferson*, ed. Saul K. Padover (New York, Tudor, 1943). In giving an answer to what should be done for those who do not possess the moral sense given by God, Jefferson writes:

    These are the correctives which are supplied by education, and which exercise the functions of the moralist, the preacher, and legislator; and they lead into a course of correct action all those whose disparity is not too profound to be eradicated.

23. See Thomas Jefferson to Francis W. Gilmer, June 7, 1816, *The Works of Thomas Jefferson*, vol. 11, ed. Paul Ford (New York, Putnam's Sons, 1904–05). Jefferson writes the following regarding the adoption of Hobbes' understanding of human nature:

    He promises a future work on morals, in which I lament to see that he will adopt the principles of Hobbes, or humiliation to human nature; that the sense of justice and injustice is not derived from our natural organization, but founded on convention only. I lament this the more, as he is unquestionably the ablest writer living, on abstract subjects. Assuming the fact, that the earth has been created in time, and consequently the dogma of final causes, we yield, of course to this short syllogism. Man was created for social intercourse; but social intercourse cannot be maintained without a sense of justice; then man must have been created with a sense of justice.

24. See Thomas Jefferson to John Adams, October 12, 1813, *The Adams-Jefferson Letters*, vol. 2, ed. Lester J. Cappon (Chapel Hill: University of North Carolina Press, 1959), 384. Jefferson communicated to John Adams that Jesus' precepts are superior to all others. Jefferson wrote:

    We must reduce our volume to the simple evangelists, select, even from them, the very words only of Jesus, paring off the Amphibologisms into which they have been led by forgetting often, or not understanding, what had fallen from him, by giving their own misconceptions as his dicta, and expressing unintelligibly for others what they had not understood themselves. There will be found remaining the most sublime and benevolent code of morals which has ever been offered to man. I have performed this operation for my own use, by cutting verse by verse out of the printed book, and arranging, the matter which is evidently his, and which is as easily distinguishable as diamonds in a dunghill. The result is an 8 vo. of 46. pages of pure and unsophisticated doctrines, such as were professed and acted on by the unlettered apostles, the Apostolic fathers, and the Christians of the 1st. century.

25. Kramnick and Moore, *Godless Constitution*, 179. The authors claim that this text is for a general audience. As such, they have dispensed with scholarly jargon and the use of footnotes.

26. Ibid. 14.

27. Ibid.

28. Ibid. 57–58.
29. Philip Hamburger, *Separation of Church and State* (Cambridge, Harvard University Press, 2002), 52–53.
30. Ibid. 51.
31. Kramnick and Moore, *Godless Constitution*, 46.
32. Ibid. 47.
33. Ibid. 46.
34. Ibid. 48.
35. Ibid. 50. By their own words Kramnick and Moore describe integration of church and state as a "bad" thing. They openly admit that their use of both the title of the book and the contents is deliberately "pejorative." This book operates and reinforces the schema of the theologico-political problem. It also reinforces a particular schema of medieval Christianity as evil, oppressive, and ignorant.
36. Ibid. 53.
37. Hamburger, *Separation*, 50.
38. Ibid. 39–40.
39. Methodological naturalism (MN) is the view that statements about that which exists, as well as what can be known about what exists, must be described in physical terms. MN entails the belief that everything that exists is physical. It also entails the belief that all knowledge about the world must be verifiable through the senses. Thus, according to MN, God being non-physical does not exist. Or at best, one cannot know that God exists, since He is not verifiable through the senses.
40. Roger Williams, "The Hireling Ministry None of Christ's, or a Discourse Touching the Propagating the Gospel of Christ Jesus," *The Complete Writings of Roger Williams*, vol. 7, ed. Perry Miller (New York, Russell & Russell, Inc., 1963), 149.
41. Ibid.
42. Ibid.
43. See Kitzmiller v. Dover Area School District, No. 04CV2688 (2005). Laws that are motivated by religion trigger the Establishment Clause.
44. Strict separationists believe religious reasoning to be outside of public reason.
45. Kramnick and Moore, *Godless Constitution*, 73.
46. Ibid.
47. Ibid. 72.
48. Ibid. 73.
49. Ibid. 75.
50. Ibid. 86.
51. See Thomas Jefferson to Roger Weightman, June 24, 1826, http://www.loc.gov/exhibits/jefferson/214.html. Jefferson writes:

All eyes are opened, or opening, to the rights of man. The general spread of the light of science has already laid open to every view the palpable truth, that the mass of mankind has not been born with saddles on their backs, nor a favored few booted and spurred, ready to ride them legitimately, by the grace of god.

52. Kramnick and Moore, *Godless Constitution*, 69.
53. Ibid. 76.
54. Ibid. 68.
55. Thomas Jefferson to Benjamin Rush, 1800, *The Works of Thomas Jefferson*, vol. 9, ed. Paul Ford (New York, Putnam's Sons, 1904–05). See also Thomas Jefferson to Benjamin Rush, April 21, 1803. http://memory.loc.gov/master/mss/mtj/mtj1/028/0100/0191.jpg Jefferson writes:

    In some of the delightful conversations with you, in the evenings of 1798–99, and which served as an anodyne to the afflictions of the crisis through which our country was then laboring, the Christian religion was sometimes our topic; and I then promised you, that one day or other, I would give you my views of it. They are the result of a life of inquiry & reflection, and very different from that anti-Christian system imputed to me by those who know nothing of my opinions. To the corruptions of Christianity I am indeed opposed; but not to the genuine precepts of Jesus himself. I am a Christian, in the only sense he wished any one to be; sincerely attached to his doctrines, in preference to all others; ascribing to himself every human excellence; & believing he never claimed any other.

56. Kramnick and Moore, *Godless Constitution*, 90.
57. Ibid. 96.
58. Rather than serve as a polemic, as Kramnick and Moore's text, Sheldon's book does not seem to be written from the position of an activist. It appears to be merely a descriptive account of Jefferson's work.
59. Sheldon, *Political Philosophy*, 169.
60. Ibid. 110 footnote 29. Though many argue that Jefferson was a deist—and they may be correct—he was part of the local Episcopal congregation.
61. Ibid. 58
62. Ibid. 143.
63. Ibid. 110
64. This is not a claim that Jefferson was an evangelical in the contemporary sense of the term. Nor, is it even to say that he affirmed the propositions of Jesus' death, burial, and resurrection. It is merely the statement that Jefferson believed that there is such a thing as religious truth, and that it is publically accessible through discourse; much as with "all the useful sciences." Ibid. 62.
65. Ibid. 56.
66. Ibid.
67. Ibid. 57. Taken from Jefferson to John Adams, October 14, 1816, A-JL, 2:492.
68. Ibid. See Jefferson to Francis W. Gilmer, June 7, 1816, WTJ 15:25.
69. Ibid. 61
70. Ibid. 67. See Jefferson to Gov. Wilson C. Nicholes, April 2, 1816, WTJ, 14:84.
71. Ibid. 58. See also, Jefferson to John Adams, October 14, 1816, A-JL, 2:492.
72. Jefferson to Thomas Law, June 13, 1814, CJ, 1032–33.

73. Sheldon, *Political Philosophy*, 142.
74. Ibid. 143.

Chapter Four: Autonomy, Neutrality, and the Diminishing of Religious Conviction

1. In the previous chapter, I gave examples of two radically different construals of the framers' original intent.
2. Michael Sandel, "Freedom of Conscience or Freedom of Choice," in *Articles of Faith, Articles of Peace: The Religious Liberty Clauses and the American Public Philosophy*, ed. James Davison Hunter and Os Guinness (Washington D.C., The Brookings Institution, 1990).
3. Ibid. 84. Many believe the courts have not shown neutrality. There is an asymmetric relation between what the court sees as public reason and religious private reason. The secular public reason is unencumbered, but the private religious reason is constrained. Secularists are free to affect the private religious beliefs of those in the public square. However, religionists are disallowed to affect the private beliefs of others in the public square.
4. Edward Bean Underhill, a biographical introduction to *The Bloudy Tenent (sic) of Persecution for Cause of Conscience Discussed and Mr. Cotton's Letter Examined and Answered*, by Roger Williams (London, J. Haddon, Castle Street, Finsbury, 1848), ix–x.
5. Ibid. x.
6. Ibid. x.
7. Ibid.
8. Isaac Backus, *An Appeal to the Public for Religious Liberty Against the Oppressions of the Present Day*, (Boston, John Boyle, 1773).
9. During his debate against Republican nominee John McCain at Saddleback Community Church in 2008, the then presidential candidate Barack Obama deferred the question "at what point does a baby get human rights, on your view?" to one's pastor or counselor. Candidate Obama answered that this answer is "above my pay grade." This is consistent with both the notion that certain moral beliefs are tied to religious beliefs, and that governments should not make decisions over such things. However, as I will note later in this book, this answer is more consistent with the notion that the church should not inform the state rather than the state informing the church.
10. Everson v. The Board of Education, 330 U.S. 1 (1946) at 9.
11. Engel v. Vitale, 370 U.S. 421 (1962).
12. Ibid.
13. Ibid.
14. One question that will be broached in chapter six is whether it is religious reasoning alone that creates the violence.
15. Sandel, "Freedom," 81.
16. Wallace v. Jaffree, 472 U.S. 38 (1985).
17. The debate over doxastic voluntarism considers to what extent belief is an act of the will. For example, one can hardly disbelieve in his own existence.

18. Sandel, "Freedom," 88.
19. This is in reference to Justice Black's argument that "a union of government and religion tends to destroy government and to degrade religion." See Sandel "Freedom," 84.
20. Sandel, "Freedom," 91.
21. Ibid.
22. Ibid. 95.
23. Ibid. 85.
24. Ibid. See also David A. J. Richards, *Toleration and the Constitution* (New York, Oxford University Press, 1986), 140. Richards writes:

> The concerns of the two religion clauses, free exercise and antiestablishment, are, I believe, coordinated by their basis in equal respect for our twin moral power at three relevant stages: the formation, the expression, and the revision of conscience. From this perspective, the moral basis of the free exercise clause, properly understood, is a negative liberty immunizing from state coercion of the exercise of the conceptions of a life well and ethically lived and expressive of a mature person's rational and reasonable powers.

25. The liberal position is that coercion must be justified.
26. Leo Strauss, *What Is Political Philosophy?: And Other Studies* (Chicago, The University of Chicago Press, 1959), 9–10.
27. See, Aristotle, *Politics*, translated by Benjamin Jowett (Oxford, Clarendon Press, public domain, I 1253a2). I believe that Aristotle had it right when he wrote:

> Hence it is evident that the state is a creation of nature, and that man is by nature a political animal. And he who by nature and not by mere accident is without a state, is either above humanity, or below it; he is the "Tribeless, lawless, hearthless one", whom Homer denounces—the outcast who is a lover of war; he may be compared to an unprotected piece in the game of draughts.

28. This reasoning is question begging; it presupposes the existence of a good that should not exist until one autonomously chooses it.
29. "Bad" in this case means that an action somehow violates rights that flow from one's personal autonomy.
30. Sandel, "Freedom," 85.
31. Wallace v. Jaffree, 472 U.S. 38 (1985).
32. I am implying here that Alvin Plantinga is correct that a properly functioning mind results in true beliefs. See Alvin Plantinga, *Warrant and Proper Function* (New York, Oxford University Press, 1993).
33. Sandel, "Freedom," 87.
34. Ibid. 87.
35. Ibid. 87.
36. Thomas Jefferson, "The Virginia Act for Establishing Religious Freedom" (1786). http://religiousfreedom.lib.virginia.edu/sacred/vaact.html.

37. John Locke, "A Letter Concerning Toleration" (1685). http://www.constitution.org/jl/tole rati.htm.

38. James Madison, "Memorial and Remonstrance" (1784). http://archive.org/details/amemori alandrem00madigoog.

39. Sandel, "Freedom," 88.

40. Madison, "Memorial and Remonstrance." The courts use the framers' words to justify their belief that religious reasoning should not be used to coerce other citizens. This is problematic because the courts use the framers' conclusions, which are the result of religious reasoning. Thus, they are using religious reasoning to coerce others to not use religious reasoning to coerce others. The courts are intellectually cutting off the very branch upon which their argument sits. For if religious reasoning is off limits for public use, then this would rule out arguments for separation from thinkers such as Roger Williams, John Locke, and Thomas Jefferson. Yet, it is upon these thinkers' religious premises that the courts' conclusion of separation sits. The courts tend to focus in on the separationist conclusion and overlook the religious reasoning.

41. See Ward v. Wilbanks, No. 09-CV-11237 (2010). See also Keeton v. Anderson-Whiley, No. 10–13925 (2011).

42. Sandel, "Freedom," 90.

43. United States vs. Seeger, 380 U.S 163 (1965), at 166. See also Universal Military Training and Service Act §6 (J), 1965, which states:

Nothing contained in this title shall be construed to require any person to be subject to combatant training and service in the armed forces of the United States who, by reason of religious training and belief, is conscientiously opposed to participation in war in any form. As used in this subsection, the term "religious training and belief" does not include essentially political, sociological, or philosophical views, or a merely personal moral code.

44. Welsh v. United States, 398 U.S. 333 (June 15, 1979).

45. John Witte Jr., *Religion and the American Constitutional Experiment: Essential Rights and Liberties* (Boulder, CO, Westview Press, 2000), 156.

46. See Justice Clark's opinion in Abbington School District v. Schempp, 374 U.S. 203.

47. Joseph Story believed that neutrality results in official disapproval by the state. This was as early as 1851. See Donald Drakeman, *Church and State and Original Intent* (New York, Cambridge University Press, 2010), 65.

48. Ibid., footnote 10.5.

49. John Witte contends that since the 1980s—as a result of the principle of neutrality—the *free speech* clause provides more religious freedom than does the *free exercise clause*. Witte, *Religion*, 9.

50. Lemon v. Kurtzman, 403U.S. 602 (1973), at 612–614.

51. Frothingham v. Mellon, 262 U.S. 447 (1923).

52. Witte, *Religion*, 151.

53. Ibid.

54. Ibid.

55. See Ronald Dworkin, *Life's Dominion: An Argument About Abortion, Euthanasia, and Individual Freedom* (New York, Vintage Books, 1993), 162–163. Dworkin makes the case that religion is subjective, and thus, the government has no obligation to take up debates concerning competing moral claims that originate from it. However, he says that governments are not required to stay out of moral debates, since this would "paralyze government altogether." Dworkin argues that overlapping moral conclusions by government are not an endorsement of the religious belief; it is wholly separate. The religious believers are not correct because of the justificatory power of religion. He believes that government has no obligation to entertain religious arguments. The federal courts tend to hold this view.

56. Roe v. Wade, 410 U.S. 113 (1973).

57. See the Atheist and Agnostic Pro-Life League, http://www.godlessprolifers.org/home.html.

58. Kristine Kruszelnicki, "Pro-Life Atheists Invade the American Atheist Convention," *Lifesite News*, http://www.lifesitenews.com/news/pro-life-atheists-invade-the-american-atheist-convention (2012).

59. J. Hodgson, "The Rise of Pro-life Atheism," *Poletical*, http://www.poletical.com/pro-life-atheism-rising.php.

60. See Windsor v. United States, 12-2335.

61. See Reynolds v. United States, 98 U.S. 145 (1879). The Supreme Court admitted that Reynolds was free to believe whatever he wanted. However, his actions concerning marriage could be limited by the court. In this case the court had an objective understanding of marriage that did not change with differing opinions.

62. Ronald E. Long, "In Support of Same Sex Marriage," *Philosophia Christi* 7, no. 1 (2005), 29–39. See also Francis Beckwith, "Marriage, Sex, and the Jurisprudence of Skepticism: A Response to Ronald E. Long," *Philosophia Christi* 7, no. 1 (2005).

63. See Sherif Girgis, Robert P. George, and Ryan T. Anderson, "What Is Marriage," *Harvard Journal of Law & Public Policy* 34, no. 1 (2011). This view is what Girgis, George, and Anderson refer to as the "conjugal" view. The conjugal view states:

Marriage is the union of a man and a woman who make a permanent and exclusive commitment to each other of the type that is naturally (inherently) fulfilled by bearing and rearing children together. The spouses seal (consummate) and renew their union by conjugal acts—acts that constitute the behavioral part of the process of reproduction, thus uniting them as a reproductive unit. Marriage is valuable in itself, but its inherent orientation to the bearing and rearing of children contributes to its distinctive structure, including norms of monogamy and fidelity. This link to the welfare of children also helps explain why marriage is important to the common good and why the state should recognize and regulate it.

64. http://www.news-gazette.com/news/religion/2010-07-09/e-mail-prompted-complaint-over-ui-religion-class-instructor.html.

65. Ibid.

66. http://www.news-gazette.com/news/religion/2010–07–09/e-mail-complaint-student-about-ui-religion-instructor.html.

67. The following chapter will give examples of the federal courts applying the construal of moral claims as religious.
68. Ibid.
69. Windsor v. United States, 12-2335. On October 18th, 2012, Judge Jacobs ruled that the Defense of Marriage Act (DOMA) is unconstitutional.
70. Sandel, "Freedom," 89.
71. See Genesis 3:22–24 (NASB).

> Then the Lord God said, "Behold, the man has become like one of Us, knowing good and evil; and now, he might stretch out his hand, and take also from the tree of life, and eat, and live forever"—23 therefore the Lord God sent him out from the garden of Eden, to cultivate the ground from which he was taken. 24 So He drove the man out; and at the east of the garden of Eden He stationed the cherubim and the flaming sword which turned every direction to guard the way to the tree of life.

> See also, Hamburger, *Separation*, 29.

> Early and medieval Christians found in the distinction between the enclosed garden and the wilderness a profound image of their church and its purity. They read Genesis of the Garden of Eden, and, more commonly, they read in the Song of Songs (4:12) of the enclosed garden of *hortus conclusus*: "A garden included is my sister, my spouse; a spring shut up, a fountain sealed." Whether imagining the garden surrounded by a hedge, fence, or wall, Christian perceived this enclosure as significant, seeing it as a type or intimation of their walled monasteries and convents, of their faith and inner life, of Mary's virginity, and of the church itself—each of these being distinct from the world and its pollutions.

72. See Francis Beckwith, "Gimme That Ol' Time Separation: A Review Essay, Philip Hamburger, Separation of Church and State," *Chapman Law Review* 8, no. 309 (2005): 312. Concerning Jefferson's letter to the Danbury Baptists, Beckwith writes:

> Because Jefferson is one of America's Founding Fathers, this letter, which Jefferson wrote while President, has the status of a sacred text in separationist circles. In fact, among some Christian church-state separationists, Jefferson's Letter to the Danbury Baptists carries with it an authority not unlike Paul's Letter to the Galatians. And, yet, Jefferson's letter is, after all, a type of communication that presidents produce at least several times a day to a wide range of constituencies. Given that, it seems somewhat dubious to base constitutional doctrine on what amounts to nothing more than a note to political allies seeking the president's support for their religious liberty. This note was not part of an executive order, proposed legislation, or even a directive offered by the president to the attorney general as a suggested way to interpret the Establishment Clause.

Chapter Five: Rawlsian Liberal Democracy, Religious Reason, and the Disputed View of the Good

1. Though John Rawls is essential to the conversation concerning justificatory liberalism, he arguably did not hold to such a strict form of it as I will be discussing.
2. John Rawls, *A Theory of Justice* (Cambridge, The Belknap Press of Harvard University Press, 1971).
3. See John Rawls, *Political Liberalism*, 2nd ed. (New York, Columbia University Press, 1995). While Rawls' *A Theory of Justice* (TOJ) and *Political Liberalism* (PL) endeavor to accomplish two different things, PL uses the same original position scenario to offer up a "thin theory of the good" to answer for the diversity of comprehensive doctrines in a free society.
4. Ibid. 11.
5. Though John Locke may have accepted the social contract to preserve existent rights, he grounded these rights in God. On this topic, Locke wrote:

   …for men being all the workmanship of one omnipotent, and infinitely wise maker; all the servants of one sovereign master, sent into the world by his order, and about his business; they are his property, whose workmanship they are, made to last during his, not one another's pleasure: and being furnished with like faculties, sharing all in one community of nature, there cannot be supposed any such subordination among us, that may authorize us to destroy one another, as if we were made for one another's uses, as the inferior ranks of creatures are for ours.

   John Locke, *Second Treatise of Civil Government* (http://www.constitution.org/jl/2ndtr02.htm 1690), 2:5.
6. Rawls, *Political Liberalism*, 11.
7. Rawls, *A Theory of Justice*. Rawls explains that there is a "thin theory of the good," from which we arrive at the "full theory of the good." 396. Rawls writes:

   In contrast with teleological theories, something is good only if it fits into ways of life consistent with the principles of right already on hand, But to establish these principles it is necessary to rely on some notion of goodness, for we need assumptions about the parties' motives in the original position. Since these assumptions must not jeopardize the prior place of the concept of right, the theory of the good used in arguing for the principles of justice is restricted to the bare essentials. This account of the good I call the thing theory: its purpose is to secure the premises about primary goods required to arrive at the principles of justice. Once this theory is worked out and the primary goods accounted for, we are free to use the principles of justice in the further development of what I shall call the full theory of the good.

8. Rawls, *Political Liberalism*, 11.

9. Rawls, *A Theory of Justice*, 226.
10. Ibid.
11. Ibid.
12. Ibid.
13. "*Sitz im leben*" is German for "setting in life." It is usually used in literary studies to determine the historical or sociological context of a given passage.
14. Ibid. 12.
15. Ibid. 13.
16. Ibid.
17. Ibid. 136–137.
18. Rawls, *Political Liberalism*, 137.
19. The principle of justificatory liberalism (JL) states that governments must justify the enactment of coercive legislation to the citizens they serve.
20. Rawls, *Political Liberalism*, 225.
21. Rawls argued that comprehensive worldviews in general were outside of public reason. These include metaphysical positions, religious doctrines, and so forth.
22. Rawls, *A Theory of Justice*, 132. Whereas, with Locke, the social contract protected one's rights, for Rawls the social contract creates rights.
23. See Patrick Neal, "Political Liberalism, Public Reason, and the Citizen of Faith," *Natural Law and Public Reason*, ed. Robert P. George and Christopher Wolfe (Washington D.C., Georgetown University Press, 2000), 172. Even Rawls' critics recognize that he was not as restrictive on religious reasoning as were others who followed in his footsteps. Patrick Neal writes:

> Rawls is generally portrayed, along with Bruce Ackerman and Ronald Dworkin, as supporting the idea that religious discourse has no proper place in the public realm of a liberal democracy. This simple description of his position is not entirely inaccurate, but it is inaccurate in some ways. Rawls's views on the relation between religion and liberal public reason are highly complex, and also quite qualified and limited in terms of the nature of the restriction they would impose upon religious believers.

> See also Francis Beckwith, *Fides, Ratio et Juris: How Some Courts and Some Legal Theorists Misrepresent the Rational Status of Religious Beliefs*, (2012), 1. Beckwith wrote, "Rawls, himself, concedes that many of these comprehensive doctrines, including the religious ones, are reasonable."

24. See Ronald Dworkin, *Is Democracy Possible Here* (Princeton, Princeton University Press, 2006), 68. Regarding the consequences of religious reasoning, Dworkin writes:

> That story is familiar: the terrible religious wars in Europe in the sixteenth and seventeenth centuries demonstrated the tragic consequences of imposed religious orthodoxy, and religious freedom was the best and perhaps only means to stop civil war and slaughter. Our founders were particularly conscious of religion's bloody history: religious dissent was not only instrumental in settling several American colonies but a source of division and even violence within them.

25. Stephen Macedo, "Liberal Civic Education and Religious Fundamentalism: The Case of God v. John Rawls," *Ethics* 105, no. 3 (April, 1995), 470.

26. Ibid., footnote 9, 470.

27. Stephen Macedo, "The Politics of Justification," *Political Theory* 18 (1990), 280.

28. Ibid.

29. Ibid., 295.

30. Ibid. 473.

31. See Kitzmiller v. Dover Area School District, Case No. 04cv2688 (2005), at 89.

32. Macedo, "Politics of Justification," 472.

33. Ibid. 474.

34. Ibid. 474–475.

35. Ibid., footnote 30, 474.

36. See Varnum v. Brien, 763 N.W. 2d 862 (Iowa 2009), at 63. The Iowa Supreme Court wrote: Now that we have addressed and rejected each specific interest advanced by the County to justify the classification drawn under the statute, we consider the reason for the exclusion of gay and lesbian couples from civil marriage left unspoken by the County: religious opposition to same-sex marriage. The County's silence reflects, we believe, its understanding this reason cannot, under our Iowa Constitution, be used to justify a ban on same-sex marriage.

37. Ibid. 470.

38. Stephen Macedo, "In Defense of Liberal Public Reason: Are Slavery and Abortion Hard Cases?," *Natural Law and Public Reason*, ed. Robert P. George and Christopher Wolfe (Washington D.C., Georgetown University Press, 2000), 11.

39. Ibid. 11–12.

40. Ibid.

41. Ibid.

42. Ibid. 16.

43. Kitzmiller v. Dover Area School District, Case No. 04cv2688 (2005), at 89.

44. Dworkin, *Is Democracy Possible Here* (Princeton, Princeton University Press), 64. Dworkin writes:

For some time many liberal academic philosophers in America have tried to insulate their discussion of political policy from more general issues of ethical and moral philosophy and in particular from issues of theology. That strategy is based on an attractive hope: that reasonable people in political community will wish to live together on terms of mutual respect and accommodation and will therefore accept the constraints of what the very influential philosopher John Rawls called public reason. They will accept that they must justify collective political decisions to one another in terms that each can understand and whose force each can appreciate given his own comprehensive religious, moral, and ethical beliefs. That constraint would rule out appeals to even an ecumenical religious faith in a community some of whose members reject all religion. It would command a tolerant secular state. So we might try to frame our debate around the question whether we should all accept that constraint of public reason.

45. The courts may not be aware of much of the literature concerning what counts as public justification. However, they to some degree act in accordance with many concepts espoused by Macedo and others.

46. Francis J. Beckwith, "The Court of Disbelief; The Constitution's Article VI Religious Test Prohibition and the Judiciary's Religious Motive Analysis," *Hastings Constitutional Law Quarterly* 33 (Winter and Spring, 2006), 336–337. This article is not specifically interacting with Macedo. However, the principles that Macedo argues for are present in the Supreme Court's reasoning as Beckwith describes their treatment of religious motives.

47. Beckwith argues that motives are types of beliefs. Ibid., 346.

48. Ibid. 349.

49. See Stephen Macedo, *Liberal Virtues: Citizenship, Virtue, and Community in Liberal Constitutionalism* (New York, Clarendon Press, 1991).

50. Ibid. 12.

51. Ibid. 63–64.

52. Robert P. George and Christopher Wolfe, "Natural Law and Public Reason," *Natural Law and Public Reason*, ed. Robert P. George and Christopher Wolfe (Washington D.C., Georgetown University Press, 2000), 53.

53. Ibid.

54. Ibid. 54.

55. Ibid.

56. See St. Thomas Aquinas, *Summa Theologica*, article 2, Benziger Bros. Edition, trans. Fathers of the English Dominican Province (1947). By natural law I mean—as St. Thomas Aquinas says—"certain axioms or propositions are universally self-evident to all." These laws are not determined by cultures, but instead they are discovered and adhered to. For example if A=B, then it is self-evident that A has all the same features that B has and vice versa. Further, Aquinas argues that there are also natural laws that are self-evident to only to the wise. This entails the understanding of the meaning of terms contained in certain propositions as well as their logical extensions. These laws do not depend on special revelation through scripture or from clergy. For example, the intentional, unjustified killing of a human being (otherwise known as murder) is understood by all cultures without having to refer to scripture. Moreover, once these terms are understood, they can be applied to special cases to determine whether a murder has in fact taken place. Many argue that it is self-evident that abortion is murder based on that criterion.

57. Ibid. 65–66.

58. Ibid. 65.

59. Ibid. 67.

60. Ibid. 68.

61. Ibid.

62. Zorach v. Clauson, 343 U.S. 313 (1952).

63. George and Wolfe, "Natural Law," 69–70.

64. Ibid. 69.

65. Ibid.

66. Francis Beckwith, "Justificatory Liberalism and Same Sex Marriage ," *Ratio Juris: An International Journal of Jurisprudence and Philosophy of Law*, 26.4 (December 2013): 487–509. Justificatory liberalism is another term for public reason as I discussed it previously.

67. See Varnum v. Brien 763, N.W. 2d 862 (Iowa 2009), at 63.

68. See Dworkin, *Is Democracy Possible Here?*

69. See Judith Jarvis Thomson, "A Defense of Abortion," *Philosophy of Public Affairs* 1, no. 1 (Autumn, 1971), 47–66; Ronald Dworkin, *Life's Dominion: An Argument About Abortion, Euthanasia, and Individual Freedom* (New York, Vintage Books, 1994).

70. See Lawrence v. Texas, 539 U.S. 558 (2003).

71. Dworkin, *Is Democracy Possible Here?*, 71.

72. Ibid. 72.

73. California Senate Bill 48–2011–2012, http://legiscan.com/gaits/text/74798 (2012).

74. Ibid.

75. James C. McKinley, "Texas Conservatives Win Curriculum Change," *New York Times*, March 12, 2010, http://www.nytimes.com/2010/03/13/education/13texas.html?_r=1. Since Texas is such a large market, public schools in other states will be affected by these decisions. This is because the publishers will add the content that the larger Texas market will demand. Schools in other states (with less influence over publishers) use these same books; thus, the curriculum in smaller states is somewhat dictated by the state of Texas.

76. Ibid.

77. Ibid.

78. Pacific Justice Institute, Press Release: "Students Told, 'America the Beautiful' Is Lesbian Anthem," (September 25, 2012).

79. William Jefferson Clinton, Presidential Proclamation: Gay and Lesbian Pride Month, http://usgovinfo.about.com/library/weekly/blgaylesproc.htm (2000).

NOW, THEREFORE, I, WILLIAM J. CLINTON, President of the United States of America, by virtue of the authority vested in me by the Constitution and laws of the United States, do hereby proclaim June 2000 as Gay and Lesbian Pride Month. I encourage all Americans to observe this month with appropriate programs, ceremonies, and activities that celebrate our diversity and recognize the gay and lesbian Americans whose many and varied contributions have enriched our national life.

80. Barack Obama, Presidential Proclamation: Lesbian, Gay Bisexual, and Transgender Pride Month, http://www.whitehouse.gov/the-press-office/2011/05/31/presidential-proclamation-lesbian-gay-bisexual-and-transgender-pride-mon (2011).

NOW, THEREFORE, I, BARACK OBAMA, President of the United States of America, by virtue of the authority vested in me by the Constitution and the laws of the United States, do hereby proclaim June 2011 as Lesbian, Gay, Bisexual, and Transgender Pride Month. I call upon the people of the United States to eliminate prejudice everywhere it exists, and to celebrate the great diversity of the American people.

81. See Wallace v. Jaffree, 472 U.S. 38 (1985).

82. See Kitzmiller v. Dover Area School District, No. 04CV2688 (2005).

83. Francis Beckwith, Justificatory Liberalism," 2.
84. See *Catechism of the Catholic Church*, 2nd ed., 2357. On the topic of homosexuality the catechism reads:

> Homosexuality refers to relations between men or between women who experience an exclusive or predominant sexual attraction toward persons of the same sex. It has taken a great variety of forms through the centuries and in different cultures. Its psychological genesis remains largely unexplained. Basing itself on Sacred Scripture, which presents homosexual acts as acts of grave depravity, tradition has always declared that "homosexual acts are intrinsically disordered." They are contrary to the natural law. They close the sexual act to the gift of life. They do not proceed from a genuine affective and sexual complementarity. Under no circumstances can they be approved.

85. Beckwith, "Justificatory Liberalism," 23.
86. Ibid., 24.
87. Elane Photography LLC. v. Willock, Docket No. 30, 203 (2012).
88. Beckwith, "Justificatory Liberalism," 27.
89. Parker v. Hurley, 514 F.3d 87, 90 (1st Cir. 2008), cert. denied, 129 S.Ct. 56 (2008). The court opined that though the children were exposed to literature that endorsed same-sex relations and that it is in fact repugnant to the parents, beliefs, the children were not the victims of indoctrination.
90. Linda de Haan and Stern Nijland, *King and King* (Berkeley, Tricycle Press, 2000). This children's book depicts a prince who desires to marry another prince rather than marrying a princess.
91. See Wallace v. Jaffree, 472 U.S. 38 (1985). Jaffree's children were subjected to moments of silence that Jaffree believed would unjustly coerce his children through peer pressure. Analogously, the Parkers argued in Parker v. Hurley that their children were subjected to a high level of indoctrination against their religious beliefs.
92. Geddy Lee, Alex Lifeson, Niel Peart, Rush: "Free Will," *Permanent Waves*, Epic Records (1980).
93. See Robert Audi, *Religious Commitment and Secular Reason* (Cambridge, Cambridge University Press, 2000).
94. Ibid. 86.
95. Robert Audi, "Natural Reason, Natural Rights, and Governmental Neutrality Toward Religion," *Religion and Human Rights*, 4, (2009), 158.
96. Audi, *Religious Commitment*, 86.
97. Audi, "Natural Reason," 166.
98. Audi, *Religious Commitment*, 103.
99. Nicolas Wolterstorff and Robert Audi, "Liberal Democracy and Religion in Politics," *Religion in the Public Square: The Place of Religious Convictions in Political Debate* (New York, Rowman and Littlefield Publishers Inc., 1997), 32.
100. Ibid.

101. Audi, "Natural Reason," 165. Audi writes: "I do not wish to assume—and, more important, no constitutive commitments of a liberal democracy should presuppose—that the appeal to natural reasons cannot yield knowledge of God."
102. Ibid.
103. See Rawls, *Political Liberalism*, 217–218. Rawls writes:

> And since the exercise of political power must be legitimate, the ideal of citizenship imposes a moral, not a legal, duty—the duty of civility—to be able to explain to one another on those fundamental questions how the principles and policies the advocate and vote for can be supported by the political values of public reason…[Citizens] should be ready to explain the basis of their actions to one another in terms each could reasonably expect that others might endorse as consistent with their freedom and equality.

104. Nicholas Wolterstorff, "Nicholas Wolterstorff on Faith in Liberal Democracy," interviewed by Miroslav Volf, *Yale University: Faith and Global Initiative* (2009).
105. Wolterstorff and Audi, *Religion in the Public Square*, 97. Wolterstorff argues that:

> …the actual political culture of a country such as the United States, for example, is a mélange of conflicting ideas. Among those ideas are the various strands that go to make up the Idea of liberal democracy. But those are far from universally embraced.

106. Ibid. 77.
107. Wolterstorff, "Nicholas Wolterstorff."
108. Ibid.
109. Ibid.
110. Wolterstorff and Audi, *Religion in the Public Square*, 77.
111. See William P. Alston, *Perceiving God: The Epistemology of Religious Experience* (London, Cornell University Press, 1991).
112. See Alvin Plantinga, *Warrant and Proper Function* (New York, Oxford University Press, 1993).
113. Wolterstorff, "Nicholas Wolterstorff."
114. Ibid.
115. See Robert Audi, *Epistemology: A Contemporary Introduction to the Theory of Knowledge*, Routledge Contemporary Introduction to Philosophy (London, Routledge, 2000), 271.
116. Ibid., 270–276. Audi contrasts evidentialism with experientialism. The latter "grounds the justification of some very important religious beliefs in experience rather than in evidential beliefs or direct rational apprehension." 270. Audi seems to land on the side of evidentialism; however, the result of religious knowledge is affirmed by both positions.
117. It seems to me that if one is *prima facie* justified to believe that a proposition is true, then one is also justified in using that belief in public discourse. It seems to me that restraint of religious beliefs is not self-evident; thus, the burden of proof is on those who want religionists to operate with restraint.

118. Audi, "Natural Reason, Natural Rights," 158.

119. Ibid. 159. Emphasis Audi's.

120. Ibid.

121. Ibid.

122. Wolterstorff and Audi, *Religion in the Public Square*, 128.

123. Ibid. 30.

124. Audi, "Natural Reason," 170.

125. Wolterstorff, "Nicholas Wolterstorff"

126. Martin Luther King Jr., "I Have a Dream," www.archives.gov/press/exhibits/dream-speech. pdf (1963).

127. Ibid.

128. Ambra Nykol, "How Liberal and Gay Rights Activists Have Hijacked the Legacy of Martin Luther King Jr," *The New Black Magazine*, at http://www.thenewblackmagazine. com/view.aspx?index=477 (2012).

129. Wolterstorff and Audi, *Religion in the Public Square*, 112–113.

130. Wolterstorff, "Nicholas Wolterstorff"

131. Ibid.

Chapter Six: Intellectual Revolutions

1. Thomas Kuhn, *The Structure of Scientific Revolutions*, 2nd ed. (Chicago, University of Chicago Press, 1970), 92.

2. Kuhn used the famous duck/rabbit gestalt to make his point about paradigms. Whereas Kuhn used the term "paradigm," I use the term "schema."

3. Ibid.

4. Ibid. 93.

5. Ibid. 103.

6. See Kitzmiller v. Dover Area School District, Case No. 04cv2688 (2005).

7. See Michael Novak, *On Two Wings: Humble Faith and Common Sense at the American Founding* (San Francisco, Encounter Books, 2002), 110. Novak referred to the proponents of this paradigm as "intellectual and artistic elites."

8. "Weltanschauung" refers to one's worldview.

9. Novak, *On Two Wings*, 8.

10. Ibid.

11. John Adams, "To the Officers of the First Brigade of the Third Division of the Militia of Massachusetts, October 11, 1776," ed. William Bennett, *Our Sacred Honor* (New York, Simon and Schuster, 1997), 370.

12. Novak, *On Two Wings*, 8.

13. Thomas Jefferson, *"Declaration of Independence,"* http://www.archives.gov/exhibits/charters/declaration_transcript.html (1776).

14. Ibid. 114.

15. Stephen L. Carter, *God's Name in Vain, the Wrongs and Rights of Religion in Politics* (New York, Basic Books 2000), 95.

16. Arthur Conan Doyle, "The Adventures of Silver Blaze," *The Adventures of Sherlock Holmes* (Ware, U.K., Wadsworth Edition Limited, 1992), as quoted by Donald L. Drakeman, *Church, State, and Original Intent* (New York, Cambridge University Press, 2010), 326.

17. Ibid.

18. Phillip Hamburger, *Separation of Church and State* (Cambridge, MA, Harvard University Press, 2002), 28.

19. Novak, *On Two Wings*, 110.

20. Isaak Kramnick and R. Laurence Moore, *The Godless Constitution: The Case Against Religious Correctness* (New York, W.W. Norton & Company, 1997).

21. Novak, *On Two Wings*, 111.

22. Ibid. 112.

23. Leo Pfeffer Speech, 8th National Convention of the Freedom from Religion Foundation (Minneapolis, September 29, 1985). Pfeffer stated, "the Orthodox consider me to be the worst enemy they've had since Haman in the Purim story!" See also philosopedia.org/index.php/Leo_Pfeffer, "Philosopedia Lauds Leo Pfeffer as 'the 20th Century's Leading Legal Proponent of the Separation of Church and State'"; see also Torcaso v. Watkins, 367 U.S. 488. Pfeffer argued that atheist Roy Torcaso's religious freedom was infringed upon when his license as a notary public was revoked because he refused to declare his belief in the existence of God.

24. Since 1947, Americans United for the Separation of Church and State has defended strict separation of church and state. See http://www.au.org/our-work/legal/lawsuits. AU lists over one hundred court cases on its website, dating during 2003–2012, in which they fought to prevent school prayer (see A.M. ex rel. McKay v. Taconic Hills Central School District, 2nd Cir., 2012); to prevent the donation of land to Catholic schools (see, Wirtz v. City of South Bend, 7th Cir., 2011), and to challenge the placement of the Ten Commandments monument in a public park (see Chambers v. City of Frederick, U.S. District Crt. Maryland, 2003).

25. See http://www.aclu.org/aclu-history.

One of the ACLU's earliest battles was the Scopes Trial of 1925. When the state of Tennessee passed a law banning the teaching of evolution, the ACLU recruited biology teacher John T. Scopes to challenge the law by teaching the banned subject in his class. When Scopes was eventually prosecuted, the ACLU partnered with celebrated attorney Clarence Darrow to defend him. Although Scopes was found guilty (the verdict was later overturned because of a sentencing error), the trial made national headlines and helped persuade the public on the importance of academic freedom.

26. Novak, *On Two Wings*, 113.

27. Ibid.

28. On June 14, 2000, Representative Souder of Indiana addressed Congress regarding a letter that he received from eight science professors from Baylor University. The professors' goal was to prevent the teaching of intelligent design and to enforce the teaching of what they called "scientific materialism" in the classroom. Their motive for this was William Dembski's work on intelligent design that critiques Darwinism and posits a theory that possibly

proves that God designed the universe. They argued that Dembski's work is pseudo-science since it does not follow materialistic science. In this case, part of the scientific community is attempting to enforce their paradigm of liberal democracy that includes a particular paradigm of science.

29. The τελος is in relation to one's design or end. This is something the principle of autonomy usually rejects. That is, according to Rawlsians, the individual determines this for herself.

30. Ronald Dworkin, *Life's Dominion: An Argument About Abortion, Euthanasia, and Individual Freedom* (New York, Vintage Books, 1994), 162–163. Rights, for Dworkin, are applied when one becomes a "constitutional person."

31. See Alvin Plantinga, *Where the Conflict Really Lies: Science, Religion, and Naturalism* (New York, Oxford University Press, 2011).

32. Francis Beckwith, "Must Theology Always Sit in the Back of the Secular Bus?: The Federal Courts' View of Religion and Its Status as Knowledge," *Journal of Law and Religion* 24, no. 2 (2008–2009).

Chapter Seven: Analysis of Two Competing Schemas

1. I recognize that correlation entails neither causation nor identity. Many federal court judges may never have even heard of John Rawls, much less have read his work. My point here is that whether the courts were directly or indirectly influenced by Rawls is irrelevant. The relevance is that the courts have shown Rawlsian tendencies in their interpretation and application of the law.

2. Rawlsian thought has greatly influenced the United States federal courts. However, this does not mean that they embrace these views in their entirety. Moreover, it is important to note that this is not a claim that all of the courts' decisions have been consistent in the Rawlsian model. It is merely the claim that there is a trend to a significant degree towards the Rawlsian positions of Stephen Macedo and Ronald Dworkin.

3. This is especially true in cases concerning ethical claims and education. The courts have tended to embrace empiricism, which is the epistemological position that knowledge requires sense perception. See Kitzmiller v. Dover Area School District, Case No. 04cv2688 (2005).

4. See chapter six of this book. This is well established in the case of Kitzmiller v. Dover Area School District.

5. In chapter three of this book I compared two accounts of the American founding; the federal courts are consistent with an account of history that rejects religious reasoning.

6. The privatization of religious belief is argued for by Rawls (chap. 5), historians interpret the formation of the Establishment Clause through this lens (chap. 3), and the courts enforce this schema from the bench (chap. 2).

7. See J. P. Moreland, *Christianity and the Nature of Science: A Philosophical Investigation* (Grand Rapids, Baker Book House, 1989). See also J. P. Moreland, "Theistic Science and Methodological Naturalism," *The Creation Hypothesis; Scientific Evidence for an Intelligent Designer*, ed. J. P. Moreland (Downers Grove, Inter Varsity Press, 1994).

8. Stephen L. Carter, *God's Name in Vain: The Wrongs and Rights of Religion in Politics* (New York, Basic Books, 2000), 89. See also Ezra Stiles Gannett, *Relation of the North to Slavery: A Discourse Preached in the Federal Street Meetinghouse*, in Boston (Boston, Crosby, Nichols & Company, 1854), 6.

9. It is conceivable that one could apply Ronald Dworkin's argument to suggest that as long as the black race had no ability to express interests in rights, that they would not possess the constitutional rights of life, liberty, and the pursuit of happiness.

10. Irving M. Copi, "Induction: Science and Hypothesis," *Introduction to Logic*, 7th edition (New York, Macmillan Publishing Company, 1986), 508.

11. As I have enlisted Alston's and Beckwith's work to show that empiricism and methodological naturalism limit the scope of answers to moral claims, it is conceivable that these philosophical commitments are taken up to protect one's actions from moral judgment.

12. Letter from Thomas Jefferson to John Adams, October 14, 1816, A-JL, 2:492. I mentioned this letter in chapter three.

13. I mentioned earlier in this book that doxastic voluntarism is not applied to math or science. To universally apply doxastic voluntarism would suggest that no matter how obviously true a statement is one could unbelieve it at will. The legal community relies on the reliability of the laws of logic; yet, if the courts applied the principle of doxastic voluntarism to this source of justification, they would not be able to adjudicate cases. Whereas the courts treat religious beliefs as something one can pick up or put down at will, they do not do so with other disciplines. This is consistent with the legal culture's perception of religious reason as wishful thinking, rather than justified belief.

14. Ronald Dworkin argues something akin to a natural right to abortion. He suggests that if a fetus is not a person, then one may have a natural right to abortion. However, Dworkin's understanding of natural rights is not the same as how the typical natural lawyer understands natural rights. For Dworkin, rights are not the consequence of the sort of being one is; they are the consequence of what sort of powers you may be able to exercise as a being. See Ronald Dworkin, *Life's Dominion: An Argument About Abortion, Euthanasia, and Individual Freedom* (New York, Vintage Books, 1994).

15. This is not an argument for pragmatism. Instead, it is a claim that equivocal language gets in the way of the convergence upon truth.

16. Moreland, *Christianity and the Nature of Science*, 53.

17. This is not a denial of free will; it is merely a statement that the good is not something at which one arbitrarily arrives.

18. One could argue that secular public reason was adequate to justify the civil rights movement, and this may be true. However, my point is to show that it was not inappropriate for the reverend to use religious reasons or language for his demands; they did nothing but strengthen his argument.

19. See Alvin Plantinga, *Where the Conflict Really Lies: Science, Religion, and Naturalism* (New York, Oxford University Press, 2011); see also Michael Novak, *On Two Wings: Humble Faith and Common Sense at the American Founding* (San Francisco, Encounter Books, 2002), 81. Novak writes:

> To the extent that the Enlightenment depends upon the principle of "created equal," it depends upon Jewish metaphysics and Christian faith.
>
> Locke's contention that by nature no man is intended to be ruled by another comes not from observation, not from history, and not exactly from philosophical argument, but from an appeal to a biblical metaphysic.

20. Francis Beckwith, "Dignity Never Been Photographed: Scientific Materialism, Enlightenment Liberalism, and Steven Pinker," *Ethics and Medicine* 26, no. 2 (Summer, 2010), 94.

21. Ibid.

22. Steven Pinker, "The Stupidity of Dignity," *The New Republic* 238, no. 9 (May 28, 2008), 28–31.

23. Beckwith, "Dignity," 96.

24. Ibid.

25. Ibid.

26. Ibid. 97. Beckwith used this song to illustrate his point that SM is inadequate to answer for human dignity. "Lookin' for Love" "Stupidity," by Johnny Lee (1980).

27. Pinker, "Stupidity," 31.

28. Beckwith, "Dignity," 103.

29. Ibid.

30. Ibid.

31. Ibid.

32. Ibid.

33. Ibid.

34. Steven Pinker, *How the Mind Works* (New York: W. W. Norton, 1997), 55, 56.

35. William Lane Craig and Sam Harris, *The God Debate II: Harris vs. Craig* (http://www.youtube.com/watch?v=yqaHXKLRKzg, 2011). This debate is over whether God is necessary for objective moral values. Craig argues that atheism lacks the adequate foundation to ground objective moral values. In the same way, I believe Rawlsian liberalism by itself lacks adequate foundation to ground objective rights and duties.

36. The privatization of religious belief is argued for by Rawls (chapter five), historians interpret the formation of the Establishment Clause through this lens (chapter three), and the courts enforce this schema from the bench (chapter two).

37. See Rodney Stark, *For the Glory of God: How Monotheism Led to Reformations, Science, Witch-Hunts, and the End of Slavery* (Princeton, Princeton University Press, 2003), and *God's Battalions: The Case for the Crusades* (New York, Harper One, 2009). Stark uses these two works to challenge the portrayal of religious history (particularly Christian history) in a negative light. Stark writes the following about the crusades:

> The thrust of the preceding chapters can be summarized very briefly. The Crusades were not unprovoked. They were not the first round of European colonialism. They were not conducted for land, loot, or converts. The crusaders were not barbarians who victimized the cultivated Muslims. They sincerely believed that they served in God's battalions. 248.

38. Jay Winter and Blaine Baggett, *The Great War: And the Shaping of the 20th Century* (New York: Penguin Books, 1996), 97.

39. Malcolm Brown and Shirley Seaton, *Christmas Truce: The Western Front 1914* (Pan Grand Strategy Series, 1999), i.

40. See Vikram Jayanti, *The Christmas Truce* (The History Channel, 2002).

41. http://www.youtube.com/watch?v=Izb459vJ-8Q.

42. See John T. McGreevy, *Catholicism and American Freedom: A History* (New York, W.W. Norton & Company, 2003).

43. Pope Eugene IV, "Sicut Dudum: Against the Enslaving of Black Natives from the Canary Islands," (1435). http://www.papalencyclicals.net/Eugene04/eugene04sicut.htm. At the end of this papal bull, the pope commands the following:

> And no less do We order and command all and each of the faithful of each sex, within the space of fifteen days of the publication of these letters in the place where they live, that they restore to their earlier liberty all and each person of either sex who were once residents of said Canary Islands, and made captives since the time of their capture, and who have been made subject to slavery. These people are to be totally and perpetually free, and are to be let go without the exaction or reception of money. If this is not done when the fifteen days have passed, they incur the sentence of excommunication by the act itself, from which they cannot be absolved, except at the point of death, even by the Holy See, or by any Spanish bishop, or by the aforementioned Ferdinand, unless they have first given freedom to these captive persons and restored their goods. We will that like sentence of excommunication be incurred by one and all who attempt to capture, sell, or subject to slavery, baptized residents of the Canary Islands, or those who are freely seeking Baptism, from which excommunication cannot be absolved except as was stated above.

44. See Fr. Joel S. Panzer, "The Popes and Slavery: Setting the Record Straight," http://www.cfpeople.org/apologetics/page51a003.html. Fr. Panzer writes:

> From 1435 to 1890, we have numerous bulls and encyclicals from several popes written to many bishops and the whole Christian faithful condemning both slavery and the slave trade. The very existence of these many papal teachings during this particular period of history is a strong indication that from the viewpoint of the Magisterium, there must have developed a moral problem of a different sort than any previously encountered.

45. McGreevy, *Catholicism and American Freedom*, 55.

46. Ibid.

47. George M. Marsden, *Religion and American Culture*, 2nd ed. (Belmont, CA, Wadsworth, 2001), 77.

48. In 1854, Senator Mason argued for the silencing of the religious abolitionist movement. He argued:

...I understand this petition to come from a class who have put aside their character of citizens. It comes from a class who style themselves in the petition, ministers of the Gospel, and not citizens....Sir, ministers of the Gospel are unknown to this Government, and God forbid the day should ever come when they shall be known to it. The great effort of the American people has been, by every form of defensive measures, to keep that class away from the Government; to deny to them any access to it as a class, or any interference in its proceedings.

See Senator Mason, "Statement in the Senate, March 14, 1854," *Right of Petition: New England Clergymen* (Washington, D.C.' Buell and Blanchard, 1854), 5.

49. Isaak Kramnick and R. Laurence Moore, *The Godless Constitution: The Case Against Religious Correctness* (New York, W.W. Norton & Company, 1997), 76.

50. See R. W. Southern, *Western Society and the Church in the Middle Ages*, The Penguin History of the Church, vol. 2 (London, Penguin Books, 1990).

51. Paul F. Crawford, "Four Myths About the Crusades," *The Intercollegiate Review: A Journal of Scholarship and Opinion* (Spring, 2011), 13–22.

52. "Justice and Peace: Because Broken Promises Fueled Islamic Militancy, the Road to Stability Must be Paved with Good Faith; A Conversation with J. Dudley Woodberry," *Christian History*, 74, no. 21, (2002), 43.

53. William T. Cavanaugh, "A Fire Strong Enough to Consume the House: The Wars of Religion and the Rise of the State," *Modern Theology* 11, no. 4 (October 1995).

54. Georg Von Rauch, *A History of Soviet Russian*, trans. Peter and Annette Jacobsohn, revised ed. (New York, Frederick A. Praeger Publishers, 1957), 238.

55. Ibid. 141–143. Rauch included the following description of the treatment of religious believers in Soviet Russia:

The complete separation of State and Church marked the beginning of a number of other measures which thoroughly isolated the life of the Church and excluded it from public affairs. The clergy were deprived of its civil rights. Religious instruction of the young was prohibited in 1921; the Criminal Code of 1926 decreed forced labor as the punishment for any violation of this prohibition. The state's hostile attitude toward religion was clearly expressed in the new school text books. All religious literature was banned and parochial schools, seminaries and monasteries were closed.

56. Randall L. Bytwerk, "The Magic of the Spoken Word: The National Socialist Approach to Rhetoric," *Landmark Speeches of National Socialism*, ed. Randall L. Bytwerk (College Station, Texas A&M University Press, 2008), 2.

57. Richard Weikart, *From Darwin to Hitler: Evolutionary Ethics, Eugenics, and Racism in Germany* (New York, Palgrave Macmillan, 2004), 3.

58. This is not to say that Darwinism is sufficient for Nazism; however, it may be argued that it is a necessary condition to justify the types of acts committed by the Nazis against their enemies. By this I mean to say that the Nazis justified their treatment of Jews, Gypsies, and the handicapped on grounds that these groups were less than human or at least malformed and detrimental to the advancement of the species.

59. Erwin W. Lutzer, *Hitler's Cross: The Revealing Story of How the Cross of Christ Was Used as a Symbol of the Nazi Agenda* (Chicago, Moody Publishers, 1995), 114.

60. See John S. Conway, *The Nazi Persecution of the Churches 1933–45* (London, Weidenfeld & Nicholson, 1968), 15. Conway wrote that Hitler's intentions were to rid Germany of Christianity. Hitler stated that "making peace with the church won't stop me from stamping out Christianity in Germany, root and branch. One is either a Christian or a German. You can't be both."

61. This is not to say that public reason leads to communism or fascism. I am only showing that what counts as public reason in American federal courts was used in these two instances of mass violence.

62. See J. Daryl Charles, *Between Pacifism and Jihad: Just War and Christian Tradition* (Downers Grove, Intervarsity Press, 2005).

Chapter Eight: Conclusion

1. See Lee v. Weisman, 505 U.S. 577 (1992), at 625.

2. See Roger Williams, "The Bloudy Tennant of Persecution for Cause of Conscience," *The Complete Writings of Roger Williams*, Vol. 7, ed. Perry Miller, (New York, Russell &Russell, Inc., 1963): Rogers used theological reasoning to arrive at his separationist attitudes. While contemporary separationists agree with Williams separationist attitude, they would have to reject his reasoning. Williams writes:

Truth. Dear Peace (to ease thy first complaint), 'tis true, thy dearest sons, most like their mother, peacekeeping, peacemaking sons of God, have borne and still must bear the blurs of troublers of Israel, and turners of the world upside down. And 'tis true again, what Solomon once spake: "The beginning of strife is as when one letteth out water, therefore (saith he) leave off contention before it be meddled with. This caveat should keep the banks and sluices firm and strong, that strife, like a breach of waters, break not in upon the sons of men."

Yet strife must be distinguished: It is necessary or unnecessary, godly or Ungodly, Christian or unchristian, etc. It is unnecessary, unlawful, dishonorable, ungodly, unchristian, in most cases in the world, for there is a possibility of keeping sweet peace in most cases, and, if it be possible, it is the express command of God that peace be kept (Rom. 13).

3. See Francis Beckwith, "Gimme That Ol' Time Separation: A Review Essay, Philip Hamburger, Separation of Church and State," *Chapman Law Review* 8 (2005), 312–313. Beckwith writes:

…the Danbury Baptists were known as dissenters—those who opposed religious establishment but did not oppose the influence of religion on government. In fact, because it was assumed that the moral ecology of a society could not be maintained without the influence of religion, dissenters had to constantly deal with the false charge that they were really separationists wanting to remove any vestiges of religion from the public square.

4. See chapter three.
5. Garrett Ward Sheldon, *The Political Philosophy of Thomas Jefferson* (Baltimore, Johns Hopkins University Press, 1991), 143.
6. Ibid. Sheldon writes:

> Thomas Jefferson's conception of a virtuous American republic presumed the existence of a social ethics appropriate to a naturally social being possessing a divinely ordained moral sense. This was the religion of Christian ethics, which conformed to man's natural sympathies and fostered a sense of duty to his fellow citizens. (103).

7. Michael Novak, *On Two Wings: Humble Faith and Common Sense at the American Founding* (San Francisco, Encounter Books, 2002), 147.
8. Michael Sandel, "Freedom of Conscience or Freedom of Choice," in *Articles of Faith, Articles of Peace: The Religious Liberty Clauses and the American Public Philosophy*, ed. James Davison Hunter and Os Guinness (Washington D.C., The Brookings Institute, 1990). 84.
9. This is not to say that the garden and wilderness metaphor has never been employed before or by the courts. It is merely to say that it is noticeably absent from the majority of the cases that make use of the wall of separation metaphor.
10. See Roe v. Wade, 410 U.S. 113 (1973). Justice Blackmun made a distinction between religious belief and secular policy as though the two cannot speak to the same issue.
11. See Francis Beckwith, "Justificatory Liberalism and Same Sex Marriage," *Ratio Juris: An International Journal of Jurisprudence and Philosophy of Law*. 26.4 (December 2013). Explaining a Rawlsian position concerning coercive legislation, Beckwith writes:

> ...because citizens, including religious citizens, have an evidential set—source of authority, background beliefs and reason—not shared by their neighbors, they should restrain from employing those sources as the basis for the reasons why they enact laws that limit a constitutionally essential liberty of their fellow citizens who do not share those sources of authority. (1)

12. There are several rationally defensible arguments for the existence of God. Two of these are the Kalam cosmological argument and the teleological argument. Though the Kalam cosmological argument dates back to medieval times, it has been further developed by philosopher of religion William Lane Craig. See William Lane Craig, *The Kalam Cosmological Argument* (Eugene, OR, Wipf and Stock Publishers, 2000).
The argument states:

> (1) Everything that has begun to exist has a cause of its existence.
> (2) The universe began to exist.
> Therefore:
> (3) The universe was caused.

(4) If the universe was caused, then that cause must be God. This is because a being wholly other from the physical universe, i.e. spaceless, timeless, self-existent, powerful, intelligent, etc…, is required to cause the universe.
Therefore:
(5) God exists.

The teleological argument is the argument from design. It is this argument that drives the intelligent design debate, and it also played a large role in atheist philosopher Anthony Flew's conversion to theism.
See Anthony Flew, *There Is a God: How the World's Most Notorious Atheist Changed His Mind* (New York, Harper One, 2007). Flew writes:

Science qua science cannot furnish an argument for God's existence. But the three items of evidence we have considered in this volume—the laws of nature, life with its teleological organization, and the existence of the universe—can only be explained in the light of an Intelligence that explains both its own existence and that of the world. Such a discovery of the Divine does not come through experiments and equations, but through an understanding of the structures they unveil and map. (155)

Flew further states:

As I see it, five phenomena are evident in our immediate experience that can only be explained in terms of the existence of God. These are, first, the rationality implicit in all our experience of the physical world; second, life, the capacity to act autonomously; third, consciousness, the ability to be aware; fourth the power of articulating and understanding meaningful symbols such as are embedded in language; and, fifth, the human self, the "center" of consciousness, thought, and action. (161–162).

13. For an argument for the knowledge of God's general will see J. Budziszewski, *Written on the Heart: The Case for Natural Law* (Downers Grove, Intervarsity Press, 1997). Budziszewski suggests that general revelation comes in five forms:

(1)The testimony of creation, which speaks to us of a glorious, powerful and merciful Creator; (2) the fact that we are made in the image of God, which not only gives us rational and moral capacities but also tells us of an unknown Holy One who is different from our idols; (3) the facts of our physical and emotional design, in which a variety of God's purposes are plainly manifest; (4) the law of conscience, written on the heart, which, like the law of Moses, tells us what sin is but does not give us power to escape it; (5) the order of causality, which teaches us by linking every sin with consequences. (180–181).

14. For the argument for God revealing Himself in history through Jesus of Nazareth, see William Lane Craig, *Assessing the New Testament Evidence for the Historicity of the Resurrection of Jesus* (New York, Edwin Mellen Press, 2002). See also C. Steven Evans, *The Historical*

Christ and the Jesus of Faith: The Incarnational Narrative as History (New York, Oxford University Press, 1996). Evans writes:

…though I discuss the prospects for arguments designed to convince unbelievers of the historicity of the story, this is not itself such an argument. Rather, the book aims to give a convincing account as to why knowledge of the story is important, and also argues that ordinary people who claim to have knowledge of the truth of the story of Jesus of Nazareth may be quite reasonable in making such a claim. Specifically, I claim that the reasonableness of such a claim is not undermined by modern critical biblical scholarship. It should be obvious that an argument such as mine is quite different from the kind of argument that would need to be offered to try to change the minds of those who do not accept the biblical story.…My hope is that a non-Christian who understands my account will gain a new respect for the integrity and intellectual vitality of Christian faith in the contemporary world. vii.

15. I am not suggesting here that laws may never violate one's conscience. My argument is that legislators should not dismiss the rationality of religious arguments.

Bibliography

Abington v. Schemmp, 374, U.S. 203.

Adams, John. "To the Officers of the First Brigade of the Third Division of the Militia of Massachusetts, October 11, 1776," ed. William Bennett, *Our Sacred Honor* (New York, Simon and Schuster, 1997).

Allegheny v. American Civil Liberties Union, 492 U.S. 573.

Alston, William P. *Perceiving God: The Epistemology of Religious Experience* (London, Cornell University Press, 1991).

Americans United for Separation of Church & State v. Porter, 485 F. Supp. 432; 1980 U.S. Dist. LEXIS 11719.

Aristotle. *Politics*, translated by Benjamin Jowett (Oxford, Clarendon Press, public domain, I 1253a2).

Audi, Robert. *Epistemology: A Contemporary Introduction to the Theory of Knowledge, Routledge Contemporary Introduction to Philosophy* (London, Routledge, 2000).

———. *Religious Commitment and Secular Reason* (Cambridge, Cambridge University Press, 2000).

———. "Natural Reason, Natural Rights, and Governmental Neutrality Toward Religion," *Religion and Human Rights* 4 (2009).

Backus, Isaac. An Appeal to the Public for Religious Liberty Against the Oppressions of the Present Day (Boston, John Boyle, 1773).

Beckwith, Francis. "Gimme That Ol' Time Separation: A Review Essay, Philip Hamburger, Separation of Church and State," *Chapman Law Review* 8 (2005), 309.

———. "The Court of Disbelief; The Constitution's Article VI Religious Test Prohibition and the Judiciary's Religious Motive Analysis," *Hastings Constitutional Law Quarterly* 33 (Winter and Spring, 2006).

———. "Rawls' Dangerous Idea?: Liberalism, Evolution and the Legal Requirement of Religious Neutrality in Public Schools," *Journal of Law and Religion* 20, no. 2, (2004–2005).

———. "Must Theology Always Sit in the Back of the Secular Bus?: The Federal Courts' View of Religion and Its Status as Knowledge." *Journal of Law and Religion* 24, no. 2 (2008–2009).

———. "Justificatory Liberalism and Same-Sex Marriage." *Ratio Juris: An International Journal of Jurisprudence and Philosophy of Law* 26.4 (December 2013): 487–509.

———. "Fides, Ratio et Juris: How Some Courts and Some Legal Theorists Misrepresent the Rational Status of Religious Beliefs." In *Reason, Revelation, and the Civic Order: Political Philosophy and the Claims of Faith*. Edited by Paul R. DeHart and Carson Holloway. DeKalb, IL: Northern Illinois University Press, 2014. Pp. 173–202.

Brown, Malcolm, and Seaton, Shirley. *Christmas Truce: The Western Front 1914* (Tuggerah, Pan Grand Strategy Series, 1999).

Budziszewski, J. *Written on the Heart: The Case for Natural Law* (Downers Grove, Intervarsity Press, 1997).

Bytwerk, Randall, L. "The Magic of the Spoken Word: The National Socialist Approach to Rhetoric," *Landmark Speeches of National Socialism*, ed. Randall L. Bytwerk (College Station, Texas A&M University Press, 2008).

California Senate Bill 48-2011-2012, available at: http://legiscan.com/gaits/text/74798 (2012).

Capitol Square Review and Advisory Board v. Pinette, 515 U.S. 753 (1995).

Carter, Stephen L. *God's Name in Vain: The Wrongs and Rights of Religion in Politics* (New York, Basic Books, 2000).

Cavanaugh, William T. "A Fire Strong Enough to Consume the House: The Wars of Religion and the Rise of the State," *Modern Theology* 11, no. 4 (October, 1995).

Charles, J. Daryl. *Between Pacifism and Jihad: Just War and Christian Tradition* (Downers Grove, Intervarsity Press, 2005).

Clinton, William Jefferson. Presidential Proclamation: Gay and Lesbian Pride Month, http://usgovinfo.about.com/library/weekly/blgaylesproc.htm (2000).

Clouser, Roy A. *The Myth of Religious Neutrality: An Essay on the Hidden Role of Religious Belief in Theories* (South Bend, IN, Notre Dame University Press, 2005).

Conway, John S. *The Nazi Persecution of the Churches 1933–45* (London, Weidenfeld & Nicholson, 1968).

Craig, William Lane. *Assessing the New Testament Evidence for the Historicity of the Resurrection of Jesus* (New York, Edwin Mellen Press, 2002).

———. *The Kalam Cosmological Argument* (Eugene, OR, Wipf and Stock Publishers, 2000).

Crawford, Paul F. "Four Myths About the Crusades," *The Intercollegiate Review: A Journal of Scholarship and Opinion*, Spring, 2011.

Davis, Derek H. *Religion and the Continental Congress 1774–1789: Contributions to Original Intent* (New York, Oxford University Press, 2000).

Doe v. Tangipahoa Parish Sch. Bd, United States District Court for the Eastern District of Louisiana (2005) U.S. Dist. LEXIS 3329.

Doyle, Arthur Conan. "The Adventures of Silver Blaze," *The Adventures of Sherlock Holmes* (Ware, U.K., Wadsworth Edition Limited, 1992).

Drakeman, Donald. *Church and State and Original Intent* (New York, Cambridge University Press, 2010).

Dworkin, Ronald. *Is Democracy Possible Here?: Principles For a New Political Debate* (Princeton, Princeton University Press, 2006).

———. *Life's Dominion: An Argument About Abortion, Euthanasia, and Individual Freedom* (New York, Vintage Books, 1994).

Elane Photography LLC. v. Willock, Docket No. 30, 203 (2012).

Engel v. Vitale, 370 U.S. 421 (1962).

Elk Grove Unified School District v. Newdow, 542 U.S. 961 (2004).

Evans, C. Steven. *The Historical Christ and the Jesus of Faith: The Incarnational Narrative as History* (New York, Oxford University Press, 1996).

Everson v. Board of Education of Ewing TP, 330 U.S. 1 (1947).

Eugene IV, Pope. "Sicut Dudum: Against the Enslaving of Black Natives from the Canary Islands" (1435). http://www.papalencyclicals.net/Eugene04/eugene04sicut.htm.

Flew, Anthony. *There Is a God: How the World's Most Notorious Atheist Changed His Mind* (New York, Harper One, 2007).

Frothingham v. Mellon, 262 U.S. 447 (1923).

George, Robert P. "A Clash of Orthodoxies," *First Things*, August, 1999.

George Robert P. and Wolfe, Christopher. "Natural Law and Public Reason," *Natural Law and Public Reason*, ed. Robert P. George and Christopher Wolfe (Washington D.C., Georgetown University Press, 2000).

Goldman v. Weinberger, 475 U.S. 506 (1986).

Haan, Linda de, an Nijland, Stern, *King and King* (Berkeley, Tricycle Press, 2000).

Hamburger, Phillip. *Separation of Church and State* (Cambridge, MA, Harvard University Press, 2002).

Hitchcock, James. *The Supreme Court and Religion in American Life: Vol.1, The Odyssey of the Religion Clauses* (Princeton, Princeton University Press, 2004).

———. *The Supreme Court and Religion in American Life: Vol. II, From "Higher Law" to "Sectarian Scruples"* (Princeton, Princeton University Press, 2004).

Jayanti, Vikram. *The Christmas Truce* (The History Channel, 2002).

Jefferson, Thomas. "Declaration of Independence" (1776). http://www.archives.gov/exhibits/charters/declaration_transcript.html.

Jefferson to Francis W. Gilmer, June 7, 1816, *The Works of Thomas Jefferson*, Vol. 11, ed. Paul Ford (New York, Putnam's Sons, 1904–05).

Jefferson to Gov. Wilson C. Nicholes (April 2, 1816).

Jefferson, Thomas. The Virginia Act for Establishing Religious Freedom (1786).

Jefferson to Thomas Law, June 13, 1814, *The Complete Jefferson*, ed. Saul K. Padover (New York, Tudor, 1943).

Jones v. Wolf, 443 U.S. 595 (1979).

Kedroff v. Saint Nicholas Cathedral, 344 U.S. 94 (1952).

Keeton v. Anderson-Whiley, No. 10–13925 (2011).

King Jr., Martin Luther. "I Have a Dream." www.archives.gov/press/exhibits/dream-speech.pdf (1963).

Kitzmiller v. Dover Area School District, Case No. 04cv2688 (2005).

Kramnick, Isaak and Moore, R. Laurence. *The Godless Constitution: The Case Against Religious Correctness* (New York, W.W. Norton & Company, 1997).

Kuhn, Thomas. *The Structure of Scientific Revolutions*, 2nd ed. (Chicago, University of Chicago Press, 1970).

Lawrence v. Texas, 539 U.S. 558 (2003).

Lee v. Weisman, 505 US 577 (1992).

Lemon v. Kurtzman, 403 U.S. 602 (1971).

Locke, John. "A Letter Concerning Toleration," 1685.

———. Second Treatise of Civil Government, http://www.constitution.org/jl/2ndtr02.htm (1690).

Lutzer, Erwin W. *Hitler's Cross: The Revealing Story of How the Cross of Christ Was Used as a Symbol of the Nazi Agenda* (Chicago, Moody Publishers, 1995).

Macedo, Stephen. "The Politics of Justification," *Political Theory* 18 (1990).

———. *Liberal Virtues: Citizenship, Virtue, and Community in Liberal Constitutionalism* (New York, Clarendon Press, 1991).

———. "Liberal Civic Education and Religious Fundamentalism: The Case of God v. John Rawls," *Ethics* 105, no. 3 (April, 1995).

———. "In Defense of Liberal Public Reason: Are Slavery and Abortion Hard Cases?," *Natural Law and Public Reason*, ed. Robert P. George and Christopher Wolfe (Washington D.C., Georgetown University Press, 2000).

Madison, James. Memorial and Remonstrance. http://founders.archives.gov/documents/Madison/01-08-02-0163.

Marsden, George M. *Religion and American Culture*, 2nd ed. (Belmont, CA, Wadsworth, 2001).

Mason, James. "Statement in the Senate, March 14, 1854," *Right of Petition: New England Clergymen* (Washington, D.C., Buell and Blanchard, 1854).

McCollum v. Board of Education, 333 U.S. 203 (1948).

McGowan v. Maryland, 366 U.S. 420 (1961).

McGreevy, John T., *Catholicism and American Freedom: A History* (New York, W.W. Norton & Company, 2003).

McKinley, James. "Texas Conservatives Win Curriculum Change," *New York Times*, March 12, 2010.

Moreland, J. P. *Christianity and the Nature of Science: A Philosophical Investigation* (Grand Rapids, Baker Book House, 1989).

———. "Theistic Science and Methodological Naturalism," *The Creation Hypothesis; Scientific Evidence for an Intelligent Designer*, ed. J. P. Moreland (Downers Grove, Inter Varsity Press, 1994).

Neal, Patrick. "Political Liberalism, Public Reason, and the Citizen of Faith," *Natural Law and Public Reason*, ed Robert P. George and Christopher Wolfe (Washington D.C., Georgetown University Press, 2000).

Newdow v. Congress, 292 F. 3d 597 (9th Cir. 2002).

Newdow v. Congress, 540 U.S. 962 (2003).

Novak, Michael. *On Two Wings: Humble Faith and Common Sense at the American Founding* (San Francisco, Encounter Books, 2002).

Nykol, Ambra. "How Liberal and Gay Rights Activists Have Hijacked the Legacy of Martin Luther King Jr," *The New Black Magazine*, http://www.thenewblackmagazine.com/view.aspx?index=477 (2012).

Obama, Barack. Presidential Proclamation: Lesbian, Gay Bisexual, and Transgender Pride Month, http://www.whitehouse.gov/the-press-office/2011/05/31/presidential-proclamation-lesbian-gay-bisexual-and-transgender-pride-mon (2011).

Pacific Justice Institute. Press Release: "Students Told, 'America the Beautiful' Is Lesbian Anthem" (September 25, 2012).

Panzer, Fr. Joel S. "The Popes and Slavery: Setting the Record Straight," http://www.cfpeople.org/apologetics/page51a003.html.

Parker v. Hurley, 514 F.3d 87, 90 (1st Cir. 2008), cert. denied, 129 S. Ct. 56 (2008).

Pinker, Steven. *How the Mind Works* (New York, W. W. Norton, 1997).

———. "The Stupidity of Dignity," *The New Republic* 238, no. 9 (28 May 2008).

Plantinga, Alvin. *Warrant and Proper Function* (New York, Oxford University Press, 1993).

———. *Where the Conflict Really Lies: Science, Religion, and Naturalism* (New York, Oxford University Press, 2011).

Prince v. Massachusetts, 321 U.S. 158 (1944).

Rauch, Georg Von. *A History of Soviet Russian*, trans. Peter and Annette Jacobsohn, revised ed. (New York, Frederick A. Praeger Publishers, 1957).

Rawls, John. *Political Liberalism*, 2nd ed. (New York, Columbia University Press, 1995).

———. *A Theory of Justice* (Cambridge, The Belknap Press of Harvard University Press, 1971).

Reynolds v. United States, 98 U.S. 145 (1879).

Robert, Bella. "Civil Religion in America," *Daedalus, Journal of the American Academy of Arts and Sciences* 96, no. 1 (Winter, 1967).

Roe v. Wade, 410 U.S. 113 (1973).

Sandel, Michael. "Freedom of Conscience of Freedom of Choice," *Articles of Faith, Articles of Peace: The Religious Liberty Clauses and the American Public Philosophy*, ed. James Davison Hunter and Os Guinness (Washington D.C., The Brookings Institution, 1990).

Santa Fe Independent School District, Petitioners, v. Jane Doe, 530 US 290 (1999).

Serbian Orthodox Diocese v. Milivojevich, 426 U.S. 696 (1976).

Sheldon, Garrett Ward. *The Political Philosophy of Thomas Jefferson* (Baltimore, John Hopkins University Press, 1991).

Sherbert v. Verner, 374 U.S. 398 (1963).

Southern, R. W. *Western Society and the Church in the Middle Ages*, The Penguin History of the Church, vol. 2 (London, Penguin Books, 1990).

Stark, Rodney. *For the Glory of God: How Monotheism Led to Reformations, Science, Witch-Hunts, and the End of Slavery* (Princeton, Princeton University Press, 2003).

———. *God's Battalions: The Case for the Crusades* (New York, Harper One, 2009).

Stone v. Graham, 449 US 39 (1980).

Strauss, Leo. *What Is Political Philosophy?: And Other Studies* (Chicago, The University of Chicago Press, 1959).

Thomson, Judith Jarvis. "A Defense of Abortion," *Philosophy of Public Affairs* 1, no. 1 (Autumn, 1971).

Underhill, Edward Bean. *A Biographical Introduction to The Bloudy Tenent (sic) of Persecution for Cause of Conscience Discussed and Mr. Cotton's Letter Examined and Answered, by Roger Williams* (London, J. Haddon, Castle Street, Finsbury, 1848).

Varnum v. Brien, 763 N.W. 2d 862 (Iowa 2009).

United States v. Ballard, 322 U.S. 78 (1944).

United States v. Seeger, 380 U.S. 163 (1965).

Universal Military Training and Service Act, §6(j) (1948).

Wallace v. Jaffree, 472 U.S. 38 (1985).

Ward v. Wilbanks, No. 09-CV-11237 (2010).

Weikart, Richard. *From Darwin to Hitler: Evolutionary Ethics, Eugenics, and Racism in Germany* (New York, Palgrave Macmillan, 2004).

Welsh v. United States, 398 U.S. 333 (1970).

West Virginia State Bd. of Educ. v. Barnette, 319 U.S. 624 (1943).

Winter, Jay and Baggett, Blaine. *The Great War: And the Shaping of the 20th Century* (New York, Penguin Books, 1996).

Witte, John. *Religion and the American Constitutional Experiment: Essential Rights and Liberties* (Boulder, Westview Press, 2000).

Wolterstorff, Nicholas. "Nicholas Wolterstorff on Faith in Liberal Democracy," interviewed by Miroslav Volf, Yale University: Faith and Global Initiative (2009).

Wolterstorff, Nicolas and Audi, Robert. "Liberal Democracy and Religion in Politics," *Religion in the Public Square: The Place of Religious Convictions in Political Debate* (New York, Rowman and Littlefield Publishers Inc., 1997).

Woodberry, J. Dudley. "Justice and Peace: Because Broken Promises Fueled Islamic Militancy, the Road to Stability Must Be Paved with Good Faith; A Conversation with J. Dudley Woodberry," *Christian History* 74, no. 21 (2002).

Zorach v. Clauson, 343 U.S. 313 (1952).

http://ffrf.org/outreach/awards/freethinker-of-the-year-award/ishmael-jaffree/

http://www.news-gazette.com/news/religion/2010–07–09/e-mail-prompted-complaint-over-ui-religion-class-instructor.html

http://www.news-gazette.com/news/religion/2010–07–09/e-mail-complaint-student-about-ui-religion-instructor.html

http://www.wallbuilders.com/libissuesarticles.asp?id=100766